ON THE EDGE OF REALITY

DREAM WEAVERS - THE MASTERING OF TIME AND SPACE

**Explosive Interviews With The Leading
Esoterica Thinkers of Today
Conducted, Compiled, Edited by
BRENT RAYNES
Introduction by Greg Little**

Global Communications

On the Edge of Reality
Dreamweavers – The Mastering of Time and Space
Brent Raynes

EAN: 978-1-60611-068-3
ISBN: 1-60611-068-3

Nonfiction

Timothy Green Beckley: Editorial Director
Carol Rodriguez: Publishers Assistant
Sean Casteel: Associate Editor
Cover Art: Tim R. Swartz

Printed in the United States of America

For free catalog write:
Global Communications
P.O. Box 753
New Brunswick, NJ 08903

Free Subscription to Conspiracy Journal E-Mail Newsletter
www.conspiracyjournal.com

Contents

Introduction
by Dr. Gregory L. Little

Beginning in the late 1960s, both Brent Raynes and I started on a parallel quest in hunt of the truth about UFOs. Brent's many early trips included visits and contacts with some of ufology's major figures, people who became his friends, such as Betty Hill, Dr. Berthold Schwarz, and John Keel. When he began his search Brent was only 14. Even during his stint with the U.S. Navy, which began when he was twenty, Brent never let up on his correspondence and visits with UFO personalities. Though he was once mistaken for a possible man-in-black or government agent, Brent's style and easy manner befriended many people, both researchers and those who reported strange experiences alike. People liked Brent, and not without reason. He never sought the limelight and avoided conflict and argument, gradually becoming ufology's "Gentle Giant," as he could be described today.

It was in 1985, about a year after my first UFO book, The Archetype Experience, was published that I met Brent through a mutual contact who had numerous experiences with UFOs and entities. He was then producing a nonscheduled newsletter about UFO research entitled, Para-UFOlogy Forum. I wrote a few articles for his newsletter and we collaborated in some UFO investigations together for several years. At that time both of us became interested in the many links between Native American Indian lore and the UFO phenomenon. Both of us were intrigued by the rituals and myths of "little people," unexplained lights, and out-of-body experiences reported by shamans and reported in other Native American lore, because they seemed too similar to modern UFO reports, but with a culture-specific aspect.

In 1993 Brent published the 24th issue of his then renamed newsletter (UFO Perceptions) and I came on with him as a co-editor. In issue 28 we renamed the newsletter Alternate Perceptions and changed the publication to a slick, color-covered magazine of 56 pages. After about two dozen issues, and even with a good circulation, in 2002 (issue # 56) we decided to take the publication to a monthly internet magazine and made all of the content free. The change resulted in a huge readership, generally averaging over 25,000 readers a month. Alternate Perceptions Magazine (www.mysterious-america.net) has now put out over 140 issues.

Over the years Brent has conducted hundreds of investigations of UFO reports, Native American experiences, bizarre and unexplained phenomena, crop circles in the U.S., and so many more scientific issues that it is mind-boggling. In addition, he has conducted and published interviews with a vast number of people, from the biggest names in ufology and the most prominent researchers in paranormal phenomena to some of the more obscure individuals who decided to allow him access to their bizarre and unexplained experiences. I found Brent to be one of the most caring and meticulous UFO investigators I ever met. He allowed people who had encounters with unknown phenomena to just tell their story and he withheld judgment and ridicule. He truly investigated reports even going so far as to compile a psychological profile of UFO percipients that has been widely cited by others. He faithfully reported on UFO accounts often seeking out the most interesting and unknown cases. His careful and nonjudgmental style was one reason so many people have told him some of their deepest secrets. This book contains some of the most intriguing interviews Brent has conducted. Those who are genuinely interested in unexplained mysteries will find it intriguing and insightful.

Over the years Brent became friends with many of ufology's best-known personalities including Betty Hill, Dr. Berthold Schwarz, Marc Davenport, and countless others. He has managed to interview such personalities as Dr. Jacques Vallee, many of MUFON's section directors, and a host of famous abductees and authors including Betty Hill, Dr. Rick Strassman, Andrew Collins, Mark Pinkham, Bob Pratt, Uri Geller, Raymond Fowler, Betty Andreasson Luca, Allen Greenfield, Paul Von Ward, Dr. Alexander Imich, Tom Dongo, Dr. Melvin Redfern, Lyn Halper, P.M.H. Atwater, Richard Dolan, Lucius Farish, Phil Imbrogno, Dr. Hans Holzer, Timothy Green Beckley, Dr. Edgar Mitchell, Brian O'Leary, Dr. Stanley Krippner, Anthony Peake, Christopher O'Brien, and many, many more. Native American personalities Brent has interviewed include Nancy Red Star, Sixto Paz Wells, Willie Windwalker Gibson, Jon Thunder, Priscilla Wolf, Allen Ross, Tommy Lightning Bolt, Khat Hansen, and others. His earlier book, Visitors From Hidden Realms, is a fascinating account of some of ufology's least known but most important theories, some of which stemmed from his many interviews. And it tells how Brent became one of the leading experts on the mind altering effects of ancient whistling vessels used in the Andes. In essence, what the reader of this vast array of material should conclude is that something quite intriguing is lurking under the surface and it is far more interesting and far more bizarre that aliens visiting our planet.

Within the pages of this book are portions of some of the interviews of many of these individuals as well as interviews with many people who have had bizarre and unexplained experiences. These individuals believe that what they say is the truth and are presented here without ridicule or without the inane and sometimes ludicrous explanations often given by those who seek to discount human experience. You will not find ridicule here, only the stories. It is a compelling and intriguing collection of individual stories that leads to the conclusion that something is definitely happening in the realm of human experience that is unexplained and very bizarre.

About the Author
Brent Raynes

Brent Raynes has been on the trail of UFOs since 1967, when he was only 14. Although in the beginning he embraced the mainstream "nuts and bolts" extraterrestrial hypothesis, his focus and range of interests quickly branched out to include a vast spectrum of other anomalous phenomena, ranging from all types of psychic phenomena (i.e., poltergeists, out-of-body experiences, near-death experiences, telekinesis, telepathy, etc.), to cryptozoology (i.e., Bigfoot, Mothman, Nessie, etc.), as well as spiritual manifestations like the Mother Mary apparitions and visions of Fatima, or shamanism, with a special interest and respect for Native American spirituality.

Brent is the editor of Alternate Perceptions magazine (www.mysterious-america.net) and the author of the highly acclaimed Visitors From Hidden Realms. He has appeared on various popular radio programs, including Coast to Coast AM and as a guest of Brad Steiger on the Jeff Rense Show. Brent has also done quite a few presentations, workshops, and lectures across the country, including the special UFO conference that the ARE (Association for Research and Enlightenment) sponsored at their international headquarters in Virginia Beach, Virginia, back in December 2005. Entitled "UFOs: The Full Spectrum," it included such luminaries in the UFO field as Jacques Vallee, Betty Andreasson Luca, Dr. Greg Little, and Stan Friedman.

Brent points out that the earliest and most powerful influences on the evolution of his ufological thinking were the articles and books written by such noteworthy and pioneering authors as John Keel, Jacques Vallee, and Brad Steiger.

Brent welcomes comments, observations, and personal reports from readers. He may be reached at: brentraynes@yahoo.com.

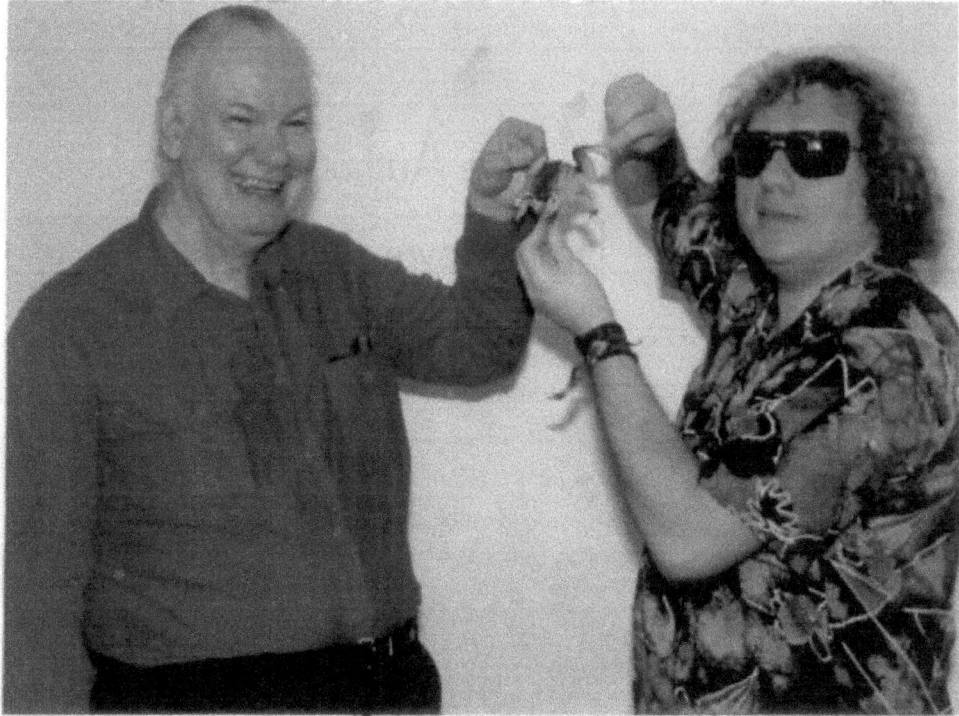

John - "*Mothman Prophecies*" - Keel presents Inner Light's Tim Beckley with the FOrtean Society Of The Year Award, its mascot pet (rubber) frog. Keel has long written about his occult experiences in the Far East. Frogs represent the strange fall -- or "teleportation" of mysterious objects from the sky as first described by historian Charles Fort (thus the term "Fortean")

Jacque Valless and Brent Raynes

Chapter 1
Gateway to Other Worlds

I had never been to New Mexico or Colorado, so I was certainly very excited about this trip, as was my wife Joan. Flying into Albuquerque, New Mexico late Thursday night, August 7th, 2008, we were met by Priscilla Wolf, an Apache medicine woman, storyteller, artist and author and her dear friend and long time companion Steve. They greeted us as we were headed to pick up our baggage. The way we conversed and laughed a stranger watching us doubtless would have assumed that we had all known each other and been close friends for years. But the truth of the matter is that we began communication with one another via the Internet, snail mail and telephone back in April of this year. I owe a solemn debt of gratitude to that indefatigable researcher and prolific writer Brad Steiger for ultimately bringing us together.

Though the trip to their home in the mountains of Tijeras, east of Albuquerque, is approximately twenty miles, it seemed like no time at all till we arrived at their beautiful mountain home/retreat. However, not long after arriving the adrenaline was beginning to wear thin from the long trip, which our gracious and perceptive hosts quickly picked up on as they introduced us to our sleeping quarters. They told us to feel at home and they certainly did indeed make us feel that way.

Powerful Earth Energies

The next morning we proceeded at a relaxed pace. A healthy and very delicious home prepared breakfast was set before us as we found an endless variety of subjects on which to converse. Day One was going to involve a trip over to Albuquerque, to the west bank of the Rio Grande where the Petroglyph National Monument is located. I had proposed this particular field trip to Priscilla a few weeks earlier and had even emailed her a copy of an interview I had done last year with New York researcher and writer John Burke, author of <u>Seed of Knowledge, Stone of Plenty</u>. Priscilla was very impressed with Burke's work and even began exchanging emails with him. Burke had visited ancient mounds, henges, pyramids, stone chambers, and known sacred spots at such diverse places as England's Silbury Hill and Avebury Henge, Guatemala's oldest Mayan city of Tikal, the Black Hills of South Dakota, to name but a few, and using a fluxgate magnetometer, a standard voltmeter, and an electrostatic voltmeter he and his colleague Kaj Halberg repeatedly detected unusual earth energies at these places. "Overwhelmingly, the ancient megalithic architects all over the world chose to build on conductivity discontinuities, and then designed and built these enormous structures in such a way as to further concentrate the natural electromagnetic energies present at these sites," Burke explained in our interview. He further expanded, "A conductivity discontinuity is simply the intersection of two zones of land, one of which conducts natural electrical ground current relatively well and the other less well. At such sites the normal daily fluctuations of the earth's geomagnetic field are magnified several hundred percent, and with them the telluric currents that flow through the ground." Burke also pointed out that Canadian neuroscientist Dr. Michael Persinger had "confirmed that the magnitude of magnetic changes we have found at these sites conforms to those he has found capable of creating visions in volunteers in his lab."

At any rate, the largest conductivity discontinuity that Burke had ever studied was (you guessed it) the Petroglyph National Monument! As he explained in our interview, "it contains thousands of rock carvings which are considered by anthropologists today to have been made by shamans illustrating their trance hallucinations. I measured very powerful and extremely odd surges of electric current in the ground there. When the ranger at the Visitor Center heard what I was finding, she said to me, 'You know, periodically I get these 'New Age types' coming in here and telling me they just love to go sit up in the rocks and feel the energy. I thought they were a bunch of flakes, but you're telling me there might be something to this."

These thousands of ancient petroglyphs are scattered across the face of a 17-mile long West Mesa escarpment that was the result of volcanic eruptions that began about 150,000 years ago. There are said to be more than twenty thousand images covering many of the countless volcanic rocks at this immense site, images said to have been created four to seven centuries ago. Most of these petroglyphs are found on south and east facing slopes. We visited the Boca Negra Canyon portion of this site, walking what is known as the Mesa Point Trail. Boca Negra Canyon was the area where Burke took most of his measurements.

While we were walking slowly up the volcanic rock-strewn hillside we were startled when Priscilla's plastic water bottle made a pop sound and she cried out that she had just gotten an electric shock. "When I was going to put the top back on the bottle it shocked me and I put the lid on and it made a loud pop, (as) you heard," Priscilla recalled later.

We came upon one large black volcanic rock on the trail that had a place in it just perfect for putting our heads inside. "It fit all of our heads," Priscilla recalled. "That was the most amazing thing." She placed her head inside, trying to get rid of a headache. With her eyes closed and her head inside the rock, Priscilla said that she could see various colors, but mainly purple. I remembered myself "seeing" a green glowing cross shape, it's four appendages appearing to be of equal distance. Later, on another part of the slope, I pulled three whistling vessels from my bag. These are fully functional replicas of the ancient Peruvian Chimu vessels, believed by a number of researchers to have been shamanic instruments of sound. I was going to use them in my presentation that upcoming weekend (August 9th and 10th) at the

UFO Watchtower Conference in Hooper, Colorado, where both Priscilla and I were scheduled to speak. They are great for inducing profound altered states of consciousness, and I was interested in observing what impressions might be produced at a site as obviously powerful as this one. After a few minutes of blowing the whistles, Priscilla had a report for me. "I seen the energy of lights, first like flashing lights, and then it was like a sun rotating itself, coming down, like moving towards me," Priscilla recalled. "I could see it just rotating around and around." I reminded her of what she had told me at the time about her back injury, to which she replied: "Oh yes. I just hurt my back a few days ago and I've been in a lot of pain and I thought, 'Oh no, we're going to be heading for this UFO place and my back is hurting so bad,' and I thought that I had probably damaged my back by lifting up the microwave. I wasn't too sure what had caused it, and on the vision today, during the whistles, I saw that I was real mad and that I had allowed an opening to come into my body, because I had been wanting that microwave moved. What happened is the anger had allowed an opening into my body to cause pain, so that's when I seen light and I used the light of the sun to close that."

Earth Spirits and Energies of the San Luis Valley and the Gates to Other Worlds!

A couple days later, late on the afternoon of Sunday, August 10th, as we were leaving the UFO gathering in Hooper, I would wonder again about unique earth energies and their possible connection to volcano sites, as in our departure from there Priscilla, in our drive into the southern San Luis Valley of Colorado, wanted to show us her childhood home and where many people had experienced many strange things down through the years. As we road down this dusty, gravel road of hills and prairie land an extinct volcano drew closer and closer. Conspicuously absent was the presence of homes and other people as we drove on mile after mile through this region. "That's a portal, what they call an opening, of Gates to Other Worlds, right here," Priscilla said. "Right in this field?" I asked. "Right in there, and the markers are one, two and three hills right there," she said, pointing out three nearby hills located around the volcano.

"And you used to come up here as a child with your brother and you used to see the disks?" I asked.

"Yeah, the black disks flying around and just totally going into the volcano, disappearing in there."

"When they disappeared into the volcano, did they go down into the top of it or did they go into the side?" I asked.

"No," Priscilla said. "I don't know where they went to but they disappeared right into it. Like when you're going straight into the mountain. Never went up or down." Priscilla recalled climbing to the top of it and looking down into a crater. "Just rock like we'd seen over there at the petroglyphs," she added. I couldn't help but wonder what sort of readings Burke's instruments would pick up at this location.

"This is all cerro do las brujas. Witch mountain," Priscilla said at one point. "Witch mountain?" I said. "Yeah," she replied. "The Catholics and all the Mexicans named it that because of the weird stuff here. Nobody will live up here. No ranchers. Nobody. A lot of land." She pointed in the distance, "There's a camp over there of sheep herders." Then she muttered aloud, "Thirty miles of nothing." As we continued on, we saw exactly what she was talking about.

Priscilla shared so many strange stories about this region that it's hard to know where to begin. Her family knew a Ute Indian who had for years been a sheep herder in the cerro de las Brujas region. This allegedly happened back in the early 1900s. "He had a lot of experience with the black UFOs," Priscilla explained. She recalled one instance where he described seeing like a "dust devil" that emerged from "this weird craft" and this "dust devil" looking thing "took him up" and then "the next thing he knew he was in these people's home. It really was like back East. They were having a big party and there were a lot of white people. There was a lot of green grass. The place looked different than what we [had]. When he moved outside they offered him food. He ate the food and everything. It was something that he thought was the future. Then, all of a sudden, he looked back and there was like a flash and he was back on the prairie, back here. He had been missing for several days and they had been looking for him, but to him he had just been there and gone and come right back."

Priscilla recalled another incident that he had described. "In the part where the volcano mountain is at, that's where they would appear at," she explained. "Another time, there were three flat white disks and he spotted them out there and they disappeared into the volcano mountain, like they went into another dimension, and then the man in black was walking around."

"Around the base? [of the mountain]" I asked.

"Around the whole area that we went to," she said. "He was just walking around after the three white disks went into the mountain."

"Like right inside the mountain like?" I said.

"Yeah," Priscilla stated. "Where they call it Gates to Other Worlds."

"Then the other time it happened to him and it was like he was taken into the past and there was a huge house," she recalled. "This huge house is not there any more. Close to witch mountain. There were a lot of people in a circle praying to the devil, doing devil worship, and this man who was half human and half goat, he said he was the devil, started dancing in the middle of the circle. Then he bent down and asked all of them to kiss his ass. When he got to him he asked God to help him, and he disappeared and all of a sudden he was just back, all dusty and dirty, with the dirt there back around his camp."

Priscilla's grandfather, also a sheep herder, recalled going down to the river to collect some fire wood one night. "This was the early 1900s," she said. "Right there across the river, on the Rio Grande, a big black dog appeared and wouldn't let him cross and the horses were backing up. He took his rifle out, and he always kept it loaded with silver bullets, and he made a cross on it and shot it and when he shot the black dog it turned into an old woman. So he said it was a brujas, a witch turned into a black dog." Priscilla recalled that the Ute Indian sheep herder "had also seen the black dog there after sightings of these weird flying objects."

I asked Priscilla to describe this mysterious "dog" a little more. "It's not a normal size," she said. "It's a huge black dog. Fire comes out of his eyes. Real red eyes. Then he vanishes. It's never been known that he hurts anybody. It's just that he appears and scares people."

Another curious anomaly described in the area are "fireballs" that come "rolling down" from the tops of nearby hills. "They look like they're coming at you and they're going to hit you, and then right before they make it to you they disappear," Priscilla said. "I had a lot of experiences with those energy balls, I call them. The ones that I saw were like red balls of fire. Some of them were white, yellowish - like electricity." In a few instances they apparently struck motor vehicles, but then they'd "just vanish." No sound and no heat, and, Priscilla added, "There was never an explosion."

Then there is the phantom faceless hitchhiker! "I know some ranchers here have seen it," she said, "I know members of my family have seen it. A lot of people have said that it's an old man in raggedy clothes barely walking and they stop to ask him [if he needs] a ride or they'd even honk at him to get off of the road, and then when he turns around his whole face is skeleton."

We also stopped and took pictures of a mound of huge boulders next to the road. People claimed that animal sacrifices to the devil had been performed there. Some even alleged human sacrifices had also been done.

All of this dark and sinister history aside, when we first entered the San Luis Valley, on our way to the UFO conference, Priscilla gave us a little history lesson about the Native American history of the region, which illustrated the area's predominantly positive characteristics. She explained, "The Ute Indians, the Comanches, the Navahos, Apaches, the Pueblo Indians, years before the white man came, would go here to hunt and fish. They had plenty of elk, deer, bear and fish. Nobody fought here. It was called The Bloodless Valley. The Great Creator would not allow any blood shed. It was a place of energy. They could kill animals, but killing human beings was not allowed." The region is surrounded by a majestic mountain range. One of these mountains, Mount Blanca, is considered very sacred to the Indians. "That's where a lot of the Navahos and the Hopis claimed that they emerged from the ground and they were taken care of by the ant people, the little people," Priscilla noted.

Before the conference, we stopped in Alamosa and I got to meet Priscilla's sister Angela. Earlier I had interviewed Priscilla about Angela's haunted home and Priscilla's skinwalker encounter there. Angela told me herself how she too had seen the entity, how she had come home from the hospital and then saw it crawling toward her, it's long black panther like body, but with a head like a man.

"I don't mind talking about skin walkers," Sister Wolf noted. "I have seen them twice in my life. It's just people with amazing powers that have learned the old ways and are more in tune with nature and God's power."

A couple of years earlier she had the encounter her sister had described. "It was August 2006," Priscilla explained. "I was very tired from my road trip from New Mexico. It was around 10 p.m. I had laid down to rest in the master bedroom when I felt something under the bed. It felt like a cat. I looked down and could see nothing. But what I didn't know (was) that something horrible had followed my sister home from her hospital stay that week. She had not told me because she wanted to see what I would pick up from my stay at her home since I could see the dead since I was a small child.

"Must be my imagination, I thought. I'm just tired. I turned toward the east side of the bed facing the wall. There it was again! Rubbing against the bed, yet I could see nothing! I got up and walked toward the front room. 'Steve, Steve,' I said in a low voice, so as not to wake up my sister. 'There's a ghost in the room.' He ignored me. He was too busy watching boxing on TV, and laying on the sofa. So I walked back. I left the bedside lamp on and went back to bed. I took a sleeping pill, so by now I was half awake and half asleep. Suddenly I felt like it was on my bed. I felt this impression on the bed next to me. I jumped out of bed and looked around, even under the bed. Nothing was there!"

"I walked into the front room and woke Steve up and told him about a ghost cat in her room. 'Change beds with me.' 'Okay,' he said.

"No sooner had I laid down to sleep, with the hall light on, and here it comes towards me! I noticed a dark shadow crawling toward me. I felt the presence getting closer and I knew it was evil! I knew right then there was a ghost in her home, something unknown to me in the form of a cat. In a flash it was on the other side of the coffee table, rubbing against it. I could see the body was long and tall as the coffee table. And suddenly it lifted its head to stare at me. It was a black cat about five feet long and had a human face. I knew I was in for a battle of my life! It was evil! I had no protection around me. By protection, I mean a cross or my medicine bag."

"My heart beat faster and hard. I had taken a sleeping pill, so I was tired, and I tried hard to stay awake. I told the Cat Man to go to Hell! And leave here in God's name. It did a horrible noise and vanished. Whatever it was, it was gone that second, but not for long! I was in for a battle, live or die! And it wasn't over. It was here to stay! Or take over someone's body. A soul taker! I fell asleep and no sooner than I did in a dream state, my second world, I was in a dark wooded area. I built a glass cage around me and no sooner I did a bunch of wild dogs attacked and a small brown cat, with such anger and force as it attacked and struck the glass cage, over and over! Seemed like forever a dream attack! First it attacked my body form, then my spirit form, testing my power! The dogs vanished but not the cat. It grew and changed colors to a gray color like a dog of anger, so much hate around it. And finally it broke the cage. I hollered 'MOM! MOM!' and I woke up. I felt a weird fear of the unknown. I got up so shaken by my ordeal and put all the lights on and got my cross and chain and put it around my neck, got my medicine bag and my grandfather's silver cross with the skull on it to protect me from evil. Whatever was in this home was not afraid of the light! It was powerful!"

"I fell back to sleep. Just two hours of good sleep. My sister got up and was shocked. All the lights were on and I was still asleep. I woke up and told her about my experience. She said she knew it was there. It had followed her home from the hospital. She showed me and Steve how it crawled and would move its head. I did a blessing of her home inside and out. She just wanted to know what I would pick up. Sometimes I feel my gift is a blessing and sometimes I feel it's from hell!"

"Next day we visited my father at the Monta Vista Nursing home and we told him about my encounter. He said it was evil! It might have been a brujo, or a Shaman with power who had died at the hospital and he didn't want to die so his spirit changed to a cat. What happened was my sister was leaving the hospital and when she opened the door it followed her home. Due to I am a medicine woman by gift, he wanted my body, or to steal my soul to continue. They do exist."

In New Mexico, Priscilla recently spoke with a real estate lady who "got real scared" when the subject of skinwalkers came up in conversation and admitted that she didn't like talking about them, but that her brother and someone else encountered one together while out riding. "The skinwalker was half man and half wolf," Priscilla recalled. "The faster they went he kept up with the car, looking at them, on the side of the car. It really scared them to death. They were going as fast as 50 and probably a higher speed than that. It's well known about skinwalkers appearing to people on Route 66. That's nothing new."

Incidentally, Priscilla lives just off Route 66.

Do the skinwalkers worry her? She says, "You've got to know how to really protect yourself. If you have the protection of a medicine bag, a silver cross, and you're religious, they can't touch you. They can't take your soul. I'm not going to say I never get scared. My God, it's a miracle I haven't had a heart attack and died right there. Because all of a sudden you see something that's half human and half animal."

Friday evening, the day we had been to the petroglyph site, we had returned and were relaxing and sitting at the dinningroom table. Steve was sitting at the other end, and Priscilla was to my left and Joan to my right. It was approximately 7:25 p.m. when I heard a male voice yell "Brent!" It seemed to be coming from outside, in through a screened window to my left. I looked at the others seated at the table close by, expecting them to comment or chuckle over this, but instead everyone gave me this puzzled look back as to why I was looking at them the way I was. I soon discovered that not one of them had heard what I had heard! I then asked Priscilla if it would be okay if I excused myself for a moment to go get my tape recorder and begin taping some of her stories. She was agreeable to doing that. Soon I returned, at which time Joan and Steve had gone into another room to talk among themselves while I questioned Priscilla about her stories. I also wanted to be prepared in case I was to hear that voice again. I was a little puzzled as to why no one else said that they had heard it. I began asking Priscilla if this sort of thing happened to her. She admitted that she occasionally heard her name called. I asked if it came from any particular side. "I usually hear it from my left side," she explained. "What's weird that's my hard of hearing side." Later, as I was transcribing this tape I came to a part of the conversation, taped that very same evening, where I thought that I had seen a cat run by the table. Priscilla seemed to think it was just one of the house cats, but then she added, "I do have a ghost cat that passes by. No really, honest to God," and then she laughs. Right after that, on the tape, you hear a female sounding voice, quite clearly say, "Brent!" But we kept talking like we didn't hear a thing, oblivious to this voice. So this time the tape recorder heard my name being called and I missed it!

I was 56 years old at the time, and I been to lots of haunted locations and spoken with a lot of psychics, and I had never had (to the best of my recollection) this experience of someone calling my name whom I could not identify. Down through the years, many people have told me about hearing someone call their name, how there's no one there or no apparent source for it, but this never happened to me. Never, that is, until the evening of August 8th, when it happened twice in the same evening (the second time as a possible EVP, Electronic Voice Phenomenon).

New Mexico Petroglyphs

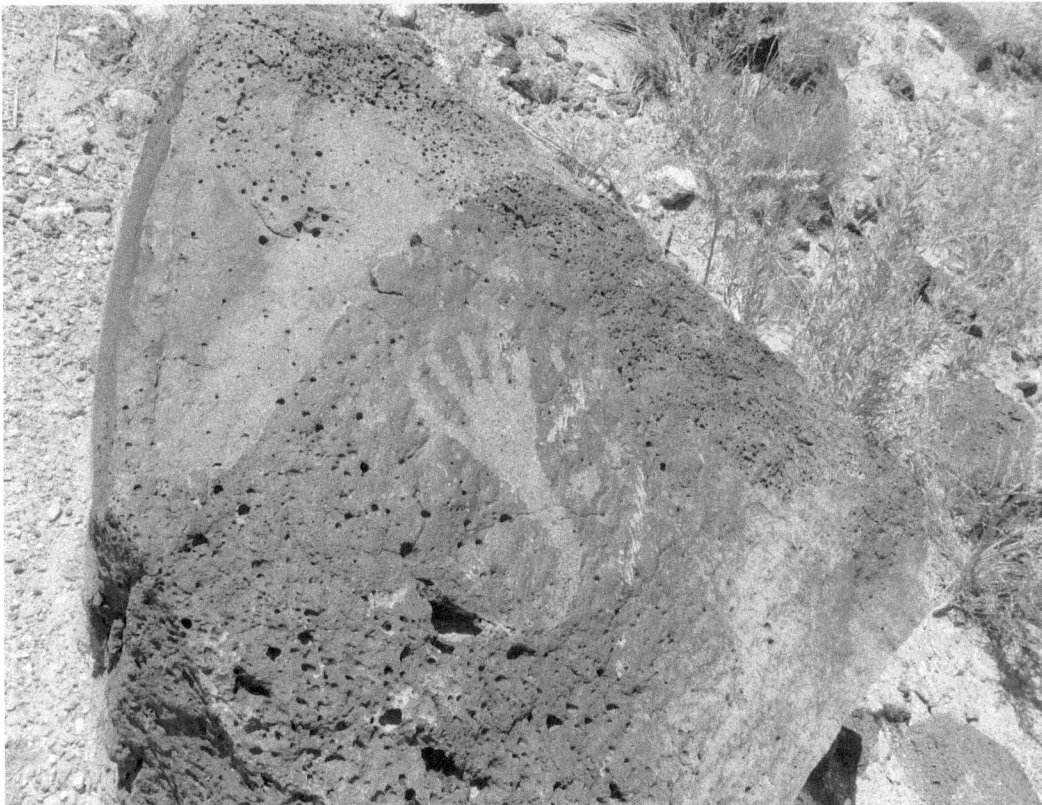

Chapter 2
Medicine Grizzlybear Lake
Saucers, Shamans, and Space-time Déjà vu!

The UFO contactee syndrome is an exceedingly challenging and bewildering mystery. Through the years, its complex psychodynamics have awed and confounded competent researchers of many different backgrounds and from many different countries. Experiencer reports of alien encounters, of strange entities and unidentified flying objects and mysterious landscapes frequently morph from physically plausible sounding extraterrestrial encounter descriptors to full-blown high-strangeness tales embodying all of the rich and colorful mythic and archetypal images and lore common to the religions and shamanic events, manifestations, and miracles of yesteryear. UFO contactees predominantly seem right-brain dominant in their awareness, frequently are talented artists, seem more psychic and intuitive than most, are deeply conscious and concerned about environmental issues, and are often of a strongly spiritual orientation.

I suspect that nothing probably illustrates this complexity and diversity of content and background any better than a survey of cross-cultural comparisons of UFO experiencer descriptions with ancient shamanic lore and accounts.

Back on Friday, December 2nd, 2005, I heard the esteemed Dr. Stanley Krippner tell an audience at a conference gathering of the ARE (Association for Research and Enlightenment) at Virginia Beach, Virginia, that UFO contact stories from shamanic people and cultures around the world was an area of exploration that anthropology had overlooked. The address had occurred in conjunction with a UFO conference occurring at that time (although Dr. Krippner's presentation and the UFO conference itself were technically two separate events). At any rate, I was to deliver a one hour talk the following day that included the word "shaman" in the title. A member of the audience asked Dr. Krippner about shamans and UFOs. As Dr. Krippner is a world renowned authority on the subject, his remarks were particularly illuminating and interesting. He had traveled the world extensively interviewing people of shamanic backgrounds, and often, he said, came across shamans with personal stories of UFO contact encounters. "I've heard many reports of UFOs from shamans over the years," he stated. "Shamans will report experiences themselves, (and) some shamans will say that they've been taken into a UFO, some will say that they have been cooperating with UFOs to help heal people, or have gotten power from UFOs."

Medicine Grizzlybear Lake
Native Healer, Indian Doctor, and UFO Contactee

Bobby Lake-Thom, a traditional Native American healer, known by many as Medicine Grizzlybear Lake, has authored such books as Native Healer (1971), Spirits of the Earth (1998), and Call of the Great Spirit (2001). Half Karuk, and part Seneca and Cherokee, Bobby Lake has apprenticed under a dozen well-known medicine men and women, including Rolling Thunder, Beeman Logan, Mad Bear Anderson, and Calvin Rube, just to name a few. For over twenty years, he has been a professor of Native American Studies at Humboldt State University (CA), Gonzaga University (WA), and Eastern Montana College.

Bobby Lake-Thom had a pretty extraordinary UFO encounter with a déjà vu twist to it. He recalled: "During the late part of winter 1974, I began to have a series of unusual dreams about silver-colored eagles. From out of the void and darkness of the dream state suddenly emerged four eagles. Each eagle came in from a different cardinal point at approximately the same time and correspondingly formed a circular flying pattern. After flying in a circle for a considerable amount of time, they then departed and eventually flew out of sight. I had the same dream on three separate occasions, but on the fourth occasion the content of the dream changed.

There was a dark void, then suddenly a strong humming noise, then the appearance of each eagle as it emerged from the east, the south, the north, and the west. They all flew in a circle but began to change form. In the place of the eagles appeared four silver-colored discs. The four silver discs then merged into one very large silver-colored flying saucer. All of the dreams were accompanied by a tremendous humming sound, and although I was asleep in each situation, I would feel my entire body vibrate to the point that it became unbearable. I would awake from the dreams shaking, exhausted, bewildered, and dizzy."

Bobby Lake-Thom was disturbed by this last dream and began seeking the opinions of others. In February 1975, a Seneca medicine man—who was one of Bobby's earlier teachers— offered an opinion about the dream experience. "The first time I had that dream Beeman Logan came out to visit me and some other Native people on the West Coast to do doctoring ceremonies and stuff," Bobby Lake-Thom recalled in a recent phone conversation with this columnist. "He stayed with me and I was talking to him about the profound dreams that I was having with the eagles changing into flying saucers and I asked him what he thought about it. He said, 'That's what's going to happen to you.' He said, 'You're connected. Those are our ancestors.' I didn't mean to embarrass Beeman but I could not help but to laugh in his face! Being a professor and dealing with UFOs ... yeah, right. I didn't really believe in it. He said, 'Well, you asked my opinion. That's what I'm telling you. That's going to come true. You're going to be contacted by them and probably share a lot of knowledge and information with you,' which they did. At that point he also told me that the Iroquois Six Nations believed that we were brought here from outer space by four ships. We didn't evolve from monkeys. ÉWe were brought here in a golden eagle ship, the hummingbird ship, the turtle ship, and the circular ship."

In March 1975, Beeman Logan's prediction came true. Bobby was living at the time in Trinidad, California. "I started having the dreams again and then I had a strong, compelling feeling to get up out of bed," Bobby told me. "I heard this loud humming noise that was just driving me crazy so I went out into the front room. There was a big picture window. I was on the second level and it was right there, just about level with the big picture window. I said, 'Oh, my God'. It was a big silver colored disc with some lights going around on it, and the next thing I know it zapped me. A big ray of light hit me and I just went right through the window, without breaking the window or anything, right up into the ship."

I began asking Bobby what he had seen onboard the craft. He laughed and said, "For Christmas, I was going to try and get my wife one of those large plasma TV sets. 45 inch or something. It's flat and you can hang it on the wall. I said, 'Look at that! That's exactly what, when I was taken up, the ancient ones, the outer space people, had me sit down in front of and look at, and I was given instructions through."

"They said that wanted me to look at that screen and they showed me the past, the present, and the future," Bobby explained. "They showed me who I was in some of my past lives, and primarily focused on the North American continent. There was some expansion into other areas, but mainly on the North American continent. After they gave me instructions and everything, they said, 'Man does not govern nature. Nature governs man. The first time the world was purified by fire, the second time it was purified by water, and the third time it will be purified by earth itself, and be forewarned of the following signs and omens.'"

Then there following a long series of predictions of future world events, such as rare and unusual diseases, a worsening of natural disasters such as floods, tornadoes, and hurricanes, predictions about assassinations, the eruption of Mount St. Helens, and many other things.

"I kept asking them who they were and finally they revealed themselves to me," Bobby Lake-Thom recalled. At first they had been four "shadowed" figures. Then, Bobby explained, "Finally they revealed themselves to me and they were four different, what appeared to me to be four medicine men from different tribes and parts of Turtle Island."

One did most of the talking and Bobby described him for me, stating: "(He) had dark hair and he had a bear claw necklace on, but he had a silver steak right through the middle of his hair. He had a bear hide slung over his shoulder. I asked them, 'Who are you?' and they said, 'Your four grandfathers. We'll be in communication with you and this is how we communicate.' I said, 'Yeah, but who are you really? Are you spirits or what?' They said, 'We're energy beings. We're your ancestors. We can take whatever form we want. .. If we were going to communicate to a black man or to a white man or to an Asian, we could take on that human form or appearance.'"

"After I had that experience I got really sick, and so I went up there on the side of the mountain, up past the Hoopa Reservation, to see my main teacher, Calvin Rube, because I was really sick. I was weak and I had these burns on the side of my body and I felt like I was losing my mind. I was going crazy. When I drove up the road he was standing outside looking up at the sky and there were a bunch of eagles all over in these trees around his house and he was looking up at the sky. I could see him talking or something, or praying or singing, and then I looked up, just as I pulled up into his yard and I started to get out of my truck. There were four flying saucers right over the top of his house. He said, "Gosh darn it, I should have known it was you. It had to be you. I don't know what you got yourself into, what kind of trouble you got into this time, but I don't think that I can help you." I was crying, I was shaking all over. I jumped out of the truck and ran up to him and grabbed hold of him and was begging and pleading with him if he could help me, and all of that was right there, and he kept trying to turn me down, kept trying to push me away. He said, 'I don't think that I can do anything about this. This is pretty heavy. Those guys have got a hell of a lot of power. I don't think that I can deal with them.' Finally I kind of like followed him into the house and shut the door myself and kept begging and pleading with him that he would doctor me and help me out. Which he finally consented to do, and then I explained the whole story and experience to him and he said, 'You've got to do exactly like what they told you to. You've got to go out there and to get that knowledge and information out there.'"

"He said, 'Sure, you're going to be laughed at and ridiculed and everything else,' which it happened. They fired me from my job, you know. I had a big meeting on campus, at noon time. I came out there, made my prayer, shared that knowledge and experience and at that time a golden eagle flew right in over. Must have been 400 or 500 people there, and this golden eagle came in screaming, and then right behind it, up in the sky, at quite some distance, but not too far away, was a big silver colored disc."

"I shared my message and everything, and of course I got reprimanded for that. It was published in some local newspaper or magazine called <u>Psychic Times</u>. My first wife wanted to leave me and divorce me because she was all embarrassed and everything, and they wanted to fire me from my job. It was a hell of a mess."

"Anyway Calvin doctored me and tried to put protective medicine on me and help me out, and he said they were good people- they were good aliens-good outer space people, and that they were our ancestors and for whatever reason I had been contacted or chosen to share that knowledge and information."

"Some people who originally criticized me and researched and followed up on all of those predictions that I was given ended up coming up with concrete proof, and a lot of people who kind of followed it and kept track of it, came out in later years and made statements like that they felt that it was more accurate than Jeane Dixon or Edgar Cayce or Nostradamus, you know, in terms of the predictions. They did have some criticism about the times that I was shown. But hey, I don't know what to say about that. I just tell them, 'Hey. It's not me. I'm not like some kind of doomsday prophet or anything like that. This is what the outer space people showed me. They deserve the credit.' So the credit has got to go there."

"Okay, one of the things on the UFO predictions was that there would be a major earthquake. -The moon would turn red with blood- and right after that there would be like a major earthquake and thousands and thousands of native people would be killed, in a major earthquake. That came true. I called up Archie Fire Lame Deer who was living down in Santa Barbara at that time, and I told him that my ex-wife Tela and I were standing out in our backyard doing a prayer ceremony and all of a sudden a great big golden mother ship (our place overlooked the Pacific ocean), right there at Trinidad, and all of a sudden this great big ship just broke through, appeared suddenly in the sky, lit up the whole damned night sky, and there were four other ships that came through behind it, and it was going real slow heading down south. Both of us were so scared that we were literally shaking. We could hardly stand up. So I tried to communicate with them and they said, 'We're going down to Mexico. We're going way down south to Mexico because there is going to be bad earthquakes going [on] down in that direction.' Going down into Southern California and then down into Mexico, so I got on the phone. -It was late at night, and I was-talking to Archie about it and he really didn't believe in them too much. He kind of laughed at me and everything a little bit and he said, 'Well, thanks for the warning. I'll talk to my spirits and make sure that we're protected here in this area.' Because I didn't know if it was going to hit his area, Santa Barbara area and then hit LA and then Mexico or what, but that's the direction the ships were going."

"Anyway, to make a long story short the next day, it was on the news, that they had the worst earthquake that ever hit Mexico City and hundreds and thousands of people were killed. Well, they were mostly native people. Mexicans down there are really more native than they are Hispanic. And there were a lot of UFO sightings up in the sky around that time also. Now what were those ships doing down there? Were they going down there to- this is the question that I posed to myself. They even had videos. So my question is what the hell are they doing down there? So I had to sit down and talk and have a discussion with my own outer space people and what they told me is that they were gathering the souls of all of those people who had been killed. Harvesting. Now I don't know if it was in a good way or a bad way. I don't know if they were gathering these souls to prepare them for like reincarnation to come back sometime in the future into other human bodies or if it was bad outer space people who were gathering them to prepare to put them into clones or androids. I kind of sense and feel, because of the description of the ship and what we saw, that these were the good guys. And I think that it had something to do with all of those ancient Mayan temples that are down in that area."

As Bobby had been trained as a traditional Native Healer and an Indian Doctor, I was interested to learn how these skills might be used or come into play in another otherworldly context like the UFO visitor presence, and how he might discern and handle the positive and negative elements of such encounter situations.

Back in the mid-1980s, there reportedly was a sudden wave of UFO activity on a certain California Indian Reservation. Witnesses described seeing a 40 foot silver disc with blue lights in the area for over an hour, flying at a mere 50 feet or so over the ground. The wave of sightings lasted for about two weeks. Right after this activity there were a lot of mysterious deaths among the elderly Indian people there (i.e., strange car accidents, suicides, and murders). Bobby was asked to do some praying in the area and the Indian population there had also brought in a well-known elderly Wintun Indian Doctor.

Bobby thinks that the disc-shaped craft "came in for protection," although he says there were other ships that were up to no good. "My wife and I were even under attack by those guys when we lived in Trinidad," he explained. He said they were beings "short in stature" and attired in monk-like outfits— "a black robe with a hood." "I could see it in my head," Bobby noted. "I could see them in their ships when they were coming and trying to attack us. So my ex-wife and I had to do a prayer ceremony. We were crying out to the Creator and to the earth powers."

Deep and Ancient Spiritual Truths

"We have a mind and we have a body," Bobby Lake-Thom explained. "This is the way that I have been taught and this is the way that I have learned both from the high spiritual medicine people that taught me and trained me, and also confirmed through my own experiences of doctoring other people. Even re-affirmed in communication with Outer Space People. Okay, we have a mind, we have a body, and we have a soul. What holds all of this together is spirit. It gets kind of confusing because a lot of people in Western Society use the word spirit and soul interchangeably. They'll even use the word spirit in relation to ghosts, things like that."

"This is real high, ancient esoteric knowledge that I'm sharing with you now. For the average person they could just consider it theoretical or philosophical, but consider the analogy of a person who was in a bad car accident and they're in the hospital. The western doctor says they're in a coma. What does that mean? Typically they'll say they're brain dead. They're being kept alive by their life support system."

"Now why is it their soul isn't in their body?" Bobby asks in a rhetorical way. He explains that the traumatic "impact of being in a car accident" essentially "could have knocked their soul out of their body." He adds, "There are certain bad spirits like shadows and demons, demonic forces if you want to call them that, that will try to capture these souls and devour them. So if that happens, and it doesn't always happen, but if that happens that person will never come back to life. They never will come back out of the coma. The only way to bring that person to a better situation, as my ex-wife Tela has, and I have too, (we've) been in situations where we doctored people. For example, I had to sit down and pray and go into a trance and travel with my wolves, because they're good hunters, or with the Ravens, and go and find that person's soul and try and defend and protect them and talk them into trusting me to bring them back to the hospital and put their soul back into the body."

Indian Doctoring, Ghosts, and the Importance of Ceremonies

"I've been doctoring a lot of people over the years who are getting hurt and sick and having accidents, sickness and problems, deaths in the family, diseases. All kinds of stuff, and sometimes I know before they come to me what's causing them to be sick. Sometimes I don't. Sometimes I don't know until I get right into actually doing the ceremony on them, whether it's right here in my house or at their house, in a sweat lodge or somewhere in nature, or whether I doctor them long distance. A lot of people have been getting sick, hurt, and tormented because they're being tormented by ghosts."

Bobby recalled a specific instance involving a college student. "He came to me to be doctored," Bobby explained. "He was a Sioux Indian." Bobby had been experiencing diagnostic type dreams or premonitions about the patient for three days prior. Even while he was preoccupied with teaching college classes, his spirits kept coming in and reporting certain information to Bobby about this patient. "When I first started doctoring him it showed up very clearly. I could see it just like I was right there. He was all drunked up and in his car and he ran over this elderly white woman. She was the one that was tormenting the heck out of him. Now Western psychiatrists or psychologists could say that was his conscience, his guilt about it. Well, that's true, but he was feeling guilt about it and being tormented because her ghost was tormenting him. The only way that he could get well was that he had to do what we call pe-gas-soy. He had to identify what might be the cause or causes of his sickness or problem and he had to confess to it, and then we had to blow that off of him and then I had to make him redeem himself with that particular person, or the Creator or spirits, and use my spirits to send her over to the spirit world."

"I don't like to bad mouth other people's religion but I'm sick and tired of cleaning up after the priests, the preachers, the ministers and the rabbis. They're going through the mechanisms of ceremony but they're not sending these people over. A long time ago, when we came onto the earth plane, we came in with spirit guides and protectors. At least one and sometimes even two. But something happened over a period of time historically as human beings became more civilized, and especially with the impact of Christianity and not doing the child birth ceremony properly to prepare for that, plus the acceptance of bringing the spirit guides over, not doing the burial ceremony properly, and knocking out the vision quest. It makes all of these people vulnerable."

"A lot of sicknesses are caused because these ghosts are going around tormenting some people, natives included. I probably doctor more white people than I do natives. I doctor black people, Hispanic people, and mixed bloods too. But many have a real hard time relating to this and understanding this because of being brought up with Christian values or Christian teachings that don't address all of these things."

"I gained the knowledge and experience because four times in my life I have been pronounced clinically dead. I have literally died four times in my life and gone over to the spirit world and was brought back to life and from that I got the knowledge and experience of how to doctor other people, to soul travel, and the connection with certain high spirits who are qualified to perform that kind of activity."

"If the reader is having a difficult time understanding this type of phenomena, in regards to ghosts tormenting certain human beings," Bobby explained, "I would suggest that they check out this new television program that deals with such issues. It is called "Paranormal States" and is found on the A&E Channel. The program's approach uses both scientific and psychic methods."

Speaking of the importance of ancient spirit ceremonies, one of my first meetings with a Native American medicine man was a Susquehannock gentleman from Pennsylvania, back in 1976. He had described to me what he called a "spirit name ceremonial" wherein his people would receive the name from spirit of an expectant mother's child. He stated that upon discovering that a woman of his clan was pregnant that every full moon the men would hold a ceremony until a spirit name was given. "We ask the Great Spirit to send an angel with name that this baby be born," he explained. As an example, he recalled for me how his son, living in

Washington, D.C., had called and announced that his wife was pregnant. So my friend began conducting the ceremonies, but was getting worried as the full moons were passing and no messenger had brought them a name, and it was a tradition with his people that if no name was given then the baby would die. The last full moon arrived in the month of March. The child was expected in April. "Spirit came in the form of a huge white turtle," my friend Lightfoot stated. "Pure white light. It came up to the fire, stood on its hind legs and then it talked. You see, they're high spirits and they come in those forms. You remember you read in the Bible about that fella's ass that talked to him? Well anyway, it said, 'The child will be a boy and you shall call him Flying Eagle.' I said 'Thank you,' and then it was gone. Two or three days after that date our son called and said "We have a baby boy." The same thing happened with our granddaughter. I held spirit ceremony except it came about six months before birth, and this time it came in the form of a little girl messenger. She said, 'Child is going to be a little girl and it will be born on the second day of April and she shall be called Little Fawn with the Heart of Love.'"

This Pennsylvania medicine man was also a UFO contactee! He described to me how tall humanoid beings had actually entered his home after a UFO landed in his backyard. He called the beings "Yuh-dush-gwa," the ancient "protectors" of his people. He told me that when he was only four years old he was instructed in the construction of a "prayer mound," which he explained was in the shape of a tortoise.

It's not everyday that you get to meet a mound builder! "I pray on mounds and commune with the Great Spirit and the Spirit of Mother Earth," he revealed to me. "Sometimes with sisters and brothers from the Sky Garden. We can communicate with powers, forces, spirits and elementals, even the spirits of trees, vegetation, stones, waters, storms, etc. Often they manifest to us in physical form. Sometimes only a voice."

Early on in Bobby's training, he learned the importance of paying attention to and working with his dreams. He had been having stomach problems and went to a medicine man for help. Suddenly in the middle of a doctoring ceremony, the elderly native healer stopped and questioned Bobby about a dream he had had of a man with a fishing harpoon who was trying to stab him in the stomach. Bobby was surprised, had honestly forgotten that indeed he had had such a dream. The healer reprimanded him about not paying sufficient attention to his dreams. He pointed out that the dream meant an act of sorcery was being directed against him. The healer told Bobby that he could learn to be aware of such dreams and to slow them down and remove potentially harmful objects. This incident is described in his book Native Healer. "That takes a lot of skill," Bobby explained, and then laughed. "I imagine" I replied.

The Sacred ET Stone of Rolling Thunder?

The noted medicine man Rolling Thunder, of Cherokee ancestry, was one of Bobby's spiritual teachers. They had become very close. In fact, Bobby claimed that back in 1984 Rolling Thunder had called him and wanted him to come to his home in Nevada. His health was very bad at the time and he wanted Bobby to doctor him. Bobby recalled that it was very difficult and that he worked on Rolling Thunder day and night. He also doctored some others, including a son of Rolling Thunder who had been injured in an auto accident. Bobby also constructed a sacred sweat lodge and performed a number of purification ceremonies during his visit. One sunset he watched in awe as a "very large silver-colored disk" flew within approximately a mile distance and hovered for about 15 minutes. At least four others saw it. As it turned out, everyone he worked on described being healed.

I had recalled reading once something to the effect that Rolling Thunder may have had a UFO contact experience, so I asked Bobby if he had shared any detailed with him. "I asked him about that and I don't know if it was because he was too busy at the time or what, but he didn't open up and share much about that with me," Bobby said. "He did tell me that he did have some kind of great big ancient artifact on his property that he got from the Cherokee in North Carolina and it had these strange designs and symbols on it. It was pretty much kind of shaped like an ancient Mayan calendar. Kind of like that. It did have like different kinds of ships on it, circular and hummingbird and turtle. Things like that, and some kind of language."

"You got to see that yourself?" I asked. "Yes, he showed it to me," Bobby replied. "He had it on his property and he said that sometime in the future that if he ever died or whatever he was going to will that down to me. He said that was directly connected to the Outer Space People, our ancestors. He said it was like some kind of historical recording of a migration here, to this earth."

"I guess it was like a circular tablet?" I next asked. "Yes, it was somewhere between 2 to 3 feet in diameter," he continued. "I drew the analogy of it looking like a Mayan calendar because that's what it kind of looked like. But it wasn't a Mayan calendar."

I then inquired as to what had ever happened to the stone and had pictures ever been taken of it? "He wouldn't let anybody do that," Bobby replied. "I went back in later years. I guess it was about ten years ago, after he died. Tried to go over there and make contact with his ex-wife, to see if I could get that object. But she wouldn't let me." At first "she acted like she didn't know anything about it," Bobby added.

I recently learned from one of my Native American contacts out in Oklahoma, who also knew Rolling Thunder quite well, that he knew about this stone too, but so far he hasn't elaborated on anything more than that acknowledgement.

Medicine Grizzlybear Lake's website can be found at:
http://www.nativehealer.net/Healer 2005/about.html.

Chapter 3
Dr. William K. Kikuchi
Kahuna Sorcery and the Akualele

In a book entitled *Kahuna Power*, which noted UFO and paranormal author and researcher Tim Beckley kindly allowed me to read in advance of its publication, he wrote of some very unusual apparitional appearances that he stated were attributed to the mysterious *akualele*. He wrote:

"In my travels through the Big Island and other Hawaiian areas, I was struck by the number of witnesses who have seen the akualele, or 'flying ghosts.' Most of the people I questioned said that they had seen these apparitions at least once, (and) that often these akualele appear as a huge red-eyed ghost dog. The flying ghosts appear as fire. Many Hawaiians carefully avoid going into areas where the ghosts have been seen. One writer by the name of J.K. Mokumai reported on a strange fireball sighting occurring in the Mauna Loa area on the Island of Oahu. He stated:

"'It was customary that when a company of people passed time away on the Ewa side of Mauna Loa, facing the edge of that hill, at eventide, a fire would be seen crawling on the edge of the cliff and drop down on that hill. It was a rocket. Your writer had seen it himself, and being too young to know better, we children shouted aloud, 'Oh, see the fire with a head in front of it and a long tail!' We children liked it, we older ones, and we were always eager to see this flying object. We questioned each other about this flying fire. We used to form a group to watch it. For two or three nights there was no sign of it, and on the fifth night every one of the boys that came, including the writer, saw its head and eyes. It was as red as fire and frightful. We screamed aloud in fear and later learned the truth. It was fed and was tame. It took the form of a man and went up there to look for food.'

"A caretaker at one of the active volcanoes states that in one of the caves along the cliffs lives an akualele and that every so often it comes out and flies about. On one occasion, a young girl with a group of people in a car was asked to chant in the area. She did so, and while she was chanting a bright ball of fire appeared and approached the car. The occupants were so frightful that they sped away—with the ball of fire flying next to them. Eventually it veered off and returned to the cave."

All of these kinds of things have potential parallels from other cultures in other parts of the world. Dr. Lyn Halper, a psychotherapist from New York, once recalled for me: "My friend and interviewee, Heshheru, a Jamaican shaman, tells me that

Jamaica vibrates with paranormal phenomena. He describes a rolling calf with glowing red eyes seen for decades by islanders that is always accompanied by a noxious odor like burning chemicals or electrical wiring." Some years back, I corresponded briefly with a ufologist over in Sweden named Hakan Blomqvist. He described one case that he had investigated wherein a Swedish couple saw "several small humanoids floating around their car. The creatures had big, hypnotic red eyes."

Back in the 19th century, at Tring, Hartford, in England, a huge spectral black dog with "eyes like balls of fire" was frequently reported. Michael Craft, in his book, *Alien Impact*, recalled a personal experience with a "huge black dog" with "burning red eyes" at a haunted house in Towson, Maryland, back in 1976.

Cherokee priests used quartz crystals to glimpse into the future. The most powerful crystal of all, called a Ulunsuti, was located on the forehead of a serpentine beast known as the Uktena. It had the appearance of a blazing diamond and could only be obtained by slaying the beast, which was a very dangerous thing to do. However, once obtained there were certain strict rules to be observed. Otherwise, it might kill its keeper! There was a description of how one of these crystals was wrapped in a whole deerskin and placed in an earthen jar and hidden in a cave in the mountains. Every seven days the blood of a small animal had to be smeared over the crystal. Twice a year the blood of a deer or some other large animal had to be smeared on it. Should one neglect or forget to perform this task, the story goes that the crystal will emerge from the cave some night in the form of a fiery manifestation, seeking out the owner or a family member to quench its thirst for blood.

In Cherokee tradition, witches were believed to have the ability to transform themselves, frequently seen as a "purplish ball of fire," or a wolf, raven, cat, or an owl. A witch was often called "owl," "raven-mocker," and "night-walker," while among the Chippewa they were called Bearwalker or Mock-wa-mosa. Practitioners reportedly were shape-shifters, often appearing as bears and owls. Balls of light and lapses into unconsciousness were also associated with their appearances.

Though on the surface of things this mysterious fireball fits the UFO MO, Hawaiian researcher Kalani Hanohano was able to identify the *akualele* as a "*supernaturally generated light phenomenon produced by Kahuna sorcery*." He furthermore wrote of how back in the 1960s, there had even been a UFO organization in Hawaii called the *Akualele Research Group*, but that when you really dig deeply into these strange stories and the local history behind them then some startling facts emerge that identify them as a specific phenomenon directly connected with *psychic*, or *supernatural forces* if you will, and again it's tied in with "*Kahuna sorcery*"! Therefore, though intriguingly similar to the UFO phenomenon, significant distinctions can be made as well.

Timothy Green Beckley was, years ago, a stringer for the <u>National Enquirer</u> and so met many celebrities. Often he'd throw in a question or two about personal beliefs or experiences involving UFOs or the paranormal. In an interview with actor and comedian Arte Johnson, formerly of TV's *Laugh In*, Mr. Beckley learned of Johnson's own "akualete" sightings during his and his wife's visits to the Hawaiian islands over the years, during which time they had made friends with some of the Kahunas who took them into their confidence regarding various core aspects of their beliefs.

In their interview, Arte Johnson told Beckley: "There's a place on the Big Island where you can see lights which the local natives believe to be the spirits of unworthy souls, those who have not found their way into the equivalent of the Hawaiian heaven. We've seen that many times. They're fireballs in the distance, and they travel from right to left over the harbor at Kona. They travel the same path all the time. The natives claim that in order to keep them away, you must swear at them. Well, since we started seeing them, we've learned to swear a lot."

"Personally, I have no idea what they could be. The only airport in the area closes at sundown, so those lights don't come from it, and we have seen these things at one and two in the morning. There certainly remains a big question in my mind. Until I find an answer, I have to think that maybe the natives are right, and that we are actually seeing ghostly apparitions. That's as good an explanation as any. Before going to Hawaii, I never thought to believe in anything along these lines, but I've since found that many of the Hawaiians' so-called superstitions have a basis in reality. For me, they've borne fruit!"

About a decade after meeting Arte Johnson, Beckley and a colleague named Maria Carta, a well-known psychic, flew to Hawaii in 1986 to personally investigate the "akualele" and other mysteries of the islands. In *Our Alien Planet: This Eerie Earth* (2005), Beckley recalled: "Early in the trip, we hooked up with Kalani Hanohano, one of the most knowledgeable experts on the folklore of the islands whose now defunct journal *Full Moon* was read by scholars and laymen all over the world. Kalani amassed a huge file of anecdotal material pertaining to the akualete, which often appear at night, taking on the form of fireballs shooting across the sky and then evaporating or exploding in midair, breaking up into small flames, each moving and withering on their own, indicating that these puffs of light are animate objects."

"Fireball witnesses are apparently plentiful," Tim Beckley wrote. "I had no trouble finding people who had seen them. One young man told me that while he was driving down Old Pali Road on Oahu a fireball passed slowly in front of his car. The engine died. But as soon as the fireball left, the engine kicked into life again.

"In another case, two men were driving along the same Old Pali Road when a fireball appeared. The driver stopped the car, got out and started to swear. The fireball broke up into small balls. The driver told me that those flaming fragments become little mythical men called *e'epa*—elemental beings no doubt!

"A 17-year-old female once saw a fireball hovering above her head at about fifty feet. It spun in flight and then crashed to the ground. A man and his wife spotted a huge luminous blue fireball that fell almost at their feet. When the wife tried to touch it, it reared up and flew away."

A good deal of the material used in Tim's book was supplied by Kalani Hanohano. Kalani also supplied me with additional answers to my own questions. Kalani, a Hawaiian himself, has researched these stories in great depth and detail. I asked him to share with us how he came about researching the akualele phenomena and what he learned. Below is a summary of key points that he provided:

What does Akualele mean?

Simply translated from the Hawaiian, *akualele* means "flying god." Akua = god; lele = to fly.

When did I become aware of this phenomenon?

When I was a young child growing up in Hawaii the most prominent parental and cultural dictate was that a child "should be seen and not heard." Knowing fully what this meant, I made sure that I quietly sat at the feet of my elders so that I could listen intently while they discussed the many strange experiences of friends and family. Among the many tales that were told were those of the Hawaiian ghost marchers, menehune sightings, kahuna practitioners, phantom hitchhikers and the hidden art of the hula and lua (Hawaiian martial arts). It was during one of these many family discussion sessions that I learned about the *akualele*. Like most children of a certain age, stories of the supernatural energized me.

During my early teen years (60s) my father introduced me to *Fate* magazine. Shortly afterward I discovered at our downtown Honolulu newsstand Ray Palmers two publications, *Flying Saucers Magazine* and *Search Magazine.*

Discovering that there were groups "out there" dedicated to solving the ufo and other paranormal mysteries galvanized me, and I began- by small steps- to formalize my borderline interests. Files were built, newsclippings clipped and my personal correspondence to pen pals increased. The *NICAP* and *APRO Bulletins* became close companions, while I yearned to save enough money to subscribe to Britain's *Flying Saucer Review.*

It was during this formative period- the early 1960s- that I became aware of Riley Crabb. He had at one time directed a local Hawaii ufo organization that he called the Akualele Research Group. When I discovered him (via a local radio station interview), he had already taken over the directorship of Meade Layne's Borderland Sciences Research Associates (California).

Although I listened to a few Hawaii radio talk show interviews with him, I never met Riley Crabb. Nor have I ever been able to obtain copies of his old *Akualele Research Group Newsletter.*

But one thing struck me immediately and changed the way that I dealt with the ufo topic: I knew from my own personal research that the akualele was a supernaturally generated light phenomenon produced by Kahuna sorcery. It was not a visiting craft from elsewhere in the universe as was so commonly believed in the 1950s and 60s.

While I certainly appreciated what Riley Crabb was doing by suggesting that the *akualele* was also a stand-in Hawaiian term for ufos, I felt strongly that this was greatly misleading. I developed the need to make a clarification of this discrepancy. The opportunity to do this would not rear its head until the early 1980s, when I left Seattle to return to Hawaii. Within 6 months of returning home I began the production of "*FULL MOON*: A Report From The Islands".

What is an akualele?

The akualele are devices manufactured by Kahuna sorcery whose main function is to harm or kill another human being.

Research during the 1980s

I returned to Hawaii in late 1979 after having lived for 11 years in Seattle. During my period of residence in Seattle I had the great fortune to work very closely with Bob Gribble, former fireman turned ufo investigator. Bob Gribble established one of the very first ufo organizations in the United States during the 1950s. This was before either NICAP or APRO came into the picture. A small group of Seattlites interested in the ufo mystery began to meet at Bob's home. The result was the formation of an organization that Bob called Phenomena Research. About a year or so later, just in time for the 1973 ufo flap that clobbered the USA, the National UFO Reporting Center was set up. We were then receiving clippings from 3 sources: Rod Dyke of the UFO Newsclipping Service; the late Gilbert Bernier, a lone ufologist who subscribed to a press clipping service; and Bob Gribble, who was then subscribing to Allen's Press Clipping Service. Today, the National UFO Reporting Center is owned and run by Peter Davenport.

As Bob Gribble's assistant, I spent many, many hours, one-on-one, discussing many aspects of the ufo phenomenon. Discussions with other members of the group, particularly Aileen Garoutte, who has known Bob Gribble for much longer than I, transformed my relationship to the ufo topic. It forced me to be far more critical of the data that I was ingesting on a daily basis, and proved to me with certainty the necessity of establishing a more functional data-base of worldwise ufo sightings.

When I returned to Hawaii in 1979, I brought with me a good deal of ufo knowledge acquired through my association with the National UFO Reporting Center.

My formal research on the *akualele* began almost immediately after my return to the islands. And then, all of a sudden, something extraordinary happened. Let me tell you about it.

In 1980, I was on the hunt for akualele information. Over the years I've developed a proficiency for library research, but my search for scholarship on the *akualele* topic was heading nowhere fast.

One beautiful afternoon- one of many in the islands- I drove to the Bishop Museum. I asked the ticket taker if she would let me in free as I wanted to see the museum's book store. What happened next is absolutely true! I will swear it with my hands on the Bible, or a used copy of George Adamski's *"Flying Saucers Have Landed."*

On entering the book store, I looked around and unconsciously reached out to a paperbound book on the shelf. I did not grasp it correctly and it fell to the floor. I could see that the book had opened to reveal an article. I bent down to pick up the book and was shocked to the core to read the following:

"The Fireball In Hawaiian Folklore"
By William K. Kikuchi
University of Arizona, Tucson

Thus began my formal and intense inquiry into the subject of this article. A gift from the gods of synchronicity. And it happened exactly as I have described it.

Dr. Kikuchi's article became the centrepiece of the first issue of my newsletter, *"Full Moon."* I received permission directly from Dr. Kikuchi to reprint his article. The response to the first issue was wonderful, particularly since some of it came from those in the anthropological and transpersonal psychology fields. I also received a great response from Bob Rickard (Fortean Times) and other British readers.

The next phase of my research began when I was introduced to, and was befriended by, the late June Gutmanis, herself an author of several books on kahuna healing and ancient Hawaiian prayers. She was aware that I worked at two jobs: one as an editor for several Hawaii magazines, and the second as an on-air technician and video editor at Hawaii's Oceanic Cablevision. She noticed that I needed to get out of the city to write and collect my thoughts so she offered me her Waianae home (located in the country area of Oahu) for weekend stayovers. I seized the opportunity and accepted her offer.

June Gutmanis was 72 when she died in the late 1990s. She was a noted historian who lectured to university students. She authored 4 books on Hawaiian themes. She had also authored several articles for National Geographic and Readers Digest. She was also a consultant on the movie "Hawaii."

June Gutmanis was born in Pawnee County, Nebraska. She was a pilot during WWII and worked alongside military meteorologists.

June had no formal college degree. Just a passion for things Hawaiian. She was a caucasion woman who had found her way home to Hawaii.

June Gutmanis was a treasure trove of information about Hawaii. And if she did not know something, she knew who did.

June was the caretaker to the late Mr. Theodore Kelsey. He was also a non-Hawaiian who had a lot of knowledge of the old Hawaiian ways.

And he spoke the Hawaiian language fluently.

June would provide care to the very aged Theodore Kelsey, and in return, Mr. Kelsey would translate Hawaiian documents or newspaper articles that would come into her possession.

In 1981, June introduced me to a remarkably interesting man by the name of Arthur Cathcart. In a series of meetings held on the lawn of the Iolani Palace in Honolulu, and at June's residence in Waianae, Arthur talked about the Hawaii of yesteryear, of ghosts, and of his personal knowledge of the *akualele*.

As I have written in a past issue of *Full Moon*, such personal testimony regarding a persons direct experience with Hawaiian sorcery rarely surfaces. Arthur's testimony of witnessing the actual processes of *akualele* arousal is a rare gem, almost impossible to find in popular literature.

Arthur Cathcart's testimony was turned into a lengthy article for the April 1982 issue of *Full Moon*. The title of that article was: *"Flying Lights: Concerning the ritual generation of a luminous phenomenon."*

What are akualele ?
The research of Dr. William K. Kikuchi

Dr. Kikuchi's ground-breaking research on *akualele*, *"The Fireball In Hawaiian Folklore"*, was published in 1976 in the book "Directions In Pacific Traditional Literature." (Bishop Museum Press).

Dr. Kikuchi's paper was aided and encouraged by the late Dr. James E. McDonald, University of Arizona. Most ufo researchers know who Dr. McDonald was and are acutely aware of his many contributions to the ufo field.

If memory serves, Dr. Kikuchi was also a student of the late anthropologist Dr. Katherine Luomala, who taught at the University of Hawaii. She was widely known for her work on Hawaiian folklore, so Dr. Kikuchi's paper uses analysis that derives from that discipline.

In his study, Dr. Kikuchi acknowledges that the fireball motif is present throughout the Pacific region: from New Zealand to Hawaii. He notes that the stories of the akualele and other tales of the supernatural were used to "instruct the listener" and to "educate in a subtle manner and instill a respect for right and wrong in selected areas of behaviour."

Social control, if you will.

Pre-european Hawaii was "stratified, integrated and cohesive." In other words, rigid and under control. The ancient Hawaiian Kapu system (a system of laws that forbade the people from doing certain things- under penalty of death) was overthrown by King Liholiho in 1819. This was done in order to undermine the supernatural foundations of Hawaiian society.

Asiatics streamed into the islands beginning in the 1800s, and the Japanese brought with them their own tales of the supernatural, including stories about the *tama-shii* (ball wind) and the *hinotama* fireball.

Dr. Kikuchi acknowledges that the akualele is derived from sorcery and quotes author Martha Beckwith:

"Sorcery had become one of the strongest forces in shaping the life and character of the Hawaiian people and in determining the careers of their leaders."

Dr. Kikuchi mentions two kinds of akualele sorcery:

The first occurred sometime during Hawaii's ancient past and the incident remains undated (although it has been discussed by Hawaii historians). According to Hawaiian tradition, on the Hawaiian island of Molokai, three "gods" nd here Kikuchi lists their names entered into a grove of previously harmless trees on the slope of Moanalua. A place with the specific name of Puuahaukina. Tradition states that their entry into this grove of trees occurred "with a horrendous flash of lighting."

The trees comprising this grove were the *nioi*, *'ohe*, *a'e* and possibly the *kauila*.

These trees become infected with a strange power. Contact with the wood resulted in death. Being hit by a chipf of wood from these trees while attempting to cut them down resulted in death.

A way was finally found to shape this poisonous wood into an image. This image was called *Kalai-pahoa*. Wood from the *nioi* tree, or images carved from the *nioi* tree were brought into contact with the *Kalai-pahoa* image and energy was transmitted from that image to the *nioi* wood.

This was the beginning of *Kalai-pahoa* fireball sorcery and it was apparently very prevalent during the reign of King Kamehameha I, around 1812.

Dr. Kikuch gives us a good description of *Kalai-pahoa* fireball generation, which was probably provided by Hawaiian historian Samuel M. Kamakau:

"*Akualele* were described as resembling 'fire rockets,' travelling great distances. When it was within the wood, the god-spirit was content. However, when (the wood was) scratched by its keeper, it would fly out, pulsating as though throbbing in anger at being hurt."

Another variation on *akualele* utilized *Kalai-pahoa mana* (probably chips of that wood) kept in a bundle. This was referred to as *akua-kumu-haka* sorcery.

Dr. Kikuchi posits five identifiable beliefs about the akualele:

1. Fireballs are sent by someone human.

2. Fireballs can be stopped by swearing.

3. Fireballs fly leaving sparks.

4. Fireballs vary in color from red, orange and white to blue.

5. Fireballs are omens.

Indeed they are omens. They are omens of someone's impending death.

Dr. Kikuchi summarizes his research on akualele as follows:

The *akualele* "is generally described as an elongated ball which in flight resembles a tadpole with a long tail leaving sparks as it flies. This is called the *pu-ali* shape. Its flight seems to be directional at above tree level, but at times haphazard at lower levels. Because of their color range, these *akualele* can be identified as to the sex of the captured spirit. Red was said to signify male, whereas all lighter shades, from yellow to blue, signified the female . . . The spirit manifests itself as a blazing, pulsating fireball, and, as it pulsates, it reaches some optimum size in its flight. The fireball can be stopped in flight and destroyed simply by searing at it. Its destruction always starts with a brilliant explosion which does not harm people standing nearby; neither does it cause secondary fires. Upon explosion, each piece moves about on the ground; and these according to one informant, are the *'e'epa* people, who scamper about to do their missions of mischief."

The Akualele according to Arthur Cathcart

As I have previously recounted, I was first introduced to Mr. Cathcart through authoress June Gutmanis. He travelled a good distance on the bus to keep his many appointments with us. He was never late. He never complained. I found him to be a truthful man, a man of enormous integrity.

Arthur Cathcart ". . . a Hawaiian-haole, was born in the palama area of Honolulu in 1903. His father was English, vice-president of Wilder Steamship Company. His Hawaiian grandparents had been invited to King Kalakaua's coronation. They took Arthur to Moloka`I at the age of four to cure a serious illness with Hawaiian medicine. After his return to Honolulu at the age of eight for schooling, he continued to spend holidays with his grandparents on Moloka`I where le learned much about his Hawaiian cultural heritage and customs.

"He attended a Catholic Seminary for approximately two years. After he dropped out, he went to work as a dance instructor and steward for Matson Line. Before he was 20, he went to Hollywood with Charlie King's music group, where performances of plays about the monarchy were put on.

"He returned to Honolulu, worked as a Hawaiian Pineapple Company security guard for 25 years until his retirement.

"Arthur attended both Prince Kuhio's and Queen Liliuokalani's funerals. He never married, and has always taken an active interest in preserving his Hawaiian cultural heritage."

Many of Hawaii's kahuna's were trained on the island of Moloka'i. Many Hawaiians were not too keen about being around these sorcerers. Arthur Cathcart told me a rather telling tale which summarizes the attitude of the common Hawaiian to these dabblers of darkness. He told me that very often, when a kahuna sorcerer completed training, he would move to a neighbordhood of his choice on one of the islands. When this happened, it would not be an unusual scene to see residents of that area pack up their belongings and move out. Such was their fear of living next to these artisans of the darkside.

My interview with Mr. Cathcart appeared in my April 19832 issue of *Full Moon*. I did not include everything he disclosed to me. There were things that were discussed, specifically about spirit capture, that stunned me.

Certain *kahunas* knew how to capture and enslave spirits (*unihipili*). These spirits were captured and placed inside ti-leaf bundles that we call *pu´olo*. I asked Arthur many questions about this. Any witnesses?

Yes, there are those who have witnessed the process. Arthur was one of them. And he described to both June Gutmanis and I how it was done. And when Arthur completed his narrative, I sat back , and after all these years, I still remember my response:

"Oh . . . my . . . god! Oh . . . my . . . god! It´s so damned simple!

Well, it´s not simple in the sense that any Tom, Dick, or Hillary could do it. It´s the "logic" of it that is stunning.

Let me put it this way. Certain kahunas, those who practiced the darkness, had a very, very deep understanding of not only the pre-death state, but the actual termination process which results in final death. And they also knew about the vulnerabilities suffered by the spirit during this period. And they exploited it.

The reader can expect no further elucidation from me on this matter. It will simply not be forthcoming. While the spiritual technology of the kahunas is absolutely fascinating, I find both the physical and spiritual enslavement of any person- much less their spirit - to be repugnant.

Once captured these enslaved souls would be kept in a *pu`olo* bundle made of *kapa* and *ti*-leaves. They needed to be fed and cared for. In an unpublished letter written to *Fate* magazine by the late Mr. Theodore Kelsey (Hawaiian translator) he has this to say about the feeding of spirits:

"The keeping of an *unihipili* incurred a grave danger to is possessor, for if prayer and offerings were neglected, the offended entity would turn against its keeper and strike him, with dire consequences."

During my research for sources of information on paranormal events in Hawaii I had the great pleasure of meeting- and speaking with- former Honolulu Police Department (HPD)Police Chief Bernard Suganuma. Enormously gracious with his time, Mr. Suganuma not only confirmed HPD involvement with high strangeness cases, but also related an experience that he had with a family in the Papakolea area of Oahu. This family kept a *pu´olo* bundle in a basket in their home. He stated that he could hear this bundle shaking and moving as if something that was trapped inside desperately wanted to get out.

I have always had an issue with the whole concept of feeding entities (spirits) and I have never fully understood the Japanese tradition of leaving fruits and other edibles on the graves of their loved ones. I come from a different set of beliefs. Let them go to where they have to go. Don't let them linger here.

Arthur Cathcart's experiences with akualele fireball-making occurred on the island of Moloka'i when he was a child of 7 or 8 years of age. He remembered clearly that the kahuna prepared a ti-leaf bundle, and into that bundle was placed awa, fingernails or bones of a deceased person and a special kind of awa that grows on a tree and has hairy roots (June Gutmanis calls this a "vining awa" and Cathcart concurred). This last awa plant with the hairy roots made up the tail of the akualele.

Each item that made up the akualele was prayed over as the device was constructed.

Hawaiian translator Theodore Kelsey also had similar knowledge of akualele manufacture and described it as follows in a letter he sent to Fate magazine back in the 1960s:

"The akualele was caused by 'keeping a bundle' (malama-pu'olo), or bones of a deceased relative or friend, generally wrapped in tapa-cloth and known as an unihipili. Through prayers and offerings this object became possessed by an aumakua, or returned spirit of the deceased, which became an entity to heal relatives and friends, or to inflict sickness or death upon enemies. Persons keeping such entities were called 'sending people' (po'e ho'ounauna), whether or not they were kahuna, or experts in hidden lore.

"Something from the body of a departed one, such as hair or fingernail, could be imbued with spiritual power (mana) if it were prayed to, calling on the name of the deceased, and sacredly and secretly kept.

"A premature birth (pu'u-koko or bloody heap) was sometimes worshipped, and thus became an unihipili, possessed by an aumakua entity."

Arthur Cathcart's description of the mid to final phase of the operation dovetails absolutely with what is known about the psychic energetics behind kahuna magic:

"The kahuna takes <u>one</u> breath and they cannot breeath after that and they pray (with that one breath) until that thing takes off."

It is only then that the kahuna can return to normal breathing, normal functioning.

June Gutmanis asked Mr. Cathcart the following question:

"When you've made the bundle and you've got it ready to and then you pray over it- if you don't stop praying you don't get hurt. What happens if you stop praying before it takes off?"

Mr. Cathcart replied that "Its apt to hurt the person that did it (i.e., the kahuna). There are some ceremonies where you take one deep breath and you (chant) all the way through otherwise if you stop, it will come back and kill you. It's so kapu (taboo) certain kinds of chants."

I asked Mr. Cathcart if the akualele fireball made any noise. He replied that one could "hear a skrrrssskkkrrr (makes a sibilant sound with his mouth). You can hear that whizzing sound going through the air."

He also described watching an akualele fireball one evening with his musician uncle. The fireball exploded over the home of the intended victim:

"You know, in a little while you can hear them (crying). You know how the Hawaiians used to cry. Loud, yea! They didn't cry softly in those days. They were loud."

Arthur Cathcart also reiterated what is known about akualele flight. The fireball heads directly for the intended and does not stop (emphasis mine). He also stated that there were still other ways to produce an akualele. The method he described to both June Gutmanis and I was the one that he witnessed personally.

I know from my discussions with Mr. Cathcart that indeed lived among the kahunas when he was a child living on Moloka'i. I asked him how it was that the kahunas allowed him to witness akualele fireball-making. His answer remains- for me- one of the most cherished responses I have ever received from anyone I've interviewed:

"Because I was young and they loved me, they let me stay and watch."

Psychodynamics

There is no room here to fully discuss the importance of mana, breathing and chanting in Hawaiian culture. However, I would like to add this little piece of information gathered from Handy and Pukui's formidable study, "The Polynesian Family System in Ka'u, Hawaii:

"Equally important in praying is the breath (ha). The mana of the prayer was in the words and names, but it was the breath that carried the words and names.

"I have seen Tutu Pa'ele, a dear old neighbor in Ka-'u, do as follows when I was a child. He used to pray over a glass of water in which there was a pinch of salt and tumeric and then, 'Ha', expelled his breath over it after the amen, to impart a mana to the water.

"A person about to die passed his knowledge to his successor by expectorating (ku-ha) or by expelling his breath (ha) into his mouth. With this, the mana he had in whatever he was an expert in, passed on to the person to whom he had given it. If he was a skilled medical kahuna, the recipient would become one in later years. So it was the knowledge passed directly from one person to a particular one and not to other members of the family in general."

During my teen years, I had the privilege of meeting with a woman who was a successor. A grandparent- at the point of death- expectorated his breath into her mouth. The gift he gave her was the ability to speak and understand the Hawaiian language. As she grew older the language grew with her until she arrived at fluency.

EM Cases

I have never come across any cases where electromagnetic effects (EM) was suffered as a result of the passage of an akualele. The akualele has a mission, and it does not waiver from its task. It is not a hunter-seeker. It knows precisely where it is going.

But there are many other cases from Hawaii where witnesses report that their car engine died as a result of a meandering globe of light. These are usually associated with spirit entities, but one cannot exclude the possibility of anomalous lights generated by tectonic stress (piezoelectric effect). Particularly on the Big Island. On the island of Oahu, meandering spirit lights and EM effects were at one time frequently reported in and around the old Pali road.

Physical Trace Cases

There are no physical traces left of an akualele event. Unless we count the body of the intended victim.

Personal Sightings

I have never had a sighting of an akualele. My father did. According to him he was in the army, stationed on the countryside of Oahu. He saw a fireball light heading straight for him. He knew what it was. There was only one action to take. Swear at the object. As he did so the object exploded over him. All he remembered was that as pieces of the fireball fell all around him, there was no sound. Dead silence.

I have had numerous ufo sightings during the course of my life. Several in Hawaii, one in Seattle, and numerous in Denver. And on September 9, 2007, my wife and I were witness to an incredible ufo event that lasted for 4 hours.

Conclusion

I have endeavored to make the case that the Hawaiian akualele is NOT a ufo in the contemporary sense of the word. It IS identifiable. And it does have a name that identifies it. I can find no Hawaiian word or term that may be associated with an aerial device identified as coming from another world, another dimension of reality. There are old legends and chants that can be interpreted as possible alien-human interaction. But that would be a liberal, if not, over imaginative rendering of the chant. Or would it?

Dreamweavers - The Mastering of Time and Space

Today, my wife (Katiuska- see her website at www.katiuska.net) and I continue our interest in things borderline. We are currently residing on the island of Tenerife, Canary Islands, Spain. We eagerly await our return to the USA . . . and to Hawaii.

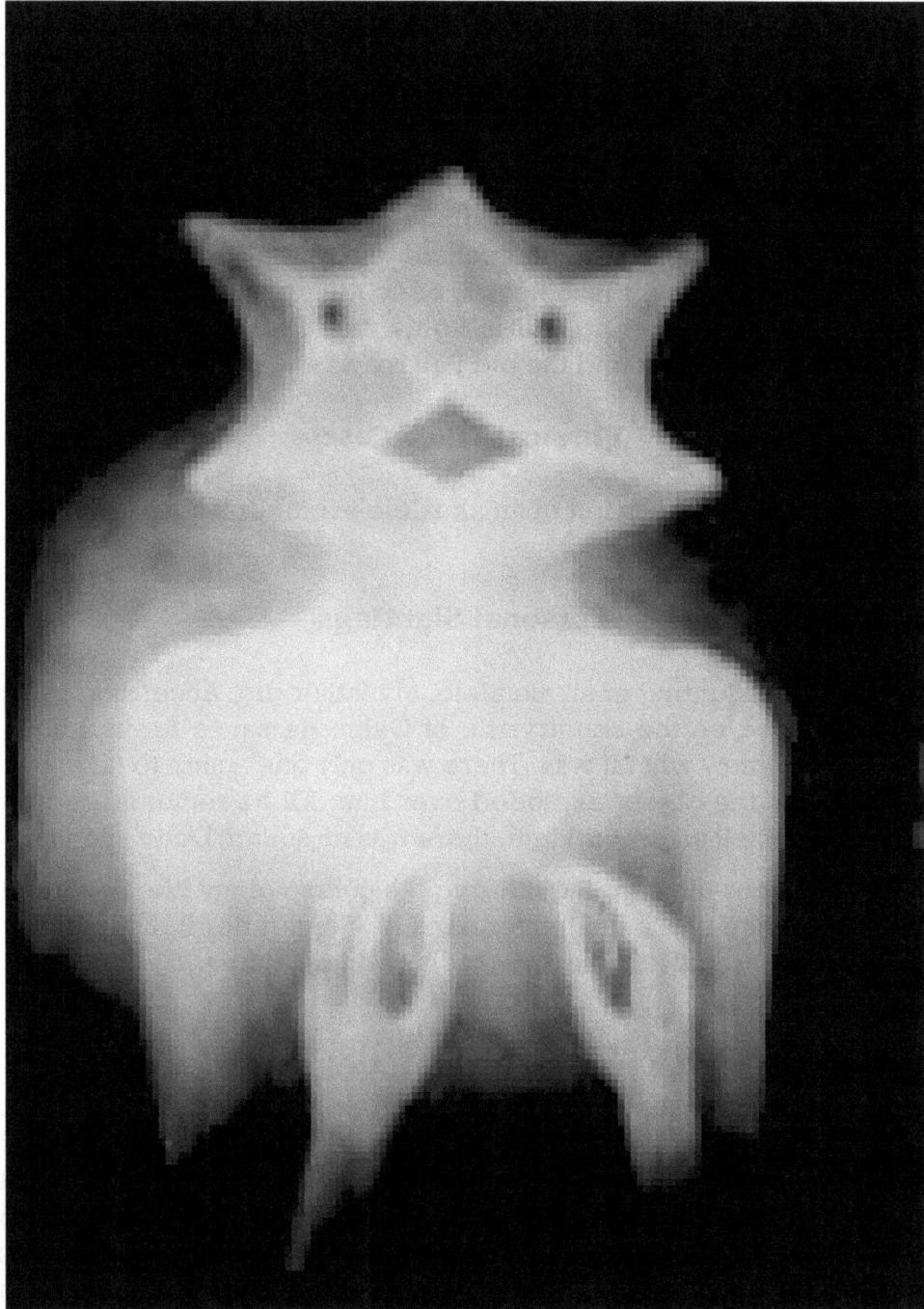

Artist's Rendering of Alien Seen in Washington State in 1937

Chapter 4
Tommy Lightning Bolt
Another Medicine Person speaks out on UFOs and Bigfoot

Of Iroquois and Abenaki ancestry, Tommy Lightning Bolt is a spiritual Native American teacher, counselor and healer who resides in the state of Oregon. Medicine Grizzlybear Lake (Bobby Lake-Thom) had shared with him an interview I had done with him in my online magazine Alternate Perceptions (www.mysterious-america.net) earlier that year (February and March 2008). Tommy informed me that he had "had many UFO encounters" and added, "You are right, there is a connection between 'Shamans' and UFOs," which is something that I had explored in my magazine column Reality Checking.

Tommy explained that several esteemed colleagues in the Mii-Dii-Wii-An (the Great Medicine Society) have told him that the Marble Mountain wilderness area of northern California is a UFO hot spot, and he admits: "Ever since the training I've done I can go out into the Marble Mountains, and the first night that I go out there a very bright light flies over my campsite. Very low, very bright. Brighter than the evening star without making any sound. It usually travels from like west to east, when all of the aerial traffic in that area goes from north to south and vice versa. I even took a photo of it one time and a friend who worked in a science lab said 'Oh my gosh! The stars don't even show up in comparison.'"

Tommy asked me if I had heard about another UFO hot spot, the Olympic National Park on the Olympic Peninsula of Washington state. "That's a place that I like to go," he said. "It's about a 6 or 7 hour drive from where I live. It's a very incredible place. I talked to Coyote about it [Coyote is Tommy's spiritual teacher], after the first time that I went there, and he was telling me that there is a race of star beings that live in there." According to Coyote, our government went into the area and was told to leave them alone or, in the words of Tommy (who was paraphrasing what Coyote had told him) "they told the government if you people don't back out of here we will make war on you." Tommy also heard that there is a "universal dimensional portal" located in that same region.

Tommy states that Coyote is enrolled in the Yurok tribe. "He has unspeakable power," he said of his teacher. "He has told me things I did 150 miles away and no one else was around and I never told anyone! He is one of the Grandfathers. Five years into the apprenticeship he revealed himself to me to be Fools Crow, revered holy man of the Lakota Nation, who had 'passed away' six years prior to the beginning of the apprenticeship. I found out after the whole thing Fools Crow is hailed in literature as 'the greatest medicine man of the last 100 years.' Yes, Beings capable of spanning time and space and even death itself. Does the U.S. Government fear Native American medicine people? You bet they do! And they really feared Fools Crow. They feared what he stood for, all people coming together in unity and harmony and the perpetuation of the 'old ways' as a living thing in everyday life and ceremony."

Tommy added: "To me, anything within the last 50 years is New Age. To Coyote, anything within the last 6000 years is New Age!! He is an Ancient."

At one point, I shared with Tommy details of my own spiritual quest and of my efforts to understand the Christian faith. "What would an 'immaculate conception' be considered in the UFO community?" he asked. "I know of women who have mysteriously gotten pregnant and several months into the pregnancy the baby is mysteriously gone. I would never try to shake your faith. It is well placed, but the writing is on the wall. In the first book of the Bible, in Genesis, the 'Sons of God' were gathered about the throne of God Adam was only one of them! Our Iroquois people say that the 'Peace Maker' Deganaweda, who came to our people was said to have been born in a Huron village of a virgin mother (sound familiar?) He won the five nations of the Iroquois to his vision of peace, democracy and unity with several displays of supernatural power including producing a solar eclipse for the Seneca! People fear the truth. People fear what they do not understand. People fear death. Jesus said, 'The kingdom of God is within you and all around you. Not within mansions of wood or stone. Split a piece of wood and you will find me, turn a stone and I am there.' He was talking about the true oneness of all things, the basic principle of the energy concept! All matter is energy! And all energy is one! My teacher, when he revealed himself to me as being Fools Crow, my skin crawled and the hackles on my neck stood on end, and I asked him, 'How did you cheat death?' He said, 'No matter what happens don't ever let go of Number One.' And I said, 'Creator?' and he said, 'Yes!' (with a big smile on his face and a twinkle in his eyes)

"I went to the desert for a day with Coyote to gather sage for ceremony and about two weeks later I noticed a 'scoop mark' on my shoulder! Kind of being a smart ass I asked Coyote, 'If they are so advanced how come they left a mark?' And he said, 'It is to remind you who's pulling the strings!'"

"The really scary part was after I noticed the mark I looked in the mirror and looked into my eyes and saw something bigger behind my eyes than what I was seeing in my physical reflection in the mirror! I burst into tears, scared to death. I wrote in my book [not yet published], 'What's scarier? Not knowing who you are? Or coming into the realization of who you are?' When I shared this insight with Medicine Grizzlybear Lake during a fairly recent visit at his home he said, 'the second is the scarier prospect.' I have learned that the highest medicine people are usually genetically modified by the good Star People because the human body was not designed to handle such extreme levels of power, and that is why they are so powerful! They are part Star Nation!"

Tommy pointed out that Coyote has moved to New Mexico. "He has shared with me that he has seen MANY Navajos that clearly are part – well - not all human! The first visible sign is when he looks in the eyes of the individual. The other sign is the energy that they emanate. He said you can feel it when you are around one (a hybrid, or a pure alien). They resonate at a different frequency than humans."

Like Khat Hansen and many other Native Americans, the legendary Bigfoot has been an absolute reality in Tommy's life. Here is an interview that we did together on this controversial and fascinating subject:

Brent Raynes: Tommy, although we've previously discussed Native American spirituality and UFOs, until I posted Khat Hansen's interview describing her Bigfoot experiences, which Coast to Coast AM put a link to on their website, I did not know that you too have had Bigfoot encounters. I appreciate you agreeing to share personal details of your own Bigfoot experiences with us. Could you begin by describing your first encounter? How you became aware of their presence and how you reacted to discovering their very existence?

Tommy Lightning Bolt: Well, this is quite a long history, going back some 15 years or so. I have never talked publicly about this experience, nor do I go out of my way to say, "Hey, I've seen Bigfoot!!!"

I understand that this is a different level of reality than most people are used to, but this is a real thing to those who have seen it as opposed to someone in New York City who has never even seen a bear in the wild. What may be a head liner to one person is yesterday's news to another person.

I have lived my entire life in the State of Oregon. I was younger than I am now. I was hiking with a friend on a Mountain in the Siskiyou Mountains in Southern Oregon on the the edge of the Oregon California border. We were hiking up the saddle of the Mountain and we were in deep Montain (not mountain, but MONTAIN) Old Growth Fir forest, trees 4-8 feet wide on an average for the old ones, at approximately 3500 feet elevation (the valley floor being at 1400 feet above sea level). We had stopped for a moment to rest at a huge boulder covered in moss. I, for no apparently conscious reason told my friend, "We are not alone, I don't know why I am saying this... But we are not alone." And then I totally forgot I even said it. We continued up the Mountain around to the right just below the edge of the ridge, and then we came up to the top of the ridge line again. Then we hiked down the other side. We came upon a huge rock that had a drop off on the front (like a small rock plateau that jetted out of the Mountain side) that was about 35 feet down to the forest floor in front of the rock, which my friend and I rested on for a smoke. When we were done I pulled out my pan flute and blew a very loud note. When the first echo went through the forest we heard an extremely loud, "Crack" below us and about 50 feet to the right, which was so loud it echoed through the forest. I looked at my friend and he was looking at me with eyes the size of silver dollars! The look on his face was definitely a Kodak Moment!!

About 5 seconds later we then heard a very loud crashing sound every 2 seconds or so which seemed to move down toward the left which actually was loud enough to echo through the timbers! I then suspected... Bigfoot! Having grown up in the Mountains I know sound, and when you hear a sound it is usually not coming from where it sounds like it is. So I looked where I instinctively know where it would of been originating from and I saw a patch of hair that was red/brown, the top of it was blond (almost like the hair on the top of his head was frosted). It was about 9 or 10 feet tall and about 2 to 2 1/2 feet thick, and it was seemingly gliding through the forest. My friend and I were both very scared, for we both knew what ever it was it was very big to make the crashing sound it made when it walked. Yes, I say, "Walked." Because it had very long strides, the length of time between each crashing sound of its foot fall. The weight sounded like 1000 pounds crashing through the forest. There is no way it was human. No way at all! No human could possibly make a sound that loud when they walk through the forest, and the friend that was with me said the same thing. I know what it wasn't, from what I saw with my own two eyes.

So, we were up on that rock, and the creature must of went behind a big old growth tree which I could clearly see just down below us and stayed for a moment, so I continued playing my flute after the initial shock of the encounter. My friend was freaked and tried to get me to stop playing my flute, and I said to him, "No Dude! I hear they like music!" So I kept playing my flute. The being must have stayed there for a good 10 to 15 minutes while I played my flute, and I felt truly honored. Then we figure it must have left then because we heard a skittering through some brush that was down and to the left of the fir tree. But it must have been focused in it's movement that time, because we did not hear the loud crashing we heard the first time. The sound seemed to get further and further away, until we could barely hear it, then we heard big branches breaking and it seemed as if it was throwing a temper tantrum. I told my friend I figured it went around the mountain far enough till it went over the ridge line and crossed the path we took hiking up... Our scent trail! It clearly was not happy that we were there, and it acted very agitated. My friend and I waited quite a while and then we high-tailed it off the Mountain. Later I played around with my own stride in walking and found the length of time between the sound of it's foot fall equaled 2 of my strides to one of it's strides. My friend concurred that it was accurate. My friend also reminded me that I had said we were not alone right before the encounter happened. I was totally blown away. I had completely forgotten about saying it. My friend and I agreed to go back up there to look for footprints in 3 days. When the day came I stopped by his house to pick him up, but he said he didn't want to go. I knew that he was scared, and I understood his feelings but nonetheless I went up there on my own, but found no foot prints. In retrospect the way we ended up at the point of the encounter, as we came around the mountain and down, it was not able to detect our scent so as not to have time to hide, as if we caught it off guard.

I was really more curious and exited than afraid. I have never been scared in the forest, as the forest is my solace. And if I was going to die I would rather die in the mountains than a building, and to die at the hands of a being of legend did not scare me, I just figured... What a way to go! I also at that point had no doubt at all that the creature known as "Bigfoot" did in fact exist, despite the arguments that there is no "tooth and bone" evidence. Cougars exist and I have never found any remains of them in the 28 years or so I lived in the Mountains, and I have done more hiking in 1 year than most people do in an entire lifetime. The same can be said for Bears, and Wolves, and Coyotes. There are mysteries that are not explained. That is why they are called "Mysteries." But Bigfoot is safer if people just think it is a "Myth."

Brent Raynes: Since then, you've had additional encounters with Bigfoot. Can you share details of what those encounters have been like, what you saw and felt, and what you have learned from these experiences?

Tommy Lightning Bolt: Yes, I have had many, many encounters with Bigfoot since then. I have found several Bigfoot "Hot spots." One time in one of the places I discovered I had caught one off guard and startled it and it projected an energy so terrifying that I wanted to run! I was within 25 feet of it when the forest exploded in thunder as it crashed off deeper into the forest. This is one of it's defense mechanisms. I was also using an open flame oil lamp to find my way in the dark because my flashlight went out. It was probably the fire that upset it. They don't like fire or "Warm" light. That same night it scared me so bad I walked all the way home off the Mountain 9 miles! When I made it home (at dawn) there was something tickling my face, and to my surprise there was a black hair about a foot long hanging off my back pack being blown by the wind into my face! The hair was coarse and kind of frizzy and it was not my hair because my hair is brown, and soft and smooth. I went back a few weeks later and offered it music and thought projected into the forest, "I am sorry if I upset you, I meant no harm, please forgive me. Here is some music for you, I hope you enjoy it." And that started a very long and meaningful relationship with them that live there. It has gotten to the point that when I am there I can hear them just over yonder shifting their weight, hanging out. I know that they are there, and they know that I am there, and I know that they know that I know they are there, and they know that I know that they are there, and we are all fine with it. At one point in an encounter in this same general area, I have been surrounded in the darkness by 5 different Beings, with 5 different spots of crashing sound in the forest around me within, 50-75 feet of me, and I was never hurt in any way. I don't go there with a chainsaw to destroy. I go there to just be, with love, respect, music, and sacred herbs, and sacred ceremony. I literally treat them like I do the Elders in my Native American family that I recognize as my Elders.

In the same area I also was hiking with one of my Wolves and he suddenly ran up the trail very fast and barking, then darted off to the right into the deep timber. When I ran up the trail to where he had ran off, the branches 8 to 9 feet up were swaying and there was no breeze, and I could hardly hear him barking! Despite popular belief Wolves do bark. I was afraid for my friends safety so I thought projected into the forest, "This is my best friend, I love him, please please don't hurt my best friend." He later came back to my and he was safe, and happy and wagging his tail, all smiles.

This same area got National attention when a few years back a therapist was hiking with his family and he observed a Bigfoot watching his family! The Therapist went on Fox News (I think it was) and told his story. The News Media of course made him out to be a crack pot! But in truth, where he had his encounter is where I have had 90% of my encounters! I genuinely believe he was telling the truth. If the location has been forgotten then let it be forgotten, I won't divulge the location because over much time and experiences I have built a relationship with them at that site. I will not jeopardize them and their safety by telling people where to go to find them. I have had extensive conversations at my home with the oregonbigfoot.com research director, who seems to me to be genuine and sincere and a good person and I won't even tell her where I have had my encounters.

There was also one time where I was at the bottom of the Mountain that I mentioned in my first encounter. I had my Alpha Wolf with me, and once again... He ran off barking. I though, "O- no! Great! Here we go again!" So I thought projected into the forest, "This is my best friend. I love him. Please please don't hurt my best friend." As I walked further into the canyon I heard a yelp. I knew it was my Alpha Wolf and I knew he was hurt, but I knew it wasn't bad. As I rounded the bend in the trail I could see him through the bushes. His tail end was visible from around an Old Growth Fir Tree about 4 feet wide. I could see his tail wagging as if he was happy and wanted to play. I knew there was something else behind that tree, but I was in no great hurry to see it. So I called my Wolf back to me, and eventually he did come back to me. When he came running back I saw on his fur coat a smear of blood on his back. I was concerned and loved him and petted him. As he was soaking up my love (Quite happily) I took my fingers and split the hair on his back to look down into his fur, and the blood was only on the surface of his coat. He was not bleeding! Whatever caused him to yelp in pain was from something strategically swatting him that had blood on its hands (Or claws). If it was a Bear, or a Cougar, they would not have stopped with one swat. He would of been killed. Whatever hit him was strategic and calculating as to encourage him to stay down, but as to not do any lasting physical harm. I know he really liked to jump up on people (as if to try to kiss them).

Another time I was in this same exact spot with a Cherokee/Choctaw partner. It was night, and I was playing my flute music and I was telling her about Bigfoot being there at that spot. I thought projected a message to the Bigfoot in the forest, "Please show her you're real." About 2 or 3 minutes later a huge tree about 2 hundred feet away was pushed over, and at that time there was no wind at all. It was a warm summer night. It was deliberate. I asked her, "Do you believe me now?" She said, "Yes."

So, if I want to hang out with Bigfoot I know where to go. I have had dozens of encounters. Building a relationship is very difficult and time consuming. There are some pretty serious trust issues on their part. They are very upset at what we as humans have done to the Earth. Bigfoot in the Pacific Northwest predominantly live in Old Growth Forest, and 97% of that forest is GONE, COMPLETELY DESTROYED! How would you feel if you were in their position? They know is it is our nature to destroy whatever we touch. If humans touch them they will be destroyed too. The Alaskan Natives have a saying, "Bigfoot is afraid of his shadow. If he can see his shadow men with guns can see him." Which leads to a point I want to make. Bigfoot is NOT nocturnal. Are you nocturnal in your home? Bigfoot are more gutsy at night because they think we can't see in the dark. But they are there night and day. They also tend to live in loose knit tribal systems, which is to say several loose knit families living in the same territory. There are tribal laws that they must follow, some of which include to not allow themselves to be seen, and to not leave any evidence of their existence, and don't do anything that will bring heat down on the tribe. They are self governing. They are also on every major continent on the face of this Earth.

It is the Bigfoot that have been kicked out of the tribe that can be the dangerous ones, because there is not anyone that they have to answer to, there are no rules they have to adhere to. Bigfoot is a shape shifter and an inter-dimensional traveler of sorts, using portals similar to the fairy portals or "Little People Portals." They are also extremely psychic and telepathic. They communicate through thought transference. I have learned that when I leave them offerings of food it needs to be 100% organic, for to expose them to the industrial world in any way is to kill them! I stress this point because I have known people who have left them store bought food with good intentions.

The Bigfoot don't always intend to be seen. They are usually seen when they are preoccupied or distracted. For them to be seen is to bring heat down on the entire tribe! When they are dealing with a specific individual in a spiritual manner they choose who sees them. They are also not vegetarian as some people think. They are just like most of us. They eat what they can get. After all it does come down to survival, and 97% of their food sources are gone. Bigfoot themselves are covered in long hair. The color can really vary from black, to brown, to reddish brown. I even spoke to an Alaskan Native who saw one walking across a swamp that was half dark brown and his top torso was, "The color of a brown paper bag." They generally have wide shoulders, and long arms. This information: "They can get up to 15 feet tall. They can get up to 3000 years old here" is passed on to me from a Yurok/Karuk Native of Northern California. These tribes have had extensive experience with the Bigfoot, including in ceremony and council. It is also noteworthy that the famous Patterson footage taken in Northern California was obtained with the help of a Yurok Indian (A Bigfoot medicine man) who performed a ceremony that lured the Bigfoot out of hiding so Patterson could get a good photo of it! And the Indian was sick for a long time afterwards for his spiritual violation. I am very careful who I bring along with me to the places I have my experiences with Bigfoot. The Bigfoot will know your intentions upon entering their environment. I have spoken anonymously with a Bigfoot research center up North and they confirmed that they had reports of Bigfoot getting to heights of 15 feet tall. They also tend to mark their territory (and I'm not talking about urinating on the trees), and compete with the bears for territorial rights. You will also not be too likely to find Little People within Bigfoot territory as the Bigfoot tend to eat them.

One of the biggest lessons I have learned about them is when you are in the forest, you had better be on your best behavior because you are in someone else's house and they are bigger, faster, and 1000 times more powerful than you are. So be respectful! I have been in situations where if they wanted to kill me they could have, and there would have been no one for miles to hear my screams! But one of the biggest things I have on my side in all of this is the medicine persons who have trained me (one of which is Yurok/Karuk Native) told me one of my spirit powers/medicines is Bigfoot medicine, so I regard them as family and sacred, and vice versa.

Brent Raynes: Many subscribe to a man-ape kind of missing link scenario with regard to Bigfoot, but you don't agree with that. Can you explain why?

Tommy Lightning Bolt: Well, it's awfully hard for them to be a missing link between Ape and Man when they are not from here in the first place! O.K., O.K., to your readers who may think this is getting far fetched, think of their abilities (the Bigfoot), then think of what Alien abductees have reported in their experiences and the abilities that they have reported the Aliens having...thought transference... telepathic communication. Lack of memory recall about an experience (this has been reported in Bigfoot encounters)... Dimensional shifting... Walking through trees, stones etc... Are you starting to get the picture?

For example, a friend of mine was up in the Mountains in the Siskiyou's and they saw a Bigfoot. The Bigfoot noticed that it had been seen, so it walked behind a tree. My friend walked up to the tree and walked around it and the Bigfoot was gone! There was no bushes it could have ducked into, it was just... Gone! This was also witnessed by a second party too! I relayed this account to the Yurok/Karuk man I trained under and he said to me, "You know what it did don't you?" I replied, "It vanished?" He said, "No. It became the tree." That is why it is so important to always give tobacco when harvesting things in the forest. You could be harvesting a Bigfoot!

To most people this kind of thing is an advanced technology, but it isn't advanced at all. It is one of the most basic, primal abilities in the Universe. It is the power of thought, of mind! For example, the original Star Gate program of the U.S. Government that is discussed in a book called "Psychic Warrior: A look into the original Star Gate Program." It wasn't with high tech machines and computers. It was all done with the human mind, traveling through time! Some people consider this a non reality, but it is in fact just a different level of reality that is still not accepted by those of the mainstream consensus reality! Are you with me on this? Are you following what I am saying?

I will give another example. I know someone who told me a true story. They said that everything is actually composed of very tiny "dots", and if you can learn to relax your vision you can start to see the dots and come to realize that nothing around us is solid. He said he knew someone who got so good with it that they accidentally put their hand through a wall! And when they realized what they had done, they panicked! And when they panicked everything froze up and became solid again and their hand got stuck in the wall! He said he knows it was real because he was the one who was called to go over to the person's house and cut their hand out of the wall!

This is some of the same technology that Bigfoot uses, and this is some of the same technology that the Alien Abductees witness!

Brent Raynes: What about UFOs?

Tommy Lightning Bolt: Well, in my reality there is a connection between Bigfoot and UFO's, albeit indirect rather than direct. All I have to say is second hand information about this issue as I have not had any first hand eyewitness accounts (Bigfoot and UFO's in the same sighting), even though the information comes from excellent, and reliable sources. There are some races of Star Beings that tinker with the Bigfoot's D.N.A. and the Bigfoot are just resigned to have to deal with it, very much the same way that humans are helpless against alien abduction. I have had conversations with several people who have seen "lights in the sky" at the same time as their Bigfoot encounters. But this certainly does not mean that if you see a Bigfoot you will see a UFO, or vice versa.

To learn more about Tommy's spiritual beliefs and his life journey visit his website at: www.lightningboltchichakos.com.

Tommy's teacher Coyote is of Yurok and Karuk ancestry. Tommy described how in front of the post office in Happy Camp, California (right over the mountain from where Tommy grew up), that this is where the Karuk Tribal Office is located, and that there is a statue of Bigfoot there. "Bigfoot is a big deal with those tribes," he pointed out to me. In the interview, Tommy described how with regard to the famous Roger Patterson Bigfoot film that the creature had been lured out into the open by a Yurok medicine man. In another email, Tommy shared that details of this aspect of the Patterson Bigfoot film are written about in Medicine Grizzlybear's book <u>Call of the Great Spirit</u>.

Jacques Vallee devoted an entire chapter to a fascinating multiple witness abduction case in California's Happy Camp (a chapter appropriately entitled "Happy Camp") in his thought-provoking classic <u>Confrontations</u>, published back in 1990. Besides Bigfoot, Vallee found lots of peculiar and fascinating UFO activity, poltergeist manifestations, and even an MIB type incident in Happy Camp. Sounds like an intriguing "window" location where a group of field investigators might wanna spend a meaningful weekend or two (or more).

All of this discussion of Bigfoot and noteworthy books to read reminds me of <u>Cryptozoology A to Z</u> by Loren Coleman and Jerome Clark. In it my old and dear friend Ramona Clark, who really deserves more than a mere footnote of recognition for her work in the Bigfoot field, was listed and briefly described in the C section of this volume. I was so proud to see her there when I first read this book. I feel that I learned a great deal from Ramona from our very first meeting back in 1973 until her passing in 1997. Ramona was both a careful, thoughtful and thorough investigator, as well as a credible experiencer herself.

Ramona and her investigative partner Duane Hibner (they married around 1974) settled in Brooksville, Florida, a virtual UFO/Bigfoot "window." (Does the John Reeves landing and entity case of 1965 ring any bells with anyone?) I periodically visited Ramona and Duane in Brooksville and even got to join them on some field assignments. Ramona was drawn into the UFO field after a close encounter back in 1967, which was soon followed by apparitional and poltergeist-type occurrences. Of Cherokee and German ancestry, I found Ramona to be quite psychic. In fact, she seemed to develop a telepathic connection with me and appeared to accurately be able to tell things about what was going on in my life, even if I was hundreds of miles away. It was Ramona who introduced me to that distinguished psychiatrist and still active paranormal investigator Dr. Berthold Eric Schwarz, author of the acclaimed UFO Dynamics (in which I have a chapter).

Yup, Ramona taught me a lot, hard headed as I can be! I valued the obvious insights and lessons I learned from her when we worked together on UFO and Bigfoot cases from Jacksonville to Brooksville, Florida from 1973 to 1975. B. Ann Slate wrote an excellent two part article on Ramona and Duane's Bigfoot field work in Saga magazines UFO Report back in 1977. UFO sightings over the Bigfoot hot spots also were noted in the second part of this article (August 77). I briefly mentioned too what they had shared with me about the UFO/Bigfoot part of their investigations in my book Visitors From Hidden Realms.

Ramona's letters to me often contained fascinating new case details, and from time to time the phenomena would again enter into her own personal life. In 1978, she wrote me: "Duane told me that during the early part of 1977, he watched a ball of light come through our bedroom window, hover for a split second over my face and head, then curve and go out another window. He said that it lit up the area quite well. I was sound asleep and had no knowledge of it till the next morning when he told me. I am aware of sparkling lights around my shoulders at times."

Chapter 5
Khat Hansen
Choctaw Medicine Woman
Bigfoot Hunter, and
All Around Expert on Multidimensional Beings!

Kath Hansen explains that she is a Choctaw medicine woman, a "Soul Eater" (a type of empathic healer) whose training as a medicine person began back at the age of three. Since age five, she has encountered various spirit beings. One of these (the main subject of this interview) is known by her people as Ste'ye'mah (what we call Bigfoot).

For more information, visit Kath Hansen's website: http://parabigfoot.ning.com/profile/1kquxwyynnzds.

Brent Raynes: To begin with, how do you wish to be identified?

Khat Hansen: My name is Khat Hansen. I am an American Choctaw Indian Medicine woman and Soul eater (it is a type of empathic healer). I have retired from the archeology field and now live quietly in the Nevada mountain range.

Brent Raynes: You have written in a blog that you've been interacting with Ki'ho'sa since age five. You explained that Ki'ho'sa means Bigfoot. You state that he's neither animal or human, and can do very incredible, if not downright supernatural sounding things. Is Ki'ho'sa a Native American term?

Khat Hansen: Yes, it is Choctaw. That is not exactly correct. Ki'ho'sa means "to forget (me)" in Choctaw. It is the name he has named himself. I have only given him this name as he gave it to me when I was 5yrs. old. He said that is what I was to call him. He is neither animal or human. He is Ste'ye'mah or Bigfoot. I do not call them sasquatch as that is a made up Indian word. It is a conglomeration of words to create one word. Ki'ho'sa calls his kind "my people" or "such as we". He has never used anything else. The Bigfoot are capable of doing many things that you or I cannot do but at the same time we are capable of doing things they cannot do. It is a balance between us in a way. They do not choose to know our way of living. For example, they do not cook or read, but they are capable of drawing and like music. They do not play music but will play with the instruments per se. They do however mimic bird whistles and song and have used them many times as a form of entertainment. I have had them steal mouth harps and slide whistles but have never heard them play them. I think they took them because they saw us playing them and were curious as to how they work. If I am playing the guitar or sitar they will come down and sit quietly in the bushes or around the area. When they are done they will leave the area and that is all I ever know. They do not tell me if they like it or experience joy or sadness. I do know that they experience anger and rage. They can also forgive, these are the emotions that I have first hand knowledge of with Ki'ho'sa and his kind.

Brent Raynes: Does being Native American open you up more to such experiences, do you think?

Khat Hansen: Maybe, maybe not. What I think opens me up to such experiences is the fact that I have been taught to respect and believe in all forms of life. I was taught that I must accept what I am being told and shown by legends and elders and other people what is true. To accept with my heart and mind that what I am being allowed to experience is a gift. I was told at an early age that not everyone can see the Bigfoot. THEY choose who will see them and what capacity it will be. For Ki'ho'sa to have chosen me was a very sacred gift to myself and my people. For him to interact with me over the years has been an even more invaluable gift. He has taught me much about myself and acceptance of things that I do not understand or comprehend.

Brent Raynes: Please tell us what you can about Ki'ho'sa and what your own first-hand experiences with him have conveyed to you about what sort of creature he is.

Khat Hansen: Ki'ho'sa is a spirit being who can assume a flesh and blood body. Which simply means: He is a being/creature that has access to this world. He comes and goes of his pleasing. This is why sometimes people say they have found footprints coming from UNDER a small rock and disappearing into a small scrub bush with nothing surrounding it or just stopping in dirt and not continuing anywhere. He can shift and leave this realm/world when he wants. He is not limited to being here as are we. He has different gifts that he uses. That we humans have not learned or been given.

For instance, Ki'ho'sa can mindspeak to people. It is a very unusual gift that took me a long time to get used to. By this I mean he can put pictures into your head and a fleeting voice that is almost like an echo. He uses this to communicate and get his meaning across to me. It is almost like flashcards strung together to create a meaning. When he does this though, it causes me terrible pain in the form of migraine type headaches and nosebleeds that sometimes last for days.

They also are able to cause humans and animals to feel certain feelings. It took me a long time to understand what this process is and a name for it. It is called infrasound or thought blasting. They use it to cause fear, terror, panic, peace, confusion or calm. It is a mind weapon of sorts. They use this when they are feeling threatened by humans to make us leave their area. In this way they will not have to physically attack us although if it did not work they would then resort to leading the person away or chasing them away. If that did not work they would attack. They are capable of anger and evil if they choose. They are not the creatures in Harry and the Hendersons. They are very intelligent and cunning. This is not a human being. Nor is it an animal. It is Ste'ye'mah or Bigfoot.

Bigfoots do not age as humans do. I always say that he is about 175 years old according to my understanding of their aging process. They age much slower than humans. It has something to do with their metabolism being different. This is also why when people have shot at them or hit them with vehicles it does not appear to hurt them. It really does hurt them, but it may take weeks or months for the wounds to manifest. This is why people have seen them just walk away from woundings without marks or blood on them. This is also why certain Bigfoot are seen over and over again for long periods like the yellowtop Bigfoot. He has been in that territory for almost a century... he does not age like us so it is a short period of time to him.

They have many different gifts such as great speed..fast as a car when they choose. The ability to become invisible (which has been explained to me as "wrapping the light around themselves"). I have pictures of this on my website. Great inhuman strength. And the ability to camouflage themselves into different forms, i.e.: stumps or trees that people do not realize are Bigfoot until they actually see it walk away or go right up to it and realize it is a Bigfoot.

Bigfoot are keepers and trackers of time here on this earth. They are waiting for man to finish his time here. Then they will resume the keeping of the earth. They will begin again and help it to heal and overcome what damages we humans have done.

They do not hold anger against us for doing the things that we have done to this planet. They just understand that it is our nature to do the things that we do. When their time comes they will again help the earth and humans and animals to balance and accept each other. For now they are here, watching and waiting.

Brent Raynes: Could you tell a little more about your background?

Khat Hansen: I am a trained archeologist that worked in South and Central America for over 20 years. My field of expertise is Pre-Columbian Civilizations.

Brent Raynes: I understand that your first Bigfoot encounter was in Oregon, by the way?

Khat Hansen: Yes, this is where I first met Ki'ho'sa. When I was 5 years old we were deer hunting and the adults had left me in camp by myself. This was a different time back then when children were safe and able to be left alone. I was playing around the camp area with my Barbie dolls (I had brought two with me) when I heard a crying sound. I listened and kept hearing it. I thought another child was left alone in their camp and was lonely. I looked for the sound and found it a ways into the forest. I came up to a fallen cedar tree and there sitting on the ground next to it was a hairy child about as tall as myself. It was crying and rocking back and forth. I just thought it was an ugly child. Maybe it lived in the woods and that is why it was so dirty? Anyway when it realized I was there it stopped crying and just stared at me. I sat down across from it and took my Barbie dolls out of my overall pockets and began to play with them while talking to the hairy child. I was asking it all sorts of questions and it finally got up and walked over to me. I offered it a Barbie and it chose the blonde one and we sat there looking at them and playing with them. Awhile later the hairy child stood up and began to whine and kind of bounce up and down and seemed to be really excited about something. As I stood up all of sudden there was this great big WHUMP! and there landed right in front of me the biggest, hairiest, ugliest thing I had ever seen. It was a male Bigfoot and it was growling this bone jarring growl and grabbing the hairy kid. I kind of screamed and peed my pants and backed away all at the same time. He pushed the hairy child back away from me and put himself between us and just looked at me. I started to scream really loud and turned and ran back to the camp. I hid in the tent the whole time until the adults came back. I told my dad what had happened and he went with me to see the area and the Bigfoot. All he found were tracks. I was very upset because the hairy child had taken my blonde Barbie doll when it left and my dad refused to buy me another one because they were 5.00 dollars.

After camping for two more days we went home which was about 60 miles away. After being home for two days I went down into the canyon below our home to play in my fort and found the Barbie doll sitting on the floor of it. As I was sitting there Ki'ho'sa came out from behind a tree and sent me the thought 'grateful' for taking care of his little one.

I was terrified of him, but he did not come close. He only sent me quiet feelings. I found out later it was a boy Bigfoot.

Brent Raynes: How neat that you did archeological work in both Central and South America for over twenty years. What were some of the most interesting, memorable places that you visited?

Khat Hansen: I have been all over the southern continent. My favorite area though is Tulum and Copan.

Brent Raynes: Are any of your archeological works published or posted online?

Khat Hansen: No, I am sorry they are not published that I know of. I worked for a private organization that had it's own agenda...religious links and such.

Brent Raynes: How about these UFOs? I seem to recall something about where you observed a strange light with consciousness once. Care to share?

Khat Hansen: I have had several instances with UFO's from the Snake people and the Ant people. I can call them down on occasion and have interacted with them on several occasions.

Brent Raynes: As a Choctaw medicine woman, could you please explain who and what the Ant people and Snake people are?

Khat Hansen: A long time ago Great Spirit created many stars and peopled them with others that are like us but are not like us. We call these people the star people. When the world was young a group of star people came to our world. At first they lived above the ground in houses that they made and interacted with our people. We called them the Ant people because they looked like small ants to us. They had big eyes and big heads, long arms and legs and were pale like the ant larvae. We lived in harmony with these people for many, many years. They offered us medicine skills and helped to develop our way of life and how to grow the food we needed. But, a time came when the world changed and grew colder and harsher. The Ant people could not survive in the cold and it was decided that they must move underground. This they did...all their cities and all their people were moved to underground cities and homes. They left us openings in the earth so that we may come to visit them or that they may come up to our world to visit and bring us messages of things that will come to pass. They are very sacred to us and deliver prophecies and medicine to our people still to this day. When they have knowledge to give to one that is chosen to hear their words, they will arrive and take the person with them to their underground cities. There they deliver the message or medicine knowledge as if you are watching moving pictures, over and over until they feel the knowledge is safely inside your head. Then they will bring you back above and leave you with the knowledge inside of you, waiting until it is time to share it with all. Sometimes at night you can see their light ships in the skies, then we know that they are coming for someone to give knowledge to and we know that it is very important to hear their words and to accept them and to not be afraid.

The Snake people are evil. They arrived here before the Great spirit created man. They claimed this planet as their own and caused great strife with Great Spirit. No matter what he did for them they were never happy. First the earth was too hot then it was too cold. There was not the type of food that they liked and all was bad. When Great spirit created man the Snake people decided that they were not as smart as they and would be used as slaves and food. The Snake people live underground too as it was easier for them to control the heat and the sun could not hurt their eyes. They dug many caverns and many cities connecting to each other around the world. They hardly ever came above ground except to steal men and women for slaves and food. The Ant people did not think it fair that they used us for such and told us to gather our weapons and to make war on the Snake people. With their help we made a truce with the Snake people and they stopped coming up from the earth to steal us men. But, the Snake people are evil and do not honor their treaty with us, and come up from the earth to steal men and women and children still. They deny that they do this and try to add witchery to their words to make us believe they do honor their treaty, but we know. When our children and men are missing we live in fear, and know that the Snake people have taken them. Snake people can look like you or I, or any animal, but for only a short time when they are using witchery to fool us.

They are more reptile than human even though they walk on two legs. We must be very careful when we are in the woods or alone where there are caves as they often lead to their world, and once in them you will become lost and captured. The Creature called Bigfoot is one such as they. That is why we must be careful when coming into contact with it as it is really an ancient reptile that can witch people and make them do as it wills. That is why so many hikers and campers disappear in their areas and why we warn our children to not be in the woods alone.

Brent Raynes: The shape-shifting Snake people sound like really bad medicine and best to be avoided if at all possible.

Khat Hansen: The Snake people are truly evil. There are a few people who claim that they have met ones that are nice and can be trusted, but we know better. They use witchery to calm you and fool you into believing their words, when in fact all that they wish to do is to entrap you and any other people you may have access to. They are liars and deceivers and strive only to cause grief and promote unease and unrest in the above world. Their appetite for humans is something they can never hide. They only want to trick humankind so that they have an ongoing food source for their people. We tried as people to befriend them, but all that they wanted from us was our bodies for food and slaves. They have not changed over the time. They are still evil now like they were then.

Brent Raynes: So at some point Bigfoot was captured by the Snake people and is under their influence today?

Khat Hansen: The Bigfoot is not captured by them. He is something else. He is a kind of reptile that existed BEFORE the snake people came. He shares a kind of kinship with them in this. He does not have the feelings of a man. His feelings are like the Snake People. Chittokaka (Great One) created him first, before humans, as a being to watch over this place. Humans can be food to him too if he were to choose, which is why we are fearful of him when he shows himself. He can be as an animal or as a devastator. We consider him attached to the Earth, almost as an arm for her to deal with humans. He delivers her words and watches over all that live here and will have us answer for what we do. He comes in many shapes and sizes. Sometimes he will come in the form of a ball of light. This is when he is the eye for the earth. He travels fast and can see for her. Other times he will be as a coyote sneaking around and peeking quietly to watch us go about our lives and making sure that we are listening and doing as the earth wants us to. His role is almost as an older brother to humanity...keeping us in line and when necessary telling the earth when we do not listen.

Brent Raynes: How about the blue people? Various traditions around the world speak of blue skinned beings. Priscilla Wolf describes meeting one. I understand that the Choctaw have traditions about them too? Are they related to the Ant people?

Khat Hansen: The blue people are another race that came to earth. They are small blue people that we call the moon people. They are big eye'd and blue, but they look like small human shaped people. I have a picture of them on my site. They are watchers like the Bigfoot (Shampe). They are everywhere and nowhere. They are another ancient race that lived peacefully on this earth until man came and started to go into their lands. We were cruel to them. We tried to take over their lands because they had already tilled them and had many plants and foods to live off of. We did not want to work when we could steal and kill them. Such is the way of man. We almost killed them all, but they left to live under the earth too as they knew that there was much space there and that humans would not follow them there. They have good hearts and still try to help humans even though there are very few left who know of them. They are nature watchers and preserve the earth. They have much magic and can make a destroyed area of the ground fertile again. They come out when the moon is full and use her magic to heal the earth where she needs it. Some people can call them... I cannot. They only come when they want to speak words of wisdom to you and you are ready to hear them. They choose who will see them just like the Bigfoot.

Brent Raynes: Can you share with us some details about your own personal encounters with so-called UFOs and what your thoughts are on the subject?

Khat Hansen: I do not believe in UFO's. They are the light ships of the Ant and Snake people. They have been here for many thousands of years and were able to bring the knowledge of how to make the ships of light with them from their homes. When we see them we know that knowledge will be delivered, or, in the case of the Snake people, bad events are about to occurÉlike kidnappings and killings. The Snake people use their ships to kidnap men and to deceive the world of their intentions. But, as a medicine woman I know their intent and try to warn others away from interacting with them. I laugh when others tell me that the ships come from outer space. They do not. There are many worlds existing beside our own and the Ant people and Snake people come and go through these doorways. This is why you see their ships vanish and emerge so fast. It is the door opening and slamming shut that amazes people. Only certain medicine people have the ability to open these doorways to other worlds, which is why the Snake people are always trying to kidnap humans so that we will not have access to their realms. But, there are many of us who DO know and keep this knowledge safe for when we as men go to war with the Snake people

Chapter 6
Johnny Sands
Singer, Songwriter, Stuntman,
Native American, and an Alien and MIB Eyewitness!

Brent Raynes and Johnny Sands

Johnny Sands gives the following abbreviated autobiographical description of himself (as it appears on his site: www.myspace.com/johnnysands). He writes: "I have been 35 years performing in the music business as a singer/songwriter, performer on shows such as NBC's 'Today Show', 'Grand Ole Opry', and Las Vegas, Nev. I worked many years with artists like Charlie Daniels, Razzy Bailey, Merle Haggard, and the late great Conway Twitty, just to name a few. I became a professional stuntman in the 60s working as a stuntman in shows like 'The Wild, Wild West', 'High Chapparel', & 'Hell's Angels 69' with Peter Fonda. I also had the great opportunity to work with Elvis Presley in two motion pictures, 'Charro' and 'Roustabout'. In 1975 I took my stunt ability & combined them with escapes. In 1983 I was inducted into the 'Houdini Hall of Fame' in Niagara Fall. That same year I broke the 'Guinness World Record' in Nashville, TN as the fastest straight-jacket escape artist in the world with a record speed of 79/100s of a second. Guinness discontinued that avenue. However they placed me on display along with Houdini's 'Water Torture Cell' which was later moved from Nashville to Gatlinburg, TN and still stands on display. Some of the avenues of escapes, dangling over Snake River Canyon without a parachute, escaping from Wells Fargo Armor Car, Las Vegas, Dunes Hotel, riding motorcycles through tunnels of fire blindfolded for TV show 'That's Incredible.' In 2004, I stayed in a stainless steel glass top casket that was submerged under 600 gallons of water and appeared at fairs throughout the eastern US for people to see me and to contribute to the Children of St. Jude's Hospital. See Johnny Sands' Underwater Stunt Lake City on Google. I am presently presenting a full pledge escape and illusion show around the country. Hoping to see you out there soon!!!"

Priscilla Wolf of New Mexico, Apache medicine woman and author, and my wife Joan, accompanied me to Nashville, Tennessee, on this evening (Wednesday, 10 June 2009) to do this fascinating interview with Johnny Sands. Johnny would like all of you to know that for free (you just pay shipping and handling) he'll send you a music CD, which includes his just released "Blue Diamond Encounter" [yes, it's about his UFO/alien encounter], along with a free booklet pertaining to this experience and an autographed 8 X 10 illustration of the alien he says that he met and communicated with.

Brent Raynes: Johnny, please tell us a little about yourself. Priscilla said that you showed her a card where you're a registered Native American. So just tell us some about yourself, where you're from and what you've done.

Johnny Sands: I'm originally from Cherokee, North Carolina. I was born there and proud to have been so. We represent, of all things, the Trail of Tears. There was a lot of hardship, pain and suffering, and I'm proud to be a part of my tribe and to represent them in a major way because over the years I think that it has been so misrepresented. They mean a lot to me. My people are a struggling people who know what pain and suffering are and know how to strive through the pain and suffering, and a lot of that was inherited into my blood. So over the years, when disaster hit, I just remember what they went through and I would think, 'Wow, if they could take it I can take it.' So I felt like a Timex watch. I felt like I could take a licking and keep on ticking. (laughs)

But I've been fortunate. I was raised up very poor and in the years of my life I was able to adopt a career as a musician and a country singer. I wrote a lot of songs, was on several major music labels and had several major chart records in the country. When I say major, we were in the top twenty around the nation, and in the '60s I became a professional stuntman, and I thought that would be the career of a lifetime because working with actors, being their main ingredients, being able to perform the stunts was a real thing with me. I was fortunate enough to work on programs like The Wild, Wild West. I was Robert Conrad's double in that television series. Then later I worked in High Chapparal with Leif Erickson, and that again was a real major opportunity for me because I was working with some real big names. I worked with Peter Fonda in a picture called The Wild Angels. I was a motor cycle stuntman and daredevil. I worked on Then Came Bronson, which was a television show with Kurt Russell and Michael Parks. So that was an honor. And then, last but not least, I worked with Elvis Presley on two motion pictures. I worked in a picture called Roustabout, where I was a motorcycle stuntman in the picture, in two different scenes, and we filmed that in A Thousand Oaks, California. Then I worked with Elvis in a picture called Charro in 1968, filmed at Apache Junction, in Arizona, at a place called Apache Movie Ranch Studios, right at the Superstition Mountains. So I was a double stunt man again.

Then I took my stunts and my career into a different mode and became an escape artist stuntman, where I break out of chains, leg irons, and handcuffs. I was a Houdini escape artist/stuntman, and in 1983 I became the fastest living escape artist in the world right here in Nashville, Tennessee, for the Guiness World Book of Records. I'm still on display at the Guiness Hall World Record in Gatlinburg, Tennessee, and I own Houdini's Chinese water torture cell.

I've added those stunts and combined them with my music career and I work with acts like Merle Haggard, Charlie Daniels, and Charlie Pride. You name somebody in Nashville and I've probably done the program with them. My insight was to be a little different, a little wilder, and put on a little bit of a performance for them.

Brent Raynes: Okay. So what happened in 1976?

Johnny Sands: Sure. Well, actually we were on the record promotion tour and I was to be in Las Vegas to appear at the Sahara Hotel. I was working on the program there and we were going to radio stations and newspapers to get this program off the ground. Las Vegas was kind of the kingdom of entertainment and so I agreed to go there, and when I got there I was interested in sites. I had been in Vegas several times before. In fact, I used to work for a place called Old Nevada, and that was a Wild West town and I was a stuntman for them

So the night that I got into town I decided that I would go and check out the Old Nevada western town, and somewhere along the way I got off track of where I was at and I realized that I was in the middle of the desert but I didn't know where. So about 14 miles out I turned the car around to come back toward town. As I turned the car around that's when I saw the lights in the sky. I noticed that it was about a thousand feet up. It looked like a cigar shaped object. At first, I thought that it was a movie set. It looked like an oversized giant blimp, but with lights rotating around it. As I seen it, my car began to malfunction. I immediately pulled to the side of the road. I lost concentration of the thing in the sky thinking about what's wrong here. I thought I was out of gas. So I got out of the car and I went back and opened the gas tank and shook the side of the car just to see if I could hear gas, which I did. When I heard the gas, I went around to the front of the car and raised the hood. As I raised the hood, I could see that the object was still hovering above me and as I looked up a flash of light descended to the ground in front of my car about (I don't know) maybe three or four hundred feet in front. As it hit, I could see from the brightness of the light two figures standing, and they began walking toward me. As they began walking toward me I realized that I was motionless. I couldn't move. It was like I was in a time lapse and nothing was functioning right for me.

They kept approaching, and as they got closer I realized that I wasn't going anywhere so I was there and so I needed to focus on what I needed to do. They got close and I could see that they were pale figures. They had no hair, no eyebrows, but they looked like human people. The only difference was that there was a growth coming out of the sides of their neck, which to me looked like fish gills. They had no ears, but they had a very wide nose. The only thing that looked funny was that their mouth looked like they had no teeth, and that was the only part of them that looked old. As far as their physique they looked good. About 5' 7"/5' 8". Very muscular looking. As he approached me, the first one came up to me close, and then he began to speak, but when he spoke I noticed that he wasn't talking from his mouth. It was like a telephone call long-distance. I looked down and he had some kind of device on his belly, like a belt, and it sounded like it was coming from it.

Still I was under the confusion and I was thinking, "Is this a movie? Is something going to happen here in a minute? Am I going to be saying, 'Wha Ha! Guess what?!'"

Brent Raynes: Smile, you're on Candid Camera!

Johnny Sands: Yeah! (Laughs)

So I didn't know. My mind was there, but at the same time I couldn't move. So the first question that I asked them was , "Where did you come from?" And he pointed up there. He didn't say a word. He just pointed. Then when he spoke to me he asked me what I was doing there and I said, "I'm doing a record. I'm a country music singer." Like he understood all of that. I don't know if he did or not, but he seemed to understand what I was saying.

Then he reached behind him and pulled out a ball, which was only about the size of a grapefruit, silver colored, and as he held it in his hand it grew into the size of a basketball. Then he let go of it and it began to rotate in a motion with the circle and as it did that he would put his fingers over the top of it and like firecrackers would go off on top of this ball, and as it went off he said, "You see, nuclear explosions are causing a problem in the solar system. These things that you're setting off on this earth are causing troubles not only for you but for us and we cannot have this kind of thing to continue because it is going to upset the balance of everything that we intend for the future."

Well, I didn't know what he was even talking about. There was no talk about nuclear stuff back in the 1970s that I was acknowledged of, and if there was it was far out of the range of what I was thinking about because I was in the music business. But I listened to what the man said. I had a question and I asked, "But are you bringing harm to us?" And his answer was: "Harm comes from evil." That was his answer.

So I felt like "I am alive, I am still standing here, so I hope and pray that you're not evil." So then I asked the question, "How old are you?" He said, "We are before the beginning of what you know as time." Well, that to me was saying a lot. I'm not a Bible scholar by any means but I've studied the Bible and understand the Bible and in Ezekiel they talk very much about a craft coming out of the sky with life-like figures on the inside. So he's talking past that type and I realized that, and then I looked back at Sodom and Gomorrah and I realized that angels come to warn the people to move out of there because it was going to be destroyed. Now those angels that came did not have wings. They were in human form. They walked as humans and they walked amongst the people that are human.

I didn't know anything about what that meant at the time but I realize now Men In Black represent that same kind of thing. They come in a human form, they look like us, they walk like us, they talk like us, but do we know whether they are from above or below?

We don't. So I asked them another question. I asked them if we were going to see them on any other occasion, and they said, "You will see us again." I said, "Why did you pick me? I'm a music guy. I don't know anything about science. I don't know anything about this." They said, "You will know, in time, the reason we picked you." I still don't know yet. But I did ask them, "Are you military?" They said, "We are not military, but your leaders know about us. They know us and know all about us."

So I believe that to be true because I talked to the Air Force in Las Vegas for a long period of time. When I got out of that desert man, I wanted to know everything and anything I could pertaining to this thing, because I thought maybe I was hallucinating. I'll be honest with you. Back years ago, I experimented a little bit with everything. I smoked a little wacky tobaccy in the past. I went to the hospital that night and I told them, straight up and straight across, I said, "Look, I smoked pot before. I'm not smoking tonight. I don't know if I'm having some kind of delusions. I don't know what's going on with me. I really want to know." They admitted me and they ran all kinds of tests and they said, "There's nothing wrong with you." They said, "It seems like you're in a little shock from the situation that you've been in, but as far as you telling what you're telling, we believe what you're telling is true."

So they suggested that I contact the Aerial Phenomenon Research Organization in Tucson, Arizona. They listened to my story and they said, "Listen, we are interested. We're going to send some people in to meet you." So my first contact was John Romero. He was the director of the Sahara Hotel. John Remara is a very brilliant man. In fact, he's a marketing director for six gaming for casinos right now in Las Vegas.

I met John and John said, "I believe what you say is true, but in order to verify what you're saying I need you to take a few tests for us." I said, "What kind of tests could I take?" He said, "Well, a polygraph would be one. A voice analysis would be another, and there's a Dr. Leo Sprinkle, who is a psychologist and a specialist in hypnosis, and we would like you to meet these three people." I said, "I'd be more than happy," because here's what I wanted. Right now, I can't promote a record because everybody would think that I'm using that as a gimmick to promote my record. I can't do nothing with my career. I'm on a stand still. Everybody wants to see me because it's hit the front page of the Las Vegas Sun, because they had had so many sightings that night, not by just me, but all over the state, New Mexico, Arizona, and Nevada. And see I didn't know this and they were all describing the same object, the same things, except they didn't meet the aliens.

Well, I'm not discriminating nobody because I'm not wanting to say that I'm the only man who has seen somebody from outer space. But I do have a little bit of problem with some of the stories that I hear because I don't think those little balloony shaped headed people with green dotted eyes and crawl around and look like piss ants. I think their intelligence is far beyond that kind of look. They're not 3 foot high. These people I seen were intelligent people. You could see wisdom in their face. You could see that strength in them. I mean, from an Indian Reservation, we know power, we know strength, and we know what the feeling of a spiritual feeling is all about, and I could feel that spiritual, that strength, that realism far beyond what most people can understand. I knew that I was talking to somebody who not only just knew what they were talking about, but knew far beyond what I could ever be talking about. I felt like a little pee on in a great big shell.

But I went through the tests. Dr. R. L. Nolan was one of the best lie detector experts. He worked with the FBI for 27 years. He came in and he said, "I'm going to just take you right quick right now. You won't even get past me because when I get done with you I'm going to wash you out and you're going to be gone." I said, "Fella, if you can wash me out and I can be gone, that means that this story is all over with and I'll be very glad." He said, "I'm going to ask you several questions. Number one, did you meet two strange creatures in the desert?" I said, "Yes sir, I did." He said, "Were those creatures pale and white, had no hair and no eyebrows, and had gills on the side of their face?" I said, "Yes sir, that's right." He said, "Let me ask you this one. This one is going to get you. Did they talk to you, and not use their mouth, and talk to you in a form of mental telepathy?" I said, "Yes sir, they did." He couldn't get past that part. There were people in another room with a glass window and he stood up and he said, "He's telling the truth. He's telling the truth." When I took the test it was a hundred percent in favor. Then Dr. Leo Sprinkle and the voice analyst gave their report as a 100 percent. Now they said that the only think that was detected in what he was telling is that he's holding back a couple of things that they had told me not to tell and he said even under the psychologist's hypnosis he won't reveal that because that was the shock to his whole program, of his life, and because of that his subconscious won't let him release that, and for 34 years I kept that a secret. Some of the things that I told you about the military, were they military, were they involved with the government, did the government know that they existed, all of these things fell around things that they had asked me not to talk about. I don't know why, but I think that it was because they just wanted to see the sincerity in what I would be and what I wouldn't be. They had me against the wall and didn't realize it because with the things that were going on, and because I was in this predicament and because I was promoting a record, I couldn't afford to make that kind of statement and jeopardize what my career was all about.

So that's where we landed, and then they took me into the Sierra Hotel, John Remara wanted to do an artist rendition of what the alien looked like, so they took me to their best artist that they brought in in the state of Nevada and they told me to describe it to him. I was there. A friend of mine named John Worth was also there. John Worth was a 17 year police officer in Philadelphia. He was a very smart man. He had busted Rinso and everybody, the Mayor, for drug stuff. So I've trusted John. He was a sparring partner with Leon Spinks out in Vegas, and quite a man. So I felt like I had a good body guard with me. So we went in to draw the picture and as the artist was laying it out he got down to the gills on the side of the face and he said, "I'm confused. They've got a nose but they have gills. Why do you think they have those?" I said, "I really don't know." And two men walked up, dressed in black. One of the men, in an awkward lean, leaned over, almost like a robot, in front of my face, and he said, "That's because of where they're from." He said, "You see, there's a planet in the solar system of a star called Sirius and that planet is an aquatic type planet, which is half the time under water and half of it is on land, and because of the heat from Sirius and the sun, it's eight and a half light years from here, and he said that they would be part time under the water so that they could resist the heat. The rest of the time they'd be on land where they'd breathe through the nose. They're kind of like a frog." I said, "Well, I don't know but it sounds good to me," and the artist said, "Well it explains it all to me," and he looked at me, this one in black, he patted me on the shoulder just like the alien did and he said, "We've got to go now, but we will see you again real soon." When he said that, John Worth was sitting beside me and he said, "Did you hear what he said?" I said, "Yeah, I heard what he said." The security guard was standing there and I said "Would you follow them please?"

Now look, we're talking about the Sahara Hotel. The halls would normally be jam packed, but for some reason there was nobody in any of the hallways. Nobody except us. These two men walked down the hallway with security right behind them. He was less than 15 feet behind them. They went out two double doors and before the doors could close he grabbed the door and was pushing it open. When he went out, I saw him lean forward, look both ways, look across the street, he turned around and walked back. He was as pale as the alien I was just showing you on the picture. He said, "You won't believe this. Them people vanished in mid air. There's no car, there's nobody on the streets." That's a broad street out there, and he said, "Let's look at this hallway. There's nobody here. Why?" He said, "They've gone."

Well, John Worth and me both began to wonder. We didn't know about any man in black stuff. We were worried about who them fellas might be, so I told John, "What should we do?" He said, "We're going to take some back alleys and get home." I was at his place. So we drove every alley, every alley, every alley all the way through Vegas out to his place and drove me into his parking lot and the minute that we stepped out of the car a long black Cadillac limousine drove down to the edge of the road, they rolled down two windows, a front one and a back one, and two men looked out the windows at us. It was those men that were in the casino. They looked at us, and then they turned their heads straight ahead, rolled the windows up and drove off. John said, "How could they have found us?" He was beginning to really wonder.

Well the next day, I got a phone call at John's house. Now nobody knew John's number. We hadn't given that out. The call was about how they'd like to meet me. They were Dave Dunn's filming production company out of Hollywood, California, and they had heard about this and wanted to do a documentary, and could they meet me. I said, "Can you get this program over with if I'll interview with you? I want it done." They said, "We think we can." I said, "Okay." So I brought John Worth with me and they told me what kind of a complex they were in and the apartment number. So me and John went down there. When I knocked on the door this Dave Dunn (or who said he was Dave Dunn) answered the door. He was dressed in a black/grayish turtleneck shirt, black pants, and as I came in the door I noticed that there were two more men. One standing in the back bedroom door looking out, not saying nothing, and one leaning against the bar. The house was completely furnished with looked like New England furniture. Heavy duty big time stuff, beautiful fireplace, a mirror with hand painted muriels on the glass. I sat down in the chair like I'm sitting here and we began to talk a little bit. He asked me about my experience and where it was at. The others were looking at him but not saying anything, and he said, "We need to write a song about this," and I said, "Well, I'm not really into a song right now." He said, "Well we need to write this about the aliens all pale white and about the headlights." He said, "You write this for me because I want to meet you tomorrow." I said, "Well I ain't never wrote a song quite that fast." He said, "Well with my help you can." He gave me some lay outs and he said "You go home and work on it and we'll see you tomorrow." So I went home and because this guy was wanting me to do something I said, "Well I'll do it." So I wrote it and I came back and he laid out this and he laid out that and he said, "Say that the object was shaped like a sphere," and I said, "Okay, I will." He said, "Talking to you without using their mouth that's very important because that's mental telepathy," and I said, "Okay, I can do that," so I re-wrote it and he said, "That's fine. That's great. That's what we want."

So he said, "What we're going to do is tomorrow night we're going to meet you at the Desert Inn, in the lobby, and then we're going to go from there out to the site where this all took place and we're going to do our filming." I said, "Okay." So the next night I didn't go in my car I got John Worth to take his and when we got to the Desert Inn the parking lot was so full it was like a football field away from the casino that we had to park in the middle of the cars because we couldn't get there and I had to meet them in the lobby. I told John that we had to hurry or we won't get there in time. So John said, "Let's go," so we opened the car doors in his vehicle and a car drove right up in front of us. A black Cadillac and out stepped Dave Dunn, or who said he was Dave Dunn, with a martini in his hand. He said, "Hello Johnny. Here's a martini for you," and he reached back in the door and he said, "And one for your friend." I said, "How did you know how to find us?" He said, "Because we were looking for you." John said, "That's a little weird there."

So what we did then we got in the back of that limousine. There was a man in the back seat and two in the front. Dave Dunn was on the passenger side. So I began to talk. I leaned forward and I looked at John. About that drink I didn't know too much about it. How could they have a drink already mixed, all fresh, coming from the casino which was way over here and find us and have it ready for us and not spill a drop was a little bit puzzling.

Brent Raynes: And he used his left hand to give you that drink?

Johnny Sands: To give me that drink.

Brent Raynes: Just like the guy with the ball.

Johnny Sands: Yes. Same thing.

So what I did was I leaned forward to talk with him and as I did I dumped the drink in the floorboard. John seen me do it so he leaned forward and dumped his. So we rode on toward the Blue Diamond Highway and as we rode out toward the Blue Diamond Highway I said, "I'll take you where it was at." He was talking up a storm. When we got to the location I said "Right here." He kept going. I said, "But right back there." But he kept going. They went on about five miles and then they made a turn like I did that night and they parked on the other side of the road, and when they did all kinds of lights hit me from all sides of the desert, and he said, "You stay in the car. We'll be right back." He got out, the driver got out, and the guy in the back seat got out. Me and John was in the car. They walked across the street and then here come these figures out of the darkness dressed in black and this one particular man was standing up in front of them all and he began to talk to Dave Dunn and he pointed at me, and he kept pointing at me. So John Worth had the window cracked and John said, "He's talking about you and he says, 'He knows too much. This has got to end here and now. He...knows...too...much!" John said, "You've got trouble." I said, "No, I don't have trouble. I'm going out there to see what the problem is." I was on the side next to the desert and I reached and grabbed the door handle and as I reached to grab it, I don't know if you've ever seen that show The Adam's Family, Cousin It, the furry thing?

Brent Raynes: Yes.

Johnny Sands: Okay. Cousin It come running at me, at my door, and I looked and it run so close to the door I slammed the door back and looked out and it stood right in front of my door. No face. Just fur. And I looked back and there was another one to the left of him, and I said, "John, do you see?" He said, "A cactus run into the door didn't it?" I said, "I don't know what it is." He said, "Are you getting out." I said, "No, I'm not." I backed up and locked the door and this thing went around the car and went over to Dave Dunn and this other man. I don't know what he said or what he done, but he came right back to my door and stood. Another words it meant don't get out. So I didn't move.

So anyway, after a long conversation they had, they came back and all got in the car and when they got in the car I said, "What's going on?" They wouldn't answer. All the way back from that 14 miles out on the Blue Diamond (the way they went it might have been twenty something miles) they did not speak one single solitary word and when we got back to John's car at the Desert Inn they let us out. They didn't say good night, thank you, good-bye, or whatever. So me and John were all confused, so I said "John, turn around real quick. Let's go back to that Blue Diamond place out there and see who all them people was." So we drove back. Now all the way out to that location there was not a car that passed us. When we got to the location there was nothing. Nobody, no nothing. Then we turned around and came all the way back and not passed one car. When we got back to the Desert Inn I said

"John, we're going to see them fellas in the morning, we're going to get to the bottom of this thing, and we're going to know what in the world is going on."

So we got up at daylight and went to that apartment and I was beating on that door and a maintenance man was coming up the hall and he said, "Excuse me, who are you looking for?" I said, "The people in here." He said, "There ain't nobody in there." I said, "Yes there is somebody in there and I want to see him right now. His name is Dave Dunn." He said, "I'm sorry, you've got the wrong apartment." I said, "No, I haven't got the wrong apartment," and John said, "No, I've got it right here written down. This is right. We've been here three times." He said, "Sir, I'm not trying to be smart but something is confusing here because that's empty." I said, "No. It ain't empy. They've got all kinds of furniture in this joint." He said, "Let me take you downstairs," so he actually woke up the landlord and I explained to her and she said, "Sir, I'm sorry, but you've got it confused. Maybe there's another apartment building." I said, "Mam, I'll tell you all about it," and I started explaining about all of this heavy duty furniture and then I got to the mantle, and when I got to the mantle being hand painted and all, she said, "Come with me," so we walked across there, went up the stairs and went in that apartment, on the second floor, and when we got there she stuck the key in the door and she said "Sir, I'm not going to tell you that you've never been here before, because you described the mantle, but the strange thing is" and she pushed that door open and she said "Where is that furniture at?" I said, "Good God. They were here last night." She said, "It's impossible. With the kind of furniture and the many rooms you're talking about here, they would have had to have had a tractor trailer in here and several men moving this stuff. There's no way in the world they could have moved that much stuff in that many hours." I said, "Mam, they were here." She said, "I believe something went on."

Look we didn't believe nobody then. We knocked on doors after doors after doors in that apartment complex. "Did you hear anything? Did you see anything?" Nobody had seen anything. They never seen these men. I said, "Did you ever see that black Cadillac?" One person said, "I thought that I might have seen it at one time." But they disappeared. Now John Worth run an investigation, APRO run an investigation, trying to locate these people. They don't exist. They didn't exist then and they don't exist today.

So the story is one hundred percent true. I just told a man on the radio today "I don't care. There are skeptics in this world. I wish I hadn't seen it because I really don't understand it but I wish that I could see it again because I would like to get an explanation and ask questions about it because I didn't know what I was asking at the time. But I would be willing to take another polygraph test on the men in black because these men in black are the most extreme thing out of all of it. They said "somebody like us" or "we will see you again soon," and I believe that somebody like them was the men in black. I don't think that they were government people because even government people can't move that quick. They're good but they're not that quick. And government people, I don't believe with all of my heart, would dress in a manner like the men in black like a Will Smith and a Tommy Lee Jones outfit every time they went to do an investigation. I think they're too smart for this. I think they come in Bermuda Shorts and sun glasses or T-Shirts, or they might come in underwear, but they wouldn't be in a man in black outfit. And I think these creatures or these aliens or whatever we call them are much smarter intelligent beings than some of these programs illustrate them to be. I believe that they're far in advance of our knowledge. When they left me in that desert, when they unfroze me and I reached my car door I looked forward and the minute I looked forward in a flash of light they were gone and they were in that craft and that craft took off from a solid stand still to 4 to 5 seconds that sucker was completely out of sight. It was gone.

He said that our government is aware of them, and I believe that they are. From the soldiers I've talked to at Nellis Air Force Base they knew that kind of thing was real. The people that they seen in Roswell, New Mexico when that ship crashed was the closest re-enactment to anything like what I'd seen. They were pale, they almost looked human, they were body figured like a man, they had fingers like a man. These other little things I'm just a little bit skeptical of. Not to call anybody a liar. Maybe they've seen something I haven't seen. But I just see these to be very intelligent, supernatural human beings. I don't know if they're from heaven. I don't know if they're from hell. But I believe they're powerful. I don't believe that they're here to do destruction to us. I believe they're here to find out our directions and I don't know where we're headed but if you're a Bible believer we're headed for destruction and I think they're well-prepared and with knowledge to see and be aware and be prepared for the times of what is to come.

I may be wrong. I'm not a genius, but I do know this. It was told to me that it was eight and a half light years to Sirius. In the time that they told me the telescope to see Sirius had just recently been invented. They didn't know what Sirius was. Yet Africa, and even before the Egyptians, talked about the star Sirius and they said that life-like aliens came from Sirius and they rotated down in a thing like an ark and whirled down to the earth. There were thoughts that there were Gods that come from the Sirius to earth, far beyond what we even knew what the star was, they knew. They knew more about our solar system than we know today actually. How did they know that? It had to be because there were creations above us and more life with knowledge than we could ever imagine that we've got.

So what I'm telling you is true. It's not something that I'm making up. Yes, I wrote the song 33 years ago and didn't put it out 33 years ago. I'm 64 now and looking for more, so yes, I think I stood the statute of limitations with them, I think I was a good host to them, I hope that they come back and see me once again. I think I've been a gentleman with them and I'd like to be that gentleman again. I'd like to answer any and all of their questions and see them on a first-hand basis. But the song told the story of my life, they helped me write it, and so I do have it. I have it on my web page: www.myspace.com/johnnysandsmusic. You can get the alien, you can get all the secrets of the story in a book that I wrote myself, and you get an 8 X 10 picture like I gave you absolutely free. I'm not selling it. All you pay is the shipping and handling. I just want all UFO collectors and people who are excited about it to see what my man looks like, to have a portrait of it, and the hope that we together and can see it sometime together.

Brent Raynes: Right after that happened, did you change in anyway spiritually, psychically, or anything like that?

Johnny Sands: Yeah. I never did believe in aliens. But since then, every day of my life, every time I see something moving in the sky, or blinking in the sky, I'm outside looking up for it. My wife says, "Won't you come on in?" I'll say, "No, I'm going out here." And I talk to them. I talk to them! I say, "If you're up there, I'm still here. I'd like to see you." I don't know. You see something and you don't realize that you've seen it then you've seen it and you know it's real and the more that they investigate it the realer it gets. I hate to see somebody destroy what's real about this thing. It's a great thing. There is knowledge inside of this that we need to be able to capture.

I don't think that they're here to harm us. If they were, they could have wiped us out a long time ago with the spirit and this power that they've got. But I believe that they are observing what we are and what we are all about.

As an Indian, we had spiritual beliefs. We seen things in animals that most people can't see. We seen gifts and reality with things that people mostly can't comprehend, but through those things there was a spiritual guidance that led us to a greater being and that greater being was a God, and that God was a God in heaven that was going to lift our spirit even through those sacred owls, or in some spiritual way to bring us to the being of the life ever lasting. And I think that these people are from that kind of a place. I don't see the devil. I know that the devil loves me because he's tried to kill me for years. He'd love to take me down and rip me up and tear me apart. These people would not do that. They helped me write a song. They took me out in the desert and kind of scared me a little bit because I had been in a place that most people haven't been. I can't walk up and down the streets everyday and say, "Hey buddy, how are you doing? Have you seen any UFOs lately?" They'd think you're a kook! (laughs)

But I've been somewhere that most men and women would like to be, but for some unfortunate reason they've never had that opportunity. Was it a gift? Yes. Would I want to do it again? Yes. Am I glad that I am the man that got to see this? Yes. Why me? They said that I'll know someday soon. I'm looking up, I'm still hoping, and I'm still going to believe that it's going to happen, and I believe that there's a reason behind any and all things. We don't get big because we're smarter or greater than anybody, we get big because life pushes us to reach certain destinations because we're meant to be for the cause. What my cause is I don't know.

Author's Note: We had finished with the interview, and then Johnny began sharing details about being miraculously healed. So I switched my tape recorder back on and caught the following details as he went from one healing incident right into another:

Johnny Sands: I just made a cross, I said "It's gone," and my wife can verify it, the next day it was gone. I went to the Bahama Islands and I got so sick I couldn't breath. I came back and they said "You've got cancer. You're dying." I said, "Oh God. I've got to get my life straightened out before I die." And I went back to the doctor and he said, "Wait a minute. Let me do this one test." He did this test and said, "You've got tuberculosis." I said, "Oh God, thanks a lot. One death to the other." He said, "No, no, no. We can cure that in eighteen months now." I said, "Oh well, good." So he brought me a sack of pills that was like a drug store and he said, "You've got to take these all day long, every day for eighteen months." I took them for two days. My wife will tell you this is the God's truth. I said I ain't telling them no more. I said, "I'm healed." She said, "That doctor ain't going to buy that." I said, "Well I mean it." I went back to the doctor and I said, "Look Doc, I brought you these pills back." He said, "For what?" I said, "Because I'm healed. It's all over and it's history." He said, "Oh I wish that it was that simple. But it isn't." I said, "Well just X-ray me." So he X-rays me, he X-rays me, he X-rays me, he X-rays me and he says, "Listen, something is wrong with this machine. I'm sending you across the street to the hospital." So he sent me to the hospital. I come back and he clipped those X-rays in and he put the pills in the trash basket and he said, "You're absolute right. You're healed. I don't know how. I don't know what done it."

How did they do it? Did they make that miracle happen in my own life? I don't know. It was from God. It was a gift. Still I'm alive today. I'm 64 years old. I've done 15,000 stunts. Hanging under helicopters, crashing through walls, been on fire. You name it, I've tried it. I walked across the Snake River Canyon, upside down, on a cable, 1200 feet in the sky without a parachute. I'm still alive. Most stuntmen my age are dead. They're not rocking, and that haven't even rode. I'm rocking and still rolling so I've been blessed. Things have been happening for the good, and I've got a wife I met 30 years ago. Everything ain't bad.

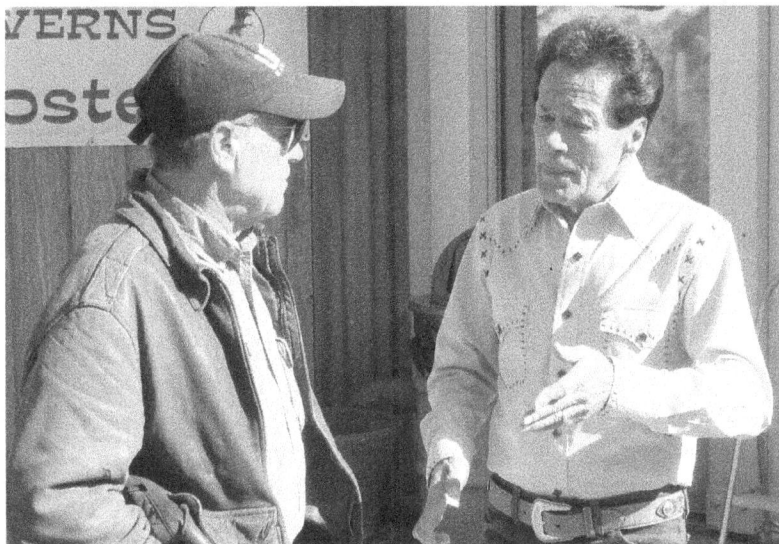

UFO magazine editor Bill Birnes chats with Johnny Sands
on the set of an episode of the History Channel's UFO Hunters series.

Johnny Sand's Alien
A bald alien with fins perhaps from a watery world came eyeball to eyeball with
country singer Johnny Sands just outside of Vegas.

Chapter 7
Anthony Peake
The Controversial World of Daemons and Ultraterrestrials

A conversation with Anthony Peake, the British author of *Is There Life After Death-The extraordinary Science of What Happens When You Die* and *The Daemon: A Guide to Your Extraordinary Secret Self* weaves about with a touch of abandon, awe, and genuine high strangeness, amid subjects like neurology, psychology, and hypnosis, that initially sound conventional enough, but before you realize what's going on you're suddenly delving deep into a wide-range of intriguing subject matter from quantum physics, Gnosticism, temporal lobe epilepsy, near death experiences, déjà vu, and precognition. The kicker is that all of these things, while interesting in and of themselves, pretty soon take on a unique Theory of Everything that revolves around a central concept of Tony's that he refers to as the *Daemon-Eidolon Dyad*.

Mythologically the Greek *daemon* was described as a guardian spirit who on occasion would help the eidolon, the lower self. To the ancient Egyptian's this mind-body split was the *ka* (guardian spirit form) and the *ba* (equivilent to the everyday self or "me"), or to the ancient Chinese *hun* and *p'o*. In modern language, or more familiar New Age terms, it's the higher self and the lower self duality of consciousness. Except in Tony's expanded theory this inner *daemon* or guardian spirit may hold highly significant clues into a dual form of consciousness that can perform incredible paranormal feats on occasion, like precognition, and may literally be part of another world (this is where quantum physics comes in), and may even allow the lower self "me" to survive bodily death.

Certain people, like temporal lobe epileptics, seem especially sensitive to and prone to these kinds of puzzling episodes. Tony believes that the acclaimed hypnotherapist Ernest Hilgard's "hidden observer" is the *daemon*, and after reading my *Alternate Perceptions* interview feature with Todd Murphy, a researcher who works closely with Dr. Micheal Persinger, he believes that their "sensed presence" is also.

Before our interview, I read in a paper that Tony had prepared for the *Journal of Near-Death* Studies (http://www.anthonypeake.co.uk/pages/ndearticle/pdf) where he wrote that the deeper one goes into a hypnotic trance state that the more likely one will encounter this "presence," the *daemon*. He recounted a case documented by the noted psychologist Charles Tart of a particularly good hypnotic subject he called William who, during one deep hypnosis session, there was an unexpected "intrusion" from a presence that was amused by the attempts of Dr. Tart and his colleagues to understand the human mind. Tony wrote that this amusement and "intrusion" is simply not a characteristic that one normally expects to encounter from a non-dominant brain hemisphere!

John Keel's hypnotic encounter with a daemon?

I found this story intriguing and shared with Tony details of John Keel's account from his book *The Mothman Prophecies* of Keel's hypnosis session with a UFO and MIB experiencer on Long Island in 1967. Jane proved to be a good hypnotic subject too, but soon, after performing tests to assure himself that she was in a deep trance state, he began to question her about her experiences. Suddenly, to Keel's amazement, he no longer had control of the session as an entity named *Apol* [pronounced Apple] began conversing with him instead. This personality explained that Robert Kennedy was in grave danger, and made specific predictions about some plane crashes.

Keel wrote: "The predicted plane crashes occurred right on schedule. I was slowly convincing myself that the entities were somehow tuned to the future." Keel also later found that he only had to ponder over a serious question and the phone would ring and Jane would be relaying a message from this *Apol*.

In our phone conversation (10-14) Tony discussed at length his overall theory and I couldn't help but notice a parallel between Keel's *Apol* and Tony's "*daemon.*" So I read that account directly out of Keel's book to get his take on it.

"*Apol*, it's the *daemon*," Tony declared. "Again it's the being inside that knows the future and he communicated directly with that higher self of Jane. The *daemon* is always in there and it's deeply rooted in the non-dominant hemisphere of the brain and in deep hypnotic trance situations people can encounter that being, and that being keeps all of the memories of the past life, and the *daemon* knows the future. It keeps itself dormant except when it's really needed, or when people are hypnotized."

Brad Steiger's strange hypnotic episodes

Years ago, when I first read of John Keel's hypnosis session with Jane, I noticed that he had made a footnote that appeared at the bottom of that page stating that noted author Brad Steiger had also had the strange experience of losing control in situations involving his own hypnotized subjects. Curious I phoned Brad (1979) and asked him about his experiences with hypnosis.

"It has turned out not to be an uncommon experience for me," Brad began. "One of the things that has been happening is people will come for things like weight control or help to stop smoking, or whatever, and we never in any way act as missionaries for our metaphysical beliefs. There are many people who come here— young athletes come here—who are strict Mormons, and they wouldn't be coming here if we made an obtrusive situation about our metaphysics. We have some of these people, when we have them in a deep state of hypnotic control, suddenly sit up and say, 'Now I know why I came here.' The first time this happened we were somewhat startled. Everything is going smoothly, and you will feel you have control and then suddenly they would sit up and say, 'Now I know why I came here.' I was working with a man, a military officer—a Naval officer—who was driving in the area, made an appointment. He was just curious about the whole matter of hypnosis. That sort of thing happened to him. He has now resigned his military commission and he is working as a healer today because he found why he really came here. He has a memory of coming here from some other place."

"They seem to recall coming here from some other place, coming here with a mission," Brad added. "Coming here because they chose to or were selected to come here."

Does Fossil Hunter Get Psychic Help?

A major archeological discovery has been made by an amateur 39-year-old fossil hunter named James Kennedy. Leading experts at the University of Florida are quite excited. One top Florida anthropologist called it "the oldest, most spectacular and rare work of art in the Americas." He's talking about a mineral hardened foot long bone fragment from what Dr.Richard Hulbert, a vertebrate paleontologist, says came from either a "mammoth, mastodon or ground sloth," creatures who have been extinct in that state for at least 10,000 years. On this ancient bone fragment is a clear etching of a walking adult mammoth or mastodon. Extensive tests have shown that the carving was executed when the bone was fresh, soon after death.

A resident of Florida's Vero Beach, James has a genuine knack for locating ancient treasures. "I've always been good at finding things, all my life," he told journalist Sandra Rawls. "I have a sort of instinct, a kind of gut feeling about whether or not something is going to turn up." The story also mentioned how James' mom is from where "some say" that "he (James) inherited a keen insight to the past and future."

Indeed there's a great deal more to that story! The distinguished Dr. Berthold E. Schwarz, a psychiatrist who retired some years ago to Vero Beach from Montclair, New Jersey, the author of the highly acclaimed two-volume book UFO Dynamics: Psychiatric and Psychic Aspects of the UFO Syndrome (1983), has written quite a bit about James's mother, a lady named Katie, a woman of impressive and documented psychic and psychokinetic abilities. He's also written some about James as well. Dr. Schwarz assures me that James "has some of his mother's abilities."

In his book Psychiatric and Paranormal Aspects of Ufology (White Buffalo Books, 1999), Dr. Schwarz wrote: "In my third year of intensive documentation and study of Katie, I also had several formal sessions with her son James, who was treated by myself during his period of stress, fugues, and then reporting nearby UFO-like lights in the orchard adjacent to his home. He also suffers temporal lobe epilepsy and is under medication. He does not use alcohol or unprescribed drugs."

"James had an episode where an ostrich skin lighter and tobacco pouch materialized under unusual, almost made-to-order circumstances. Then on November 10, 1985, while James, Katie, and a third participant were being videotaped, James attempted metal bending for the first time; he telekinetically split the stem of a silver-plated spoon so a slip of paper can be fully inserted through the crack. However, unlike Katie, James is fearful of these abilities and his potential."

"In a related vein, of applied clairvoyance, James discovered several archaeological artifacts which include a fossilized mastodon's tooth, an ancient whale skull, and very old arrowheads."

At approx. 9 p.m., February 12, 1987, James and his girlfriend Dawn were in an isolated, wooded area west of Vero Beach when they claimed they came upon something very strange and frightening. James described it as "an ape about seven feet tall, weighing an estimated three hundred and fifty pounds, had no breastsÉbut his chest had hair all over, and the arms hung below the knees." They both drew pictures of the creature (included in this book) and Dr. Schwarz went with the two witnesses to the site of this encounter the next day. Unfortunately, he found no trace evidence to support their encounter claims, though their testimony and details matched, and James did not wish any publicity over the incident.

Dr. Schwarz added: "In James' experience, he has no previous knowledge of ufology and his reading skills are not developed. His past is filled with episodes of violence, accidents, and seizures. Once, while confused and in a state of furor after a temporal lobe seizure, he actually assaulted an emergency medical technician, broke his wrist, and snapped the restraining strap while being transported in an ambulance to the hospital. Katie recalls (October 7, 1979) being told, 'ÉJames was talking backwards and in a different language. He knew what you were going to say before you said it.' Apparently this was part of an aura which progressed to tachycardia, nausea, and his convulsion. These temporal lobe symptoms are unique and not unlike those reported in the case of Vicki, another high quality, UFO-psi experient under long-term study; and to the late Joseph Dunninger, the telepathist, who in his later years told me how he 'Éknew the exact words and sentences on numerous television movies <u>before</u> these were said.'"

Dr. Schwarz provided me with a copy of a thought-provoking article that he had written for England's <u>Flying Saucer Review</u> (Vol. 31, No. 6, 1986) entitled, "Presumed Physical Mediumship and UFOs." In it, he described something very interesting about that ostrich skin lighter and tobacco pouch incident referred to a few paragraphs earlier.

He wrote: "Once during the height of telekinetic activities in the home, Katie's fifteen-year-old son observed, early in the evening, 'orange globes the size of a basketball in the orchard in the backyard.' The son was once videotaped bending spoons with his mother and a third person. The stem of one of the son's spoons split so that a sliver of paper could be inserted through the tiny crack. On another occasion, when at his home the son asked his mother if it was possible 'to go back in time.' With her approval, he immediately went into her walk-in closet, closed the door, lay on the floor and presumably entered a trance. According to what he told me in an audiotaped telephone report shortly after the event, 'I wanted to see what it was like in the 1920s and the next thing I knew I was by a Christmas tree and there was an old, bald-headed man nearby. I knocked over an oil lamp, but grabbed a cardboard box when I woke up.' Now, apparently the box returned to 1985 with him. Upon opening the box, he discovered (and I later confirmed on personal examination) that it was an 'ostrich skinned' cigarette lighter and gold leather pouch inscribed, 'Compliments Moragues Bay City, Inc., Mobile, Ala., Christmas 1928.'"

Again noted British researcher and author Anthony Peake, the author of <u>The Daemon: A Guide to Your Extraordinary Secret Self</u>, has extensively researched temporal lobe epilepsy, déjà vu, precognition, not to mention quantum physics, and has amassed a mountain of thought-provoking evidence, along with fascinating theory and speculation. His book is highly recommended and can be ordered through Amazon, or you can get a signed copy directly from the author himself from his website at: www.anthonypeake.com

I provided Anthony with the same details you've just read and he replied with the following thoughtful observations and speculations:

James is showing many of the classical "symptoms" of my Daemon-Eidolon Dyad. That is that we all consist of not one, but two, centers of consciousness. The Daemon, popularly known as the "Higher Self" has strong precognitive abilities and foreknowledge. However, this knowledge is not usually available to the Eidolon, the "lower", everyday self that calls itself "I" or "me" and perceives time in a linear fashion. However, certain neurological conditions open up a channel of communication whereby an Eidolon can fleetingly perceive the awareness of its Daemon. When this happens the "Lower Self" can show amazing, usually short-term, precognitive abilities. Sometimes these manifest as a "deja vu" sensation and at other times a complete awareness of the contents of the immediate future. Usually, but not always, this channel of communication is facilitated by such brain-states as migraine, temporal lobe epilepsy, and, in extreme circumstances, schizophrenia.

However James' case is even more fascinating. His UFO and cryptozoological experiences imply that something more complex is taking place. I suggest that this may involve an extreme case of Temporal Lobe Epilepsy whereby a particular endogenous (internally generated) chemical such as Dimethyltryptamine (popularly known as DMT) is released from his pineal gland into his temporal lobes and in doing so opens up a portal to the "reality behind the reality". This idea has been exhaustively researched by Dr. Rick Strassman. In his fascinating book "DMT: The Spirit Molecule".

To get a better understanding of Tony's fascinating theory, I recently did a fairly extensive interview with him. The following is our exchange:

Brent Raynes: Let's start with a little about your background and what stimulated you to explore these areas and to write the book that you wrote.

Anthony Peake: I've always been interested in human psychology and how the human brain works. My first degree was in sociology and history at the University of Warwick. I followed that up with post-graduate study at London's School of Economics. I've always been very much a social scientist but I have always been fascinated by particle physics and neurology. I've also always been interested in the mysteries of the mind, and one particular area has always fascinated me, and that is the phenomenon known as déjà vu.

Around about 5-6 years ago I was in the fortunate position of being able to take a year's sabbatical from my normal occupation as a management consultant to write a book. My initial plan was to write a book just about déjà vu and I started reading on the background of the déjà vu phenomenon and I was surprised to discover that there has been very scant work done on it. There was a book written by a guy in Seattle named Vernon Neppe, and in Switzerland Dr. Arthur Funkhouser has proposed some fascinating ideas with regard to déjà vu, dreams and precognition. I am also pleased to say that recently Dr. Chris Moulin from the University of Sheffield has been doing a good deal of interesting work over here in the U.K.

Effectively, there's no real explanation for it. There are various neurological based suggestions, all of which seem very, very inadequate to explain the phenomenon of the feeling that "I have lived this moment before" in some past life, or in a past incarnation. Or, the counterargument is that somehow I am perceiving the content of my immediate future. Both of which are rather strange ideas.

So I started looking into the neurology and the background to déjà vu and I was surprised to discover- and it's quite interesting because I was looking at your website and you have an interview with Todd Murphy who works with Michael Persinger- and I started to read more and more about temporal lobe epilepsy and the linking between temporal lobe epilepsy and déjà vu. I was fascinated to discover that déjà vu is part of the pre-seizure aura sensations that occur just before a temporal lobe seizure. So clearly there seems to be some form of linkage between TLE and déjà vu, and indeed I then started looking into the background of things that people in history who have had TLE, people like Alfred Lord Tennyson and Philip K. Dick, and all of them also describe other sensations, such as the slowing down of time and also the idea that they're not alone in their head, this idea that there is another presence in the brain.

This is quite interesting because then having subsequently found the work of Persinger, where Persinger has something called "the sensed presence," which they've been able to observe by stimulating the temporal lobes, clearly there is something quite peculiar happening and there seems to be a linkage between TLE and déjà vu.

But then a link was made from another source, linking it to near-death experience. The culprit seems to be a particular neurotransmitter in the brain called glutamate. It's a known fact that glutamate is the major neurotransmitter of the brain and it's particularly effective in the temporal lobes and it seems that at the point of death there is an effect called the glutamate flood whereby the brain is literally flooded by glutamate, and indeed that brings about the classic near-death experience, which, as you know, is the idea of having the out-of-body experience, of your life flashing before your eyes, and the idea again of meeting with other beings. Particularly a phenomenon known as the being of light.

So I started putting all of these together, but I didn't know where I was going with it. I genuinely didn't. There were things that I had read over the years from my interest in ufology right through to my interest in psychology, psychiatry, and this type of thing. But I didn't know where I was going with it until one day I received a phone call from a lady who ran a recruitment consulting service and she asked me if I was interested in doing any work as she had a potential contract for me, and I said, "Yes, I would be interested, but at the moment I'm taking a year sabbatical to write a book." She said, "What are you writing about?" I said, "Well, I don't know where I'm going with it, but at the moment I'm interested in temporal lobe epilepsy." She went incredibly quiet and then she said, "Look, I need to meet up with you." So I arranged a meeting near London Gatwick Airport and she said, "Tony, the reason that I needed to speak with you is that I've recently been diagnosed with temporal lobe epilepsy, and everything you were describing was sending shivers down my spine because it's effectively what happens to me." So I said, "Could you explain to me the first time that you discovered or that you realized that you had TLE?" She said that she was sitting in a restaurant at work with a friend and that as she was doing so and as that friend was about to pour a cup of tea she felt a snap over her right ear and suddenly she looked at her friend and her friend had frozen in time and space. Literally had stopped moving. She looked around the restaurant to find that everybody else in the restaurant had also stopped moving. They were literally frozen in time. She could hear this low humming sound behind her and she realized then, to her horror, that her friend had not in fact frozen but was moving incredibly slowly and she realized that the humming sound that she was hearing behind her was in fact people talking because the metabolic rate in her body had speeded up to such an extent that time had slowed down for her and she was literally trapped in this temporal fugue, for want of a better term, for hours and hours and hours. She watched her friend pour the tea and she said that she never realized what surface tension in a liquid was till she saw the tea hit the surface and watched it bounce up and down. Then after hours and hours she felt another snap over her ear and she came to and her friend looked at her and said, "Are you okay?" She had literally been away for about .5 of a second. She had a classic TLE absence, and this fascinated me, and for some reason, and I don't know why even to this day, but I said, "Do you get déjà vu's?" She said, "Oh good Lord. I get déjà vu's to kill for." She said she got déjà vu's where she knew what was going to happen for the next ten minutes. I said, "Why don't you just say something to somebody?" She said, "Because I feel that if I do I'll change the future or I'll change the way things are planned to be." It must be peculiar being in a situation where you feel you know what's going to happen next and you know that by saying something that you'll stop that event from happening.

I was quite intrigued by this because I then checked and discovered the link between déjà vu and TLE. It's quite well known, but I then found that there are other areas of TLE that are interesting, such as an area that you're interested in. Abductions, and in fact, Whitley Strieber and I have been in contact and Whitley has requested a copy of the book because he's quite intrigued about the implications of the things that I'm writing about in terms of TLE and the idea of abductees in such a light.

Brent Raynes: Right. I know that in Communion that was one of the areas that he was exploring at the very beginning.

Anthony Peake: Yes it was. Very much so and in fact he's gone much further on now into the TLE side of things, because clearly it quite fascinates him as well. I don't know if he's been diagnosed as having temporal lobe epilepsy, but it's clear that he has a lot of the symptoms.

Do you watch the TV series House, with Hugh Laurie? They had a fascinating show on a few months ago here in the U.K. where a little boy was having abductions and indeed they did experiments on the child and he had temporal lobe epilepsy.

Now, strangely enough, the thing that intrigued me, at this stage was the thing when people have a near-death experience and they say that their life flashes before their eyes, and that fascinated me so much because I thought, "What does that really mean?" I started looking into the neurology of the brain and the way that the brain records information, and I was amazed to discover that the research is very much showing that the brain records information and it buffers it, rather like a computer does or like when you're down loading files from the web. It buffers the information, gets all of the information and then presents it to consciousness. There have been a lot of experiments done on this, and the idea is that this buffering is recording reality. So the implication is that if the brain records reality then the implication is that that recording is kept somewhere in the brain. I then discovered the work of Wilber Penfield who was able to evoke memories by placing an electrode on to exposed temporal lobes of patients while they were conscious, and he was able to evoke three dimensional memories of the individuals past, to the extent that they could remember things that they had long forgotten. One lady recorded that she remembered and was reliving being in her kitchen again many years before and could hear her son calling outside and indeed reheard a whole argument that her neighbors had over the fence. Penfield, towards the end of his life, because he reproduced this particular effect on many occasions, came to the conclusion that the human brain records everything, and a neuro-surgeon named Jose Delgado continued it in the 1970s.

In fact, I was fortunate enough to be in contact with a Professor Karl Pribram at the University of Georgetown, and Karl believes that memory works like a hologram, is a holographic recording, and indeed he emailed me and said that he had many conversations with Penfield and Penfield was convinced that not only did the human brain record everything but that it recorded it on holographic principles and under given circumstances those memories could be re-evoked in a three dimensional recreation of reality that you could not distinguish from the actual events.

So I started thinking could it be that this past life review in a real life scenario, you could actually fall out of time and relive your life in a three dimensional recreation of your life, from the moment of your birth until the moment of your death. There is the old Gnostic idea and the old Stoic idea, and the old Neitschian idea of something called The Eternal Return, which is the idea that you live your life over and over again. Indeed this is what the film Groundhog Day was based upon. The film was based on a book written by a Russian philosopher Petyr Ouspensky, called "The Strange Life of Ivan Osokin."

Brent Raynes: I've seen the movie, and of course on your website you quoted the Gnostic Gospel of Thomas that said that "Two will recline on a couch. One will die. One will live."

Anthony Peake: My second book is due to go to my publishers this week and I'll be focusing in on this other aspect that I deal with in my theory, which I call the Daemon-Eidolon Dyad. And remember that I hinted before this idea that when somebody has a near-death experience, or in a temporal lobe epileptic sense that there is somebody else in their head, that they are dual beings.

It's been quite phenomenal. The book has sold over 20,000 copies worldwide in a year and I get emails from temporal lobe epileptics around the world. One young lady in Canada bought eighteen copies of the book and given to every single friend she has saying that this book is the most accurate representation of what's happening in her head.

What I argue is that at the point of death human consciousness splits into two personalities. The higher being, which I call the old Gnostic term of the daemon and the lower being, which is called a eidolon, and I believe that when we live our lives again in this three dimensional recreation of our lives, that when you live that life there is part of you that knows what is going to happen next, which is the daemon, and the daemon warns you. You know, when people have precognitive dreams or they have hunches or things like this. I have so much information that virtually proves that this is happening.

I've done about 50 talks in the U.K. and in Europe over the last six months and people come along to my talks and empirical, subjective information I've been given by regular people who for the first time have been able to talk to somebody and say, "Oh my God, that's happened to me." They hear voices in their head. There was one woman who said she was walking along one day and a voice in her head said, "That man over there you're going to marry him. Speak to him now." She did so, and she married him. She said it was amazing. She had never heard this voice before. It was something inside her that knew what she had to do.

This reality, this illusion that we could be living in, if I'm correct, the statistics show that seventy percent of the people experience déjà vu. Thirty percent of the people haven't got a clue what you're talking about. I believe that the seventy percent of us that do get déjà vu are living our lives again. The thirty percent of us who don't are putting down the memories for the first time.

I also say that the reality that we live in, this illusion, is very similar to The Matrix that's put forward in The Matrix films. I term it the Bohmian Imax. Have you ever come across the theories of Professor David Bohm?

Brent Raynes: Right. The physicist.

Anthony Peake: Right. He was a quantum physicist. He worked with Einstein and Oppenheimer, and he fell foul of the McCarthy problems in America in the 1950s, and after teaching in Brazil for a short time he moved over to the U.K. and he worked at Birkbeck College. He came up with the most phenomenal alternative theory to quantum physics, which he called the Implicate Order. Did you know that there was a very famous experiment that took place in Paris in the early 1980s, called the Paris experiment, and it proved something called the EPR paradox? The Einstein, Podolsky, Rosen paradox, and basically what it showed was that if you take two particles and you entangle them and you set them off in different directions, and you do one thing to one particle the other particle knows about it immediately. There's instantaneous communication, and what Bohm argued was that the reason why there was instantaneous communication is that at a much lower level of reality the particle is the same thing, and at a much lower level of reality everything interlinks, and that's what he calls the Implicate Order. But he also argues that the Implicate Order works upon a holographic principle, and its holograms.

Now I argue that if you take this idea about memory being a hologram and if you take what David Bohm says about reality being a hologram, you have a brain hologram processing an external hologram, which is reality, as a recording, and I believe that this recording that we all live within is that kind of principle, and I call it the Bohmian Imax because there's a famous philosophical concept called the

Cartesian Theater which was suggested by a Professor Daniel Dennett. And that's the idea that we process reality as an internal in an internal theater as it were.

You know the ideas of Rene Descartes, the French philosopher who came up with the famous phrase "I think, therefore I am" (cogito et ergo sum)? He argued that the only thing that a conscious being can know with absolute certainty is that they exist. Everything else is mere supposition. I extrapolate that idea and take it out into quantum physics and say that with quantum physics we can show that we are all living in this eternal generated reliving of our own lives, but, and this is quite important, even though we're living in inwardly generated illusion it's a recording, but we can change it. The daemon can warn us of events in our lives and make us change which route we take, and that works on the principles of another element of quantum physics called the Many Worlds Interpretation of Quantum Physics proposed by Hugh Everett III in 1957. This postulates that there are literally trillions of versions of us having this very conversation in trillions of alternative universes, and the upshot of that is that any possible event that can take place has or will take place somewhere in this temporal/macroverse. There is a version of you and a version of me who will fulfill every possible thing that we can do in our lives. It's just a question of which one of us is us. Which one of those trillions of individuals is myself, and I argue that we can swap universes, and the brain can make us do that. Therefore, every time the daemon warns you to do something or not do something, you make something like an evolutionary change and you move into a different version of yourself whereas the old version of yourself continues along the old path.

Brent Raynes: Well, that's a lot to take in. So with like the near-death experience, are you saying that at that point, when they're having the life review that actually this information is being downloaded for safe keeping for your linkage to another world?

Anthony Peake: Yeah. In effect, the theory that I've got, I call *Cheating the Ferryman*, and it postulates that at the point of death a cocktail of neurotransmitters flood the brain and in doing so it slows down the subjective experience of time. Time slows down. People report this, like in car accidents, people will say that the time slowed down. As the time slows down what happens is that the memories of your life are reconfigured again and you literally go back to the first moment of your birth and you go back to that point and you relive your life again, in real time. In the final split second of your life you live your whole life again.

Now occasionally, and I'm not sure which of these angles it is, but either there is literally a jittering in the recording process, which makes you see something twice, rather like happens to Neo in the film *The Matrix* where there's a cat which he sees going in front of him and he sees the cat going in front of him again, and he's informed by the other characters in the film that that's the changing of the matrix. That the matrix has been changed. Or, it could literally be that you have some deep rooted memory, that you remember you've done this before, so déjà vu is literally what it seems. I've done this before, and that explains it, and as you live this life again you will follow the same life pattern, because it's a recording, but there will be occasions when your own higher self, your daemon, will influence your decisions and make you possibly change.

I have case after case of people who have had precognitive dreams or have had warnings, literally voices in their heads telling them not to do something, and it saved their lives, and I think that is the point where they swapped universes. And there will be one universe where they go on and they die and there's the other universe which is the universe you're in at all times where you survive.

There is a very interesting theory being put forward by a Professor Max Tegmark. Tegmark proposes something very similar to what I am suggesting, which he calls the quantum suicide experiment. He applies the theory of Schrodinger's Cat thought experiment, and he shows that scientifically it can be proven that within your own universe you will never die because the circumstances will always arise that you will survive. The logic being that you create your own universe, so therefore the universe that you are creating and that you are observing cannot exist without you observing it.

Brent Raynes: Wow!

Anthony Peake: The theory is quite amazing. I'm getting emails from around the world. If you go on to Amazon.Com and you look at the comments that have been made by people who are reading the book you can see the enthusiasm by which my readers approach the theory. I had an email message from an Australian family about six months ago and they said the strangest thing just happened. They lived on the border of the Outback of Western Australia and they said, "We just had a knock on our front door and we opened the door and there was a Buddhist monk standing there clutching your email address," and he requested could they email me so that I could send them my address so that he could write to me. He had read the article that you had read, in his Buddhist monastery in Australia, and the article had blown him away so much that he wrote to me and he said, "Do you know that your article is scientifically proving Buddhism," and indeed he traveled over- he was coming over to England for personal reasons and he arranged to meet me in a Buddhist monastery in the Midlands, in England. We sat down for three hours and he talked through my theories and their applications to Buddhism. I've been invited to do a talk at a Sufi monastery in northern Cypress because some Sufi's consider that my theories support what they believe in about human duality. I've had people who were into the Kabbalah saying that a lot of what my book was saying was Judaic mysticism. So it seems like suddenly I'm hitting this really incredible interest and it seems the time is just right. People see different things in the book This can be seen in some of the amazing discussions that are taking place on my blogsite (http://cheatingtheferryman.blogspot.com/). This is a very exciting time right now.

The reason I like doing interviews such as this is because I feel that this theory is of profound importance and I am not alone in this belief. I want as many people to know about this as possible. Indeed in the USA the book is available for free download on www.wowio.com. It is important for people to come to their own opinion about this theory, because after all that is all it is, a conclusion drawn from observed scientific information.

Brent Raynes: And it seems to connect with so many historical and mythic tales of the Greeks, Egyptians and Gnostics.

Anthony Peake: Oh yeah. It even amazes me the amount of supporting material from the most disparate areas. A classic example is that in my next book there will be a whole chapter on the writings of Philip K. Dick, the American science fiction writer. He supposedly had temporal lobe epilepsy, and if you read his novels and watch the films that have been adapted from his writings and you read my book, it's mind blowing. He wrote a book called U Bick and in U Bick the central theme is that all of the characters are living in the final seconds of their life in a three dimensional recreation of their lives, which is what I say. But the real creepy one is that he wrote a book called *Valis*, and in *Valis* you read my book and read *Valis*, it's a fictionalized version of my book. The reason is that he was writing about his temporal lobe epilepsy. It's quite staggering.

I've read three or four of the major biographies of him, but the really freaky thing, and you'll love this, is they're making a film at the moment of the life of Dick and I think that it's going to be provisionally entitled *The Owl In Daylight*, and I'm in contact with the script writer of this film. We've swapped emails. Now one of the things that I pointed out to him is that a group of Philip K. Dick's letters went on E Bay about six or seven months ago, because towards the end of his life he started correspondence with a young student in Anchorage, Alaska, and I've managed to get hold of photocopies of these letters that were posted on the web, and they are mind-blowing. The guy was having amazing precognitions, and there was one of the letters where he says, "I'm going crazy. I'm starting to be able to see the future." And then, get this, he describes "Last night I had the most incredible dream that I saw a man lying on a floor dead, face down, between a coffee table and a couch." Literally two or three weeks later, Philip K. Dick was found, on the floor of his house in California, and he'd had a massive stroke. I argue that he had had a precognitive experience of his own death, and even the guy who was writing the screenplay was not aware of this. I wrote him, "Really you need to be aware of this, because this is exciting stuff," and he's trying to put me in touch with Phil Dick's daughter.

In *Minority Report* he has creatures which are called precogs, and in fact precogs are one of the central themes of all of his short stories and novels. Precogs are people who can see a very short time into the future, and I have people who email me now, and I've got one young lad, and I noticed this on your website something about this as well, this one young lad I'm in contact with who has a birthmark on his pineal gland and this lad gets even greater déjà vu sensations than this lady I was talking about. He tells me that when he has a potential seizure situation and starts getting déjà vu he knows what's going to be happening for the next hour or so. What he does, to stop himself from going absolutely mad, he speaks in his mind the things as people say them to him, literally word for word in his head because he remembers the last time around the things that they said to him. And again, I said to him, why do you not say something, and he said because 'I can't do it. I can't change the future, because if I do I'll change things irrevocably,' which is exactly what Philip K. Dick was writing about. Time and time again, he wrote about this sensation.

In fact, have you seen *Vanilla Sky*?

Brent Raynes: No, I haven't.

Anthony Peake: People were emailing me when *Vanilla Sky* came out and saying, "My God, have you seen this film? It's your book!" Again *Vanilla Sky*, the character, is living the final seconds of his life in this three dimensional recreation of his life. Now I am genuinely convinced that the whole of this book seems to be written for the right time. *Eternal Sunshine* and *The Spotless Mind*, people were emailing me over that, and *Fight Club*. There has been film after film. I can go on and on about the films that all seem to be dealing with my theory but in a small partition of it.

Now what I argue is that in our lives the Daemon is always in there and it is deeply rooted in the non-dominant hemisphere of the brain and in deep hypnotic trance situations people can encounter that being. And because the being keeps all of the memories of the past life, the daemon knows the future always, and it keeps itself dormant except when it's really needed or when people hypnotize. In my latest book I've got some fascinating stuff about this. Daemon and eidolon are Gnostic terms, but it carried right through into the Cathars, and they had this idea of duality. There was another Gnostic teacher called Mani who lived in Persia in the 6th century. He believed that he was two people. I believe that mystics are people who are more in tune with this higher being, this higher self. Some people can actually bring together the two, and this is what my Buddhist friend was telling me, that Buddhism has this idea. I turned around to him and said, "Buddhists believe in reincarnation," and he replied, "Yes, but we also have this concept of to die before you die."

Brent Raynes: I know that I was reading about the Hopi and this is the fourth world in which they'll live and they'll live on other planets, in other worlds, and it's a progression thing, and once they get it they don't have to come back here. They just go on to the next one.

Anthony Peake: Really. That's fascinating as well. I am a member of an organization called the Scientific and Medical Network, which is a group of scientists and doctors who are interested in bringing together spiritual beliefs and science. I did a talk in Switzerland and I met a guy over there who had been trained as a Kahuna in Hawaii. On his suggestion I started reading up about the Kuhuna and their belief system. I was amazed to discover that yet again their theology has large elements of my theory. They are convinced that all human beings in fact have three parts to them- a lower and higher self and the subconscious. It seems that the more one looks into it the more it becomes apparent that many belief systems of a lot of civilizations are aware of this incredible secret. I believe, for instance, that the Holy Grail idea is something everybody has wrong. The Holy Grail is nothing to do with the bloodline of Christ, nothing to do with Chalice. It is to do with human duality.

That's why the Cathars were such a problem. A close reading of the events that took place at Montsequr in 1244 clearly suggests that the secret of the Cathars was a belief in the real existence of two elements to the human soul.

There is now a good deal of excitement about the film "The Golden Compass" that will be released in early December. This is based upon a series of books written by British writer Philip Pullman. This film, although fiction, contains nearly all the elements of my theory. For example, in both the film and the book all the characters have a higher self called a daemon. This daemon manifests as an animal. So certain characters will have a daemon which will be a snow leopard or an owl. They're always with these people, and that's their daemon, their higher self.

Brent Raynes: Wow. I had an experience years ago where I was trying to find myself spiritually and I just said that I was going to leave it up to God to show me what I need to see and it was these little balls of light that came together as a small four legged white animal or being.

Anthony Peake: Wow, really? That's what I find so exciting about this book and I genuinely get so excited about it because everybody I speak to like yourself, discovers elements of it that relates personally to their experiences. I've done lots of radio interviews now across the U.K. and for web based sites in the states as well, and whenever I talk to people like yourself we find so much similarity of experiences. For instance, I'm re-reading Carlos Castaneda and the teachings of Don Juan. This is because somebody recently emailed me from the States to say that my book is a scientific explanation of the teachings of Don Juan and the writings of Carlos Castaneda. In fact, if you look on my blog site I think that there's something there about this.

In February I did a talk in Switzerland and in the audience were a couple of guys from CERN, the particle research laboratory. The talk was a presentation about the quantum physics behind my theory, Cheating the Ferryman. Had I known that these people were in the audience I would have died a million deaths! At the end the guys approached me and congratulated me. To my absolute relief they said, "Your science works. Your science absolutely works." In support of this I suggest that your readers take a look on Amazon with regard to the "readers reviews." Many of the comments lodged say that "the science works." But as I said the book touches a very broad spectrum of readers. I have mediums who come to my lectures ready for an argument, but because I explain about the higher self I give a possible explanation of their spirit guides. Indeed I even had a group of Mormons who attended a book signing and talk that I gave in Leicester a few months ago. Again they were prepared for an argument. After my talk they came over and said, "There's lots of what you're saying in Mormonism, you know." One of them went to his car and he annotated sections of the Book of Mormon that supported my theory. I'm going wow!

Brent Raynes: Yeah, you can't make anybody mad. (laughter)

Anthony Peake: Incredible. Scientology is another area. Scientology has this idea of something called the Operating Thetan. I argue that this being is another name for my 'Daemon.' Indeed the ultimate aim of scientology is to become a 'Clear.' For me this is the psychological joining together of the higher (Daemonic) and lower (Eidolonic) consciousnesses. The whole principle of Scientology is to try and find this inner being and get it out. It's the Daemon!

As times goes on the evidence from personal experiences of my readers becomes stronger and stronger. A guy who I'm working closely with who had a really profound near-death experience, he fell in the sea, and in doing so he became attuned to both his Daemon and the real nature of reality. He and I are planning to come over to the States at some time in the future to do a series of lectures. I will discuss the evidence from science and neurology and he will discuss the evidence from his own very real personal experience in the sea of the South Coast of England.

Brent Raynes: Well it's been a real interesting interview and I want to thank you.

Chapter 8
Lyn Halper, Ph.D.
The Energy World of Kundalini and UFOs

In Brad Steiger's *Gods of Aquarius* (1976) he quotes a statement given to him by one Gene Kieffer of New York's Kundalini Research Foundation who explored the area of UFOs and Kundalini. Kieffer had concluded that "Kundalini is responsible for most of the UFOs that abound in our times." He recalled a personal experience back in December 1968, how when meditating (and before he had any knowledge about kundalini) he observed a "luminous green, slightly pulsating, amorphous vehicle." Though he initially believed that this was a true visual sighting, he later concluded that it was a "projection of my own self." He was also given instructions, he felt, to contact a certain person at NASA in Alabama and inform him that astronauts who were about to embark upon a lunar mission were going to have a "spiritual experience" when they entered lunar orbit.

Hans Lauritzen of Copenhagen, Denmark, contracted a severe case of liver hepatitis in February 1966, when traveling in Africa. It became chronic and he had to stop working and was put on invalid pension. Then on the evening of December 7, 1967, Lauritzen went with four friends to a wooded area in Copenhagen to look for UFOs, and sure enough, at one point he observed "two great, dim, yellow globes" at an estimated distance of 100 meters. One of his friends also saw one of the "globes." For some reason, he felt compelled to walk into the forest alone, felt a "presence," and also felt as though he were in a "semi-trance like" state. He also felt as though he was in telepathic contact with this "presence," for when he sensed this "presence" he mentally asked that they let him help humanity. They told him that he had a "very strong power," Lauritzen recalled, and that it would become stronger. He came to the place where he had seen the two yellow spheres, then suddenly found himself standing in another spot nearby. He looked at his watch and discovered that over an hour had inexplicably elapsed. His friends at this point were calling for him, so he ran to meet with them. He noticed he wasn't tired anymore, he had lots of energy. Later he returned to his medical doctor who discovered that the liver condition had disappeared and the liver was of normal size again. Lauritzen wrote, "The blood tests showed that it functioned now as any normal healthy liver."

Soon after this Lauritzen began to experience classic kundalini symptoms. "Something was moving up along the spine from the bottom to the neck and back head," he wrote. "It was accompanied by a pleasurable feeling and made me stand up and make strange movements and turns. Because of the semi-trance state I just had to follow it, but afterwards I became extremely afraid what it could be. It was like something spreading in the whole nervous system." This went on for months, with a variety of different physical and psychological symptoms.

Jeremy Vaeni is a well-known UFO abductee and has been a columnist for *UFO Magazine*. I read in one of Vaeni's columns a brief entry as to where he had experienced something along these lines, symptoms and sensations similar to Lauritzen's. I emailed Mr. Vaeni and requested a more detailed description of his kundalini like experiences, to which he replied:

"I don't know how long of a statement you're looking for but briefly, this thing came into me or activated within me, however that works, not from aliens but from reading a bunch of Jiddu Krishnamurti books and finally 'getting' exactly what he was saying, which is essentially: You are thought. If you want to see if there's anything beyond thought then you have to stop thought (die while alive, basically) completely and without any motive, including the motive to see what's there. Just stop and being happens.

"So I did (or not-did) this and in that very moment my head started to rotate as if doing an exercise. It felt completely natural in spite of the fact that I was not the one rotating 'my' head. Only when pondering it and thinking 'This shouldn't be happening' does it seem unnatural. But when it's happening there's no question.

"So this evolved over time and was accompanied by psychic awakenings, chakra activation—ooooh a whole host of things I never believed in and always made fun of. In fact, I still don't believe in them. Whatever they are, they're real. I mean, it's as simple as that.

"So psychic awakenings, visions, what seemed like spiritual visitations and even possession. The details are too long to go into here but I'll add that there is ANOTHER form of energy that I've experienced since this began in 2000/early 2001. This second energy I've only experienced three times and always the same way: It feels as if a slit opens at the base of my spine going from the tail bone up horizontally. It's a hairline of a thing and it feels like it's being cut open and closed with no pain, just this feeling as if the area is numbed like a doctor would do.

"The first time it happened, this blissful energy slid in and consumed my entire backside head to toe. It was like levitating on beads of energy. (I hate using that word 'energy' because it has no real meaning but I don't know what else to call it.)

"After maybe 30 or 60 seconds, the energy slid back out the way it came, the cut sealed itself and I was back to normal. The second time it happened, same thing: Slit opens, energy washes in--only this time something rode in with it. Again, I have zero belief system for any of this I'm just reporting to you the closest thing I can compare it to—if it's not actually what it is. The 'it' in question is a demon. I could see it superimposed over my own body and feel its feelings. It didn't have thoughts, really. Seemed ancient and dumb but immensely powerful. I had the impression that whether it was good, evil or questions like that are irrelevant, all it wanted to do was bask in the glow of being alive through this body for the few seconds it had. It did so, it washed out through the slit, slit closed. I'm saying "demon" but I don't really know, just that it looked like a muddy red gargoyle and gnashed my teeth like an animal.

"But nothing evil happened so when I say 'demon,' really I'm thinking we have no clue what that word means and should rethink everything.

"The third and so far final time it happened, I had the big I AM experience. Slit opened, bliss energy, and 'I' seemed to wash out of myself. I dissolved into nothingness. The moment Nothingness became aware of itself there was a visual, like a drop of water expanding in all directions over black. I was nothingness, I was nothingness aware of itself and I was Jeremy aware of my own body all at the same time. I could feel the stretching in my brain as the visual of the 'water' stretched. It felt like it had an elasticity to it and would snap and frankly I was scared shitless that I was dying. It did snap, finally, but I didn't die. Instead, at the moment it snapped, a light flared and from this banged big the entire universe.

"I'm seeing the universe and I am the universe. Not just the macro but the micro. I am solar wind. I am hot rock forming planets. I am the stars and the debris. I am the trees and the wind zipping through them--I mean just on and on all of these awarenesses (points of view) happening AT THE SAME INSTANCE. It's indescribable.

"Curiously, when I was the sun giving life to the nearest planets that could take it, I had the impression that I was alive unto myself. That is, that stars are alive unto themselves, like mini gods. They are alive and aware and alone but not lonely. This is confusing but I'll just say it: I had the impression that I am that right now as I write this. That there is some aspect of me that is that sun even though I have no clue how that would work. It could be that I'm misinterpreting and that the Egyptians had it right: We become stars when we die. I don't know.

"Anyway, it was pretty friggen incredible and there's more to it than that but that's the basic gist.

"I've had a few experiences that lead me to believe that these creatures we call aliens, whether they are or not, are aware of this energy and know how to use it. I think they activated it at least that third time for the big 'god' experience because I had the feeling they were in the room with me doing this to my back. I never did see them but I did receive a message toward the end of this experience, when my vision rested on this giant red planet (maybe Mars; maybe not). A female voice I've spoken to but never seen during abductions said, 'Do we humans not understand that other planets cannot help us if we continue to block them out and kill ourselves?' Notice she said WE humans, not YOU humans, oddly enough."

Lyn Halper, Ph.D., formerly professor of Religious Studies at Rockland Community College of the State University of New York, holds a degree of Master of Science in Education, an Advanced Certificate in Marriage and Family Counseling, and a Doctorate in Transpersonal Psychology. For a number of years, Dr. Halper has maintained a private practice as a transpersonal psychologist, as well as acted as professor of psychology at Mercy College. She is the author of *Adventures of a Suburban Mystic* (Trafford, 2001), which recounts her personal Kundalini experiences (which are touched upon in this interview) and she also is the author of *Mystic Souls: Nineteen Remarkable People Tell Their Stories* (Universe, 2003), a compilation of stories from shamans, mystics, and clergy who relate their struggles and triumphs with the mystical life.

Here is an interview exchange that we had:

Brent Raynes: Can you please share with us some details of how all of this came about?

Dr. Halper: My story began when I became incapacitated by a bizarre allergic condition that resisted intervention by conventional medicine. As a psychotherapist, wife and mother with two young children, I was desperate to be well, and having run out of resources, agreed to have a session with a professional psychic a friend recommended. The psychic told me that the illness was a "consciousness-expanding vehicle" and I was about to embark on a huge spiritual journey. I went for readings with other psychics and they all said the same thing - get ready for a tremendous opening. A few weeks later while visiting an aunt in Clearwater, Florida I met with the great dental healers, Margaret and Willard Fuller. They told me they could "see" the oil of anointment running down my forehead and I would soon meet a "teacher of spiritual persuasion." When I asked how to find him, they smiled and said, "You'll be led to him." When I got back home I looked through college catalogues hoping to see a name that would strike me! It was funny. I knew nothing! But, as I began to immerse myself in meditation and esoteric studies, the allergic condition eased and eventually disappeared. Years later I would learn that the allergic condition was the Shamanic illness - you are made sick until you get the idea and take up the spiritual mantle. A few months after my meeting with the Fullers, I met a psychic psychotherapist - an American who had spent years in Asia and learned the secret of initiation - in Sanskrit, *Shaktipat*, transmission of energy from guru to disciple. At our first meeting, he recognized me and said he had been waiting for me to arrive. Two months later he raised the Kundalini energy in my spine and started what would become a turbulent six-year process of spiritual development - a process that nearly cost me my life.

Brent Raynes: Can you share with us what Kundalini is understood to be and what triggers it?

Dr. Halper: Kundalini energy is the psycho-spiritual energy that is latent in all of us, and to clairvoyants, looks like a coiled up serpent at the base of the spine. It is recognized by all spiritual traditions though called by different names in Christianity it is the Holy Spirit and to the !Kung people of the Kalahari it is n/um. Most people go their whole lives without being aware of it, but it can be triggered by meditation, yoga, prayer, childbirth, anesthesia, traumas like near-death experiences. When the

Kundalini begins its ascent through the body it comes in contact with spiritual centers called *chakras*. When a chakra is first activated by the kundalini energy it can cause some startling symptoms. For example, if *Anahat*, the heart chakra, is activated, the person may have chest pains, but when that chakra is cleared, be overwhelmed by outpourings of supra-human love. When the *Swadhishthana Chakra* in the genital region is activated, and this is typical when Kundalini is first revving up, there will be megavolts of sexual energy released. If it's the *Vishuddha Chakra* located at the throat, there may be spontaneous laughing, screaming, or singing. Later, the individual finds he has become an effective speaker.

Brent Raynes: I have heard that while Kundalini can be very beneficial, it can also be quite overwhelming and detrimental for people who are unprepared for such an experience.

Dr. Halper: Yes, Kundalini can be detrimental unless prepared, but how many Westerners are prepared? "Prepared" implies that we sit meditating for a decade or two and so clear the pathways the Kundalini energy will travel. Even great Eastern sages like Krishnamurti had difficulty with the energy. For most who have a sustained awakening, it will cause severe disturbances.

You see, the Kundalini is a titanic force that, when unleashed, rages through the body. It's essentially a purifying agent and where it meets with blockages such as physical toxins and emotional debris, it works away at them till they're dissolved. It's a hot energy, the !Kung call it "boiling," a "death thing," and a "fight." So, when it starts to rise - look out! The most common symptoms are tingling and vibrations, the energy can be icy cold, but mostly it is hot and one feels intense burning - and there are some who have burn marks on their skin. The process starts out explosively, there can be pains, muscle spasms, flashes of light, roaring sounds, bizarre emotional states and weird psychic experiences. Imagine a hot vibrating current moving through your body twenty-four hours a day, kicking up anger, sadness, anxiety, and your old back injury is a hundred times worse! But, in the final stage, *nishpatti*, the energy has burned a clear pathway through the organism, and those vibrations can feel like a glorious and soothing healing balm. Old physical and emotional ills disappear and there is often the emergence of psychic and spiritual gifts.

And, this was true for me, but, like most, I struggled with the process. The first arousal following the initiation lasted 18 months and was frightening, but my teacher was there to offer reassurance. The next arousal occurred spontaneously a year later as a result of meditation and provoked a crisis. My teacher had left the scene and I couldn't deal with the turbulence on my own. As the energy roared through the nervous system it caused strange mental states and I was terrified that I was losing my sanity. I saw and heard spirit guides with whom I interacted - entities that possessed utter power. I was dehydrated, drank gallons of water, and perspired so profusely my clothes were always drenched. After a while, I became physically and emotionally exhausted. I was so weak I knew that if the process continued for even another week my body would give out and I would die. I reached the nadir and felt myself to be dead and wandering an abyss. I didn't know that this psychic state is the experience of the dying of the old for the emergence of the New. With the dénoument of this cycle came psychic and spiritual gifts - notably, the spontaneous appearance of a catalytic-healing energy when working with clients in psychotherapy sessions. Still, it took months to recover from the ravages of the process. My older son, then 18 years old, went through a cleansing process around the same time that was not as difficult as mine. My younger son emerged, without a noticeable process, with strong clairvoyant abilities. Speaking of children, it's a strange thing, but two years after the final Kundalini cycle, I had visions and dreams of a child in South America, and led by synchronicities, went out and found her. That child, our daughter, is quite psychic too.

Brent Raynes: You began to locate others who had experienced Kundalini, so that you could understand it better. How common does this experience seem, and what lessons has your research and investigative work revealed?

Dr. Halper: My body knew the transformative process, but I needed to know it with my intellect. So, I grabbed my tape recorder and hung out with psychics, mystics, Hindu sages, Native Americans, Chinese healers - as diverse a group as I could find. I spent time with these people - people like David Bluewolf, the Lakota storyteller, and my daughter, then 8 years, and myself were drawn, psychically, into his world. I looked for the common threads in the narratives and found such people had a high prevalence of danger and near-catastrophic experiences, there was the frequency of Kundalini awakenings, contacts with inter-dimensional beings, a high degree of predetermination in their lives, and they had attained the spontaneous shift to the supra-conscious state.

As for the commonality of Kundalini, SEN, the Spiritual Emergence Network, a hot-line for those with Kundalini-related problems, say they receive about 150 calls a month. People who have a fully transformative Kundalini process is one out of a hundred. Today with the popularity of Eastern practices, there are many who find themselves with Kundalini raging out of control. Some people wind up being misdiagnosed with physical or mental illnesses, but even if there were more awareness in the medical profession, little can be done. The Kundalini is a self-directing, self-limiting force that will not be coaxed or forced into submission. There are people who have become casualties of the process and are left with impairments. Still, people flock to Kundalini workshops or for *Shaktipat* by a guru and that concerns me because there are risks, and besides, unless your body is genetically and astrologically coded for transformation, nothing much will happen. Conversely, if you are inherently "programmed," there is no place to run and hide, when the time comes - you must go through the process. A guru once said, people want spiritual experiences - until they get them.

Lessons? Well, certainly I have a healthy respect for the power of unseen forces - even the so-called experts are impotent in the face of the mysteries. It surprised me to discover that the world has a spiritual base - but then, who are the powers that be? Those "spirit guides," I believe, are the same phenomenon as yetis, or UFO's, and the power behind them is enormous. Incomprehensible. I am changed in that the psycho-spiritual component of myself is in operation - so I can be intuitive, have more synchronicities, get assistance from a transpersonal level of mind. My formula for living is simple: mild meditation, be aware of what you do and say so as not to hurt anyone, if help is needed, give it. Become a physician or scientist - find a cure for cancer - improve the quality of life on this earth here and now.

Brent Raynes: In what ways do you correlate or compare those spirit guides you interacted with to other phenomena out there like yeti's and UFOs?

Dr. Halper: I began to have a glimmer of the interconnectedness of the phenomena after several years of observing the odd actions/communications of my "Guides." So I began to dig into metaphysical literature, occult literature, and finally UFO literature. Gradually a picture began to emerge. There were striking parallels between my guides and other paranormal entities! It was shocking to me and it took a while to process the idea.

This is a huge subject area, but a couple of examples: The most common trait of UFOs is their vanishing act. Yeti's leave tracks that end abruptly as though they've disappeared into thin air. My friend and interviewee, Heshheru, A Jamaican shaman, tells me that Jamaica vibrates with paranormal phenomena. He describes a rolling calf with glowing red eyes seen for decades by islanders that is always accompanied by a noxious odor like burning chemicals or electrical wiring. This same phenomenon, the chemical-burn odor, is commonly reported around UFO close encounters.

There are parallels between the behaviors and communication patterns of UFO entities and spiritual entities, including the rather unsettling propensity for game playing and humor. Some contactees have noted that the space saucer and the entities were made of the same "stuff." There seem to be cyclic correlations between increases in UFO sightings and an increase in poltergeist cases. Phantoms, UFOs, Loch Ness monsters, spirit guides all have qualities that suggest they are a paraphysical phenomenon, and this theory cannot be proven or even tested. Ghosts, Nessies, Men in Black, the blood and tissue extract of Philippine healers, all dissolve before hitting the laboratory. Well, none of this is new, but the parallels are there for anyone willing to wade through the literature and/or risk personal investigation.

Brent Raynes: There have been a number of cases of people following UFO close encounters or contacts who reported having Kundalini type experiences afterwards.

Dr. Halper: Uri Geller tells how, as a young child playing alone in his backyard, he saw a metallic object descend and was knocked unconscious by a beam of light. His strange psychic abilities arose following that experience. Joey Nuzum, my interviewee, probably the greatest occultist and master of PK phenomena today, asserts that his spirit guides are interdimensional beings and that they have influenced his astounding psychic abilities. Whenever my "Guides" were around they seemed to emit a high voltage etheric energy that acted to jumpstart my own

Kundalini energy. Whether you call it "illumination" or "space-blast," high volumes of that energy can trigger psychic faculties in those with sensitive systems.

Chapter 9
Phil Imbrogno
UFOs, Poltergeists, Ancient Stones, and Magnetic Anomalies

Phil Imbrogno possesses graduate degrees from the University of Texas, Northeastern University, and the Massachusetts Institute of Technology. He has taught chemistry, astronomy and the earth sciences at both the high school and college levels. He was a keynote speaker at the first annual "UFOs: the Culture of Contact Multi-Media Festival" in New York City (June 22, 23, and 24, 2007).

Brent Raynes: During your extensive field investigations during the New York's Hudson Valley UFO wave of the mid-1980s, where you were also joined in this effort by the legendary Dr. J. Allen Hynek, your perspective on this activity changed from the mainstream nuts and bolts ET perspective to exploring the concept of theoretical windows to other dimensions. During his last years, Dr. Hynek was presumably leaning more and more in this direction as well.

Phil Imbrogno: That's true. The UFO people think of alien spaceships. I had been researching UFOs for a number of years before the Hudson Valley incident, but nothing very spectacular, or witnessed by quite a few people, so when these sightings started taking place and I had picked up a newspaper and it said "hundreds see UFOs"- and it was just on the previous night. The paper was March 25th and it was March 24th, and in the paper there were names listed, so I called some of these people to talk to them, and every person I talked to I got like 10 more names.

Now the point is that after I interviewed a countless number of people over the course of months and months, these people saw the same thing, and many of them were very good witnesses with professional backgrounds, people who normally didn't care anything about UFOs. They just saw something and they were convinced now that UFOs exist.

So I got a call from Dr. Hynek. I'll never forget his first words on the phone. He said, "What's going on up there?" Evidently, some of the sightings had made the newspapers, the AP press, and the radio. He came up and he stayed here for awhile, and he went back and forth for awhile and interviewed a lot of people. We did a lot of field research together over a couple of years, and we had a number of conversations.

Brent Raynes: Now this was what year?

Phil Imbrogno: We're talking the early 1980s. 1983, 1984, and 1985.

The descriptions of what the people were seeing, an object the size of a football field, going over the major highways all lit up at night and at a not very high altitude—you know, at rush hour, on the major highways, the cars just pulling over to the side of the road and hundreds of people getting out watching this enormous object drift over, with practically no noise, and people coming out of their homes (who lived around the highway). It's like something out of a science fiction movie.

So a lot of data and numerous conversations with Dr. Hynek, and he said, "When we're talking about an object that people are reporting that's larger than a football field, where do you put it during the day if it just comes out at night?" He said, "How do you hide something that big?" We looked at a lot of the data and people reported the object disappearing and re-appearing, there were pilot reports of the object folding down on itself, like a telescoping antenna, and Dr. Hynek said to me that he would be very disappointed if UFOs just turned out to be somebody else's spaceships. He thought that the answer was more exotic than that. He talked about parallel realities, of a multi-dimensional universe, and I asked him, "Why are there so many sightings here?" He told me to look for "windows." That there were "windows" in the space-time continuum in which these objects, which he believed were under intelligent control, came through these portals. And, of course, that led me to doing more research after Dr. Hynek passed over.

It's interesting because we had many conversations about this and he believed that, for the most part, UFOs is a very complex phenomenon, that they can't be easily explained as somebody else's spaceships.

There were other explanations. All UFOs that were being seen were not from one source, and he believed that a great number of them were from what he called a parallel reality. But the interesting thing is that in the 1960s, John Keel was proposing this theory.

Brent Raynes: Right. And, of course, his colleague Dr. Jacques Vallee was proposing similar ideas too and they were associates. I'm sure that he had some influence on him too.

Phil Imbrogno: "You know," Allen Hynek was smoking his pipe, and he said, "John Keel may have been right about this whole thing." John Keel also influenced Vallee with his ideas. So after 1986, after Allen Hynek had passed over, I called up John Keel. We're very good friends and I said, "John, you know, Allen Hynek said that you were probably right about this whole thing." He said, "I'm shocked. Allen Hynek was my greatest critic. I can't believe that he was saying that."

There's quite a bit of evidence to indicate that the sightings in the Hudson Valley may have been some sort of interdimensional phenomenon rather than so-called extraterrestrial spacecraft scanning around.

And I got a call from Budd Hopkins. Budd and I go way back, and he was interested if there were any abduction cases, and I said, "Yes, there were quite a few, but Dr. Hynek doesn't want to deal with that because we're putting together a manuscript and Allen Hynek says we have to keep respectable sightings in the book because abduction cases would make it look more cultish and more towards the paranormal. He wanted to concentrate on witnesses, the quality of the witnesses, and what they saw, evidence that you could not deny in court.

So Budd Hopkins said, "Do you know why they're flying over the area there?" I said, "Why?" He said, "They're looking for people." He may have been right also because many people who had close encounters with this object and were scanned by a brilliant light later had an abduction experience. The ones, of course, that I followed up on, which were quite a few, but definitely not the total number of witnesses who had this experience.

Brent Raynes: So it may have been that the initial experience of being hit by a beam of light was sort of a scanning process and then later the other memories would evolve?

Phil Imbrogno: What happened is that this object would drift over the highways, going really slow, like it didn't care who saw it. It would stop over an area and project down a beam of light to engulf a car, an individual, and so on. The witnesses that I talked to, that this happened to, which is probably a small percentage of the total number, later, within two years, had an abduction experience.

So I find that quite interesting. Budd may have been right in his initial analysis saying, "It's doing that not because it's wanting to be seen or looking for the geology of the area. It's looking for people." He believed, of course, that there were genetic experiments going on and that this object was going over and scanning people to see who was genetically compatible for their species.

That's what he believed. I don't know, but many of the abduction experiences of course were not totally recalled. They really didn't have positive experiences.

Brent Raynes: Now from charting the UFO activity you found a connection with lunar phases, and you also found outbreaks of paranormal activity just prior to outbreaks of UFO activity, and correlations to ancient stone chambers and carvings. Can you bring us up to speed on the significance on these aspects and what you found?

Phil Imbrogno: I received a number of phone calls saying, "Well what about all of these UFO sightings." Everybody was telling me about the lunar phase and UFOs. "Oh yeah, UFOs are seen at the new moon, the full moon," and so on, so I really got curious and I took the data and I did a number of graphs and I found out something interesting. Sightings peaked not on the full moon or the new moon but two to three days after the new and full moon. Not on the new moon and full moon itself. But the interesting part of that data is that it didn't matter if it was a new moon or a full moon, the peak occurred between two and three days, or two and a half days I'd say, after the new and the full moon. So you have a definite peak there indicating that the lunar phase did have an affect on the number of sightings. That was an interesting part of the data.

Also you have to remember that I had so many reports with times and the days, especially on March 24th, 1983 and July 24th, 1984 and October 1984, and November 1983. I had so much information that I said, "Okay, I've got to plot this." So I had two classifications of reports. I divided them into two sections. 1) Ordinary UFO reports, if you consider UFO reports ordinary and 2) high-strangeness reports. Electromagnetic phenomena, aliens, abductions, appearance of strange creatures, really bizarre close encounters with a smaller object that seemed to come out of the larger one, and so on.

So I took the normal UFO sightings, which is people seeing this enormous object passing over and I plotted it on the map, on a big wall map, and I put the times and the dates and everything and I realized that as you looked at it you'd see 8:15, 8:17, 8:18, 8:19, and you'd see the pattern of the UFO and where it was going. You could see where the first sightings were and although the UFO sightings from those particular dates were scattered over a very large area the center, the emanation point, the apex of these sightings took place in a small town called Kent Cliffs, New York. So I said that was quite interesting. The first sightings were in that particular area and the last sightings were in this particular area.

So I took the high-strangeness reports, just to see how they would fan out on another map, and I noticed that they weren't spread over a large area. They were concentrated in very small areas, they were clustered, and I said "That's bizarre. What the heck is this?" So the next thing to do was, of course, to go out to these areas and just take a look. Got a team of people together, and we went to Kent Cliffs in Putnam Valley, and Lake Carmel in Brewster. All the high-strangeness reports were of a higher concentration in Putnam Valley, New York, and Kent Cliffs, New York. At the first location, we found a stone chamber. I said, "You know, I'd heard about these things. Barry Fell wrote about them in his book *America B.C.*" Then the second location we found a big carved standing stone hidden in the grass with another stone chamber, and I said, "There's another one of those things." Then the third location and I realized that this was more than just a coincidence. So there was a direct correlation between the locations of these stone artifacts, these megaliths, these chambers, in relation to paranormal activity and the UFO sightings. And, of course, that led into further research because not only did I start investigating the paranormal phenomena, residents were contacting me saying that they saw apparitions coming in and out of these chambers, balls of lights, and UFOs seemed to be seen in very close proximity to them.

We did a number of different studies. Of course, with the geology and everything, and then we did magnetometer studies. The magnetometer studies proved to be quite interesting. They showed that these structures are located on extreme negative magnetic anomalies where the earth's magnetic field actually takes a big dip and it doesn't seem that the chamber is closing the magnetic anomaly but someone built the chamber (word unclear) to mark the magnetic anomalies, or the standing stones there. So there was a correlation between these magnetic anomalies, the UFO sightings, and so on.

And the greatest number of chambers that we found was in Kent Cliffs, New York, and of course getting into a study of this, getting into the legends, getting into the history, and so on, countless numbers of reports of strange going ons around these structures that indicate to me that they may actually be the location of Dr. Hynek's dimensional windows. We know for a fact that UFO-paranormal investigator's have in the past considered a correlation between magnetic anomalies and the appearance of UFOs, and I think that I was actually really the first one to actually document that, because the data was graphed and charted and it was analyzed by physicists at the Lamont-Doherty Observatory in New Jersey and they couldn't understand the data, how the earth's magnetic field is being deviated into like a funnel, which a psychic friend of mine calls a vortex.

So it is no coincidence that the chambers, the UFOs, the magnetic anomalies are all in these particular locations and you experience these phenomena. People go up there with cameras. Hundreds of photographs have been taken of spheres, of balls of lights, a majority of which can't even be seen by the human eye. But yet digital especially picks it up. These are things that exist outside the range of the human senses. Many of the UFOs that may appear in the area, or of UFO like phenomena, may actually be invisible to us.

So the stone chambers are a fascinating thing, unlike the UFOs where if you see a UFO in your life you consider yourself lucky because you saw something fascinating. These structures are out there. They're sitting there and have been there for centuries and they were obviously built by an ancient people who came here.

Now getting back a little bit to the location of the chambers, they're not built randomly. They're built in straight lines, they're built on lines of magnetic anomalies, and it's interesting because the geology of the area where the chamber's are built has a layer of magnetite, which is high pure iron ore, and on top of that a layer of quartzite. So you have this interesting geology, and the chambers themselves, the stones are only made of quartz, quartzite, and granite, with fine quartz in it. So they're not just stones piled upon each other. The builders put a lot of effort into selecting a certain proper stone, and you could theorize why, but obviously it was very important to the builders to construct them this way.

Brent Raynes: You eventually came to feel that, and did quite a bit of research and felt that these were connected with the Celts or Druids, that there were actual visits to this continent, which of course modern historians and mainstream archeologists haven't really acknowledged for the most part. I read where you felt that apparently there were three waves of visits in the ancient past, as described in Sean Casteel and Timothy Green Beckley's book *Our Alien Planet*.

Phil Imbrogno: Right. When I started researching these chambers back in 1984, I was completely ignorant about them. People were telling me that they were Colonial root cellars, that they were Indian sweat lodges, and so on and so forth. But I knew that there was a connection between what I was researching and the Hudson Valley stuff and these stone chambers, and Dr. Hynek's windows to another dimension. So I did a considerable amount of field work into these chambers, historically and so on.

If you go to a hard-core astronomer and want to talk about UFOs, you get the strange look and they walk away from you. The same thing happened with the chambers. When I went to a certain archeologist and archeology meetings they'd give you a look and they'd laugh at you. "Ha, ha. The stone chambers. That's Barry Fell's crazy stuff." But, you see, there's enough artifacts in the area and there are enough standing stones that nobody has really ever documented, except Barry Fell tried and another archeologist by the name of Sal Trento also started some early research, but gave up on it.

The structures of the chambers are amazing. Not only the chambers—it's carved standing stones, and also some of the large boulders, the dolmens, that are sitting on pedestal stones in the area, things that you would only think that you would find in Ireland and Scotland. The walls in the chambers go up at angles. Enormous stones were cut from the bedrock—flat stones, and placed on top, so they're not just little huts. Some of the larger ones go back 35, 40, 50 feet, and there's tons and tons of stone.

There's two types of chambers. One is cylindrical and the other one is oval. To the Celts this indicated male and female. Also the chamber openings point to the east, the southeast, the south, the southwest, and the west. None really to the north, or the northeast or the northwest. Also many of these chambers had different purposes. For example, these sites that I've been talking about with all of the paranormal stuff that takes place around them, and still does. One chamber we called the winter solstice chamber and you go in there on the first day of winter and you see the sun rising and it comes down, just about to the angle of the chamber opening, but if you went back 3000 years ago the sun would rise directly into the chamber opening, down this corridor, and project on to the back of a wall. Also, in another chamber, they found a stone that had carvings on it and I looked at the carvings and I recognized that. Somebody was trying to make an impression, in the stone, of the Pleiades (the Seven Sisters), which was very important to the Druids. The Pleiades was directly overhead at midnight. It marked the end of the old Celtic year and the beginning of the new Celtic year. That was the high holiday and it was called Samhain. Now, the Druids believed that this time there was a universe, a parallel reality that was very close to ours and at certain times of the year, and especially at that time of the year, our world merged with their world. Our reality merged with this other reality and beings from that other reality could easily come into our world and we could go into their world. Today we call this holiday Halloween, and the Druids believed in it very seriously because it was when these two worlds merged together. And that particular chamber, in Kent Cliffs, which we called a Cathedral Chamber, because it has a very high ceiling to it, was probably used for a ritualistic purpose for Samhain, because at the bottom of the stone there were carvings and writing, and the writing was Ogam. It was partially translated. Most of it was weathered away. But you do see the word "Samhain," pronounced Soween in Irish Gaelic or Saveen in Scottish Gaelic, for that time of Halloween, the end of the Celtic year, the end of the thirteen month calendar. On a number of occasions, people have reported what they called the ghost of a Druid priest seen in the chamber, coming out of the chamber and going into the chamber and so on.

Other things that we found, for example, in one chamber we called the King's Chamber we found an obsidian dagger, a dagger that was carved out of obsidian, volcanic glass, which is not indigenous to this area. When we had that analyzed it turned out that that obsidian dagger was cut from a volcanic outcrop of obsidian 2800 years ago. Now that doesn't mean that the chamber was built 2800 years ago, but it means that whoever built the chamber may have brought the dagger in there, and the chemical analysis showed that it was possibly from Iceland.

Now the Native Americans have legends about the people who built the chambers. They say they came across the sea, eighteen to a ship, their faces were of fire (red beards), their eyes were of the sky (blue eyes) and they had horns coming out of their heads (helmets). Where a chamber was built was once Native American sacred ground and if you look at a lot of the language, if you look at the Algonquin language, there are many, many words that are pronounced very similar to Gaelic words, and it could also explain why many of the Algonquins, when the colonials came over, they were the only Native Americans who had tribe members with fair skin and blue eyes. Also a lot of the Native American beliefs in the Northeast have this belief of a spirit world close to us, very similar to the old Celtic worship of the idea of another world, and there must have been a lot of infusion into the Native American society from these people who came here.

The chambers themselves are in different states of decay. For example, the very first people who built the chambers here and the last chambers that were built here, there was a great length of time between them. Probably the last people who built the chambers and in between didn't even know about the first people who came and who built the first series of chambers and the second series of chambers and so on. From what I can tell, in my analysis, is that the oldest ones (you can tell there's a different design and people are getting better as time goes on). The first series of chambers were built somewhere at the pre-Bronze Age, so we're talking about 2800 B.C. The second series of chambers was built around 500 B.C., 600 B.C. and so on, and all the way up to about 100 A.D. and so on. And the third series of chambers was built by Irish Christians in Connecticut in 500 A.D. Then there seems to have been a lapse, and then around 800 or 900 A.D. the first Vikings came over and they didn't really do much of anything, but explore and start settling into the landscape and then of course the Vikings came back and forth until about 1200 A.D., and then there was another gap where Columbus came over.

But one thing that you have to remember is that in 500 A.D. the story of Brendan the Navigator, an Irish Christian monk who sailed across the sea to go to this land, North America, because he had a vision and was told to do so by an angel. It was this voyage and the story that was written about this voyage that inspired Christopher Columbus as a boy to when he became an adult to make this journey. So there's legends way before Columbus's time about the Northeast United States being unexplored and colonized by not only the first group (who I believe were Pheonician), the second group who were the Celts from Brittainy, in Ireland, and then the third group who were Irish monks from Ireland. Then of course the Vikings came after that.

But these chambers were built by these people over a very long period of time. You also find these stone chambers and standing stones in Vermont, Massachusetts and New Hampshire. If you start in New York's Hudson Valley and go north the most northern town in Putnam County is called Fishgill. After you leave Fishgill the chambers disappear. Then they re-appear in Massachusetts, Vermont and New Hampshire. But the chambers up there are much more recent than the chambers in New York's Hudson Valley. As far as I know, NEARA, New England Antiquities Research Association actually found pieces of wood that was probably used to move one of the stones, trapped between the rocks in the massive stones that make up these chambers, and those pieces of wood were radiocarbon-dated to 1200 A.D. If you look at them and compare them to the Hudson Valley chambers, you can see that those chambers up there are much more preserved and there is much less weathering than with the chambers down here.

Brent Raynes: You stated that in legend the ancient Druids used to summon strange lights, where apparently they'd be in a circle of stones and a light would come and perhaps enter the person in the center, and that person would kind of channel information about astronomy or various things.

Phil Imbrogno: The Druids believed that there was this parallel universe. One of the translations of the word Druid means "gate opener." These standing stones, and there's a few of them up here—most of them have collapsed. Yeah, the Druid legends state that they would have these stones in the ground and they would have a person, most likely a woman, stand in the center, and these stones would channel up energy and the light would come up and bounce around the stones. The Druid priest would be controlling the whole thing and the light would go into the person and the person would pass out and wake up with ideas of medicine, astronomy, prophecy, and it would last for a certain length of time and then it would just fade away from the person, as if this person was being programmed or downloaded with information. Which is an interesting thing because people who have gone out to these chambers here and actually spent time in them, many people have claimed to have seen visions, heard voices, heard music, seen apparitions appear in front of them, and many people go out there and stay around these areas and a lot of people do it still today because of experiences that they had. They go out there and it's almost like somebody is programming information into them. Some of them are looking for answers to problems or whatever, but it seems yes, you go into these locations and you stay there for awhile and all of a sudden all of these thoughts and ideas start coming into your head. It's happened to me on a number of occasions, and it seems the more that you go into these areas the more sensitive you become to them. How or why this is happening I don't know. Perhaps the anomaly is somehow connecting synapses in the brain with some multidimensional source in the universe.

They say, according to legend, that prayer can answer your questions if you pray to a higher intelligence, God or whoever, that information can be put into you, called inspiration. How are artists inspired to creative work? Perhaps it's coming from an outside source. So these particular chambers, locations, and standing stones have this affect on people.

Someone proposed an idea to me that these magnetic anomalies are like the hard drives on computers. In a multidimensional way they kind of like store information and people can go inside, if they know how to connect to it, or are sensitive the information is downloaded into their brain. I don't know, but the phenomenon is very real. Although it's incredibly hard to document the effects on people are very, very real. People go into these areas, for example, have a physiological effect which is documented. For example, blood pressure drops considerably, pulse rate drops considerably, and some people go out there and they have emotional effects. They start bursting out in tears, and this has happened over and over again. Women actually go into these areas and have their periods. It's happened so many times. The first couple of times I kind of ignored it.

There's definitely a physiological effect also that these places have, and I believe that it's due to these magnetic anomalies that are found in the areas, and they must have a physiological effect on the human body. Animals will not go into these chambers. You never find animals (in them).

Brent Raynes: I was reading that you had stated that apparently that like with a Druid burial they would place someone in these chambers after they died and in a lot of these chambers there was a place where a body could be laid out?

Phil Imbrogno: Yes. We found a couple of chambers they call the tomb because there's a stone slab that's cut in the back that's perfect for a body. One of the legends that the Druid's had, and you've got to remember that the Druids didn't have a written language. They didn't write anything down because they were afraid that people were going to learn it. It was only passed on. The same method, by the way, that the Native Americans had. You see, they believed that when someone died they would pass over into this other dimension. There were many of these other worlds, and where you went, and what you did when you passed over depended upon your station in life, your spiritual awareness, who you were, like were you a great king, were you a great warrior, were you a great wise man, were you a priest, were you a murderer, and so on. They believed that the body would have to be placed in it, and the Druid priests were said to put a containment, say like an energy field, around the body, inside one of these chambers, whether it was Ireland or Scotland, or here probably, and that this resonation of energy would hold the spirit in, stopping it from passing over to the other side until the proper gate or doorway could be opened for this spirit to pass over to go to the right place to where it was supposed to go. Once the spirit was gone and passed over, the body was just taken out and for the most part it was just burned or recycled back into the earth. They would just strip off the meat from the body and take the bones and leave the meat for the birds. Once the spirit was gone they believed that the body was just an empty shell.

Brent Raynes: Now you've had some experiences yourself over the years. Paranormal, strange lights, things that you had experienced yourself.

Phil Imbrogno: Yeah, on three occasions I saw the Hudson Valley UFO, and on a couple of occasions with people I was researching it with. There are many people who are involved with paranormal research, but you don't really understand its reality until you experience something yourself, and then it becomes more of a reality than a hobby. You have people who are investigating UFOs who are looking for spaceships and so on, which is okay, but you see a lot of these people are doing it as a hobby or something to fascinate them or entertain their bored life, but what they don't realize is that a lot of this stuff is real and I know many people, people who I have worked with and have been part of my investigation team who have totally given up all of this because once they realized that this is a reality it scared them to death and they got out of it. It was no longer like watching TV. It was something that was in their life. It was real. "My God, this isn't just something I read about." People say, "This is real!"

Yes, I've had a number of experiences. How could I not have. I've been researching paranormal and UFO phenomena and so on, and so you're right in the center of the activity. You're bound to see or experience something sooner or later. Poltergeists, apparitions, UFOs, right across the board. But for the most part, out of all of the cases that I have investigated, and all of the paranormal cases that I have investigated, the actual percentage of these cases that actually turned up good data is very, very small. For the most part, most of it is misinterpretations. People who want to believe in something that just is not happening. People who think they're having a paranormal experience when in fact there is a logical explanation. People who claim to be channelers who are either hoaxers, people who are charlatans, or people who are just in contact with their own imaginations. But there is a small percentage of people who do this channeling who I believe are in contact with something else on a multidimensional level rather than their own imaginations. So I've seen enough to convince me that Dr. Hynek was right. We live in a very complex universe, it's multidimensional in nature, and that a lot of the phenomena that we call paranormal actually emits from these parallel universes when these windows open and close, and that includes some aspect of the UFO phenomena. Not all of it. Some of it may actually be extraterrestrial but not all of it. A good percentage of it probably is interdimensional, like Dr. Hynek, Vallee, and John Keel feel it is. From my research and what I've been involved with, I have to agree with them.

Brent Raynes: It's certainly compelling listening to you tell about this. Now the magnetometer that you used. Can you tell more about it?

Phil Imbrogno: Well the magnetometer that we used was taken from the Lamont-Doherty Observatory and you see I could do the readings myself but because the readings would be questionable I got one of their scientists [later, in an email, Phil identified this person as Dr. Bruce Cornet—editor] to come up with me and run the magnetometer and get the data. This was a magnetometer that it costs like twenty or thirty thousand dollars. Luckily, I got a sympathetic ear down at the Lamont-Doherty Observatory and a fellow who has a Ph.D. in physics came up and met with me one day, was interested in the stuff, and he came out and did the readings and was totally surprised and brought the data back to his fellow scientists down at the Lamont-Doherty Observatory. They went over the data and they were just like amazed by it saying of these anomalies how could they naturally be formed?

Brent Raynes: This John Burke was mentioning about the stone chambers in New York and he was talking about putting corn seeds in them and then later planting them, and some that were outside the chambers, but the ones that were inside the chambers grew much, much better than the ones that were outside. I wonder if you had heard of anything like that?

Phil Imbrogno: You know, I've heard different stories, but I really don't see any evidence. I mean, from what I know if you put anything in these chambers they rot. They're not like for food containment. People say root cellars, but you can't put roots and potatoes in these things. They rot.

In the recent New York state tourist guide they mention the stone chambers and they're no longer calling them root cellars. They're saying that they're possibly of ancient Celtic and Druid origin, and saying to people, "Ah, it's one of the great mysteries of the Hudson Valley, like the Headless Horseman."

Brent Raynes: Now you wrote a book on UFOs with Dr. Hynek and Bob Pratt, and then you also wrote something on your research into these stone chambers and the Druid history?

Phil Imbrogno: Right. After *Night Siege: The Hudson Valley UFO Sightings*, I wrote a book called *Contact of the Fifth Kind*. *Contact of the Fifth Kind* was all of the cases that we didn't want to deal with in *Night Siege* that involved contact and channeling and abductions and so on. It was my investigation into the possibility of: are human beings in contact with a non-human intelligence. In *Contact of the Fifth Kind* I began to mention the chambers, because they started to play a part in my research, as well as some of the underground mines that also connected with the story. In *Contact of the Fifth Kind* there's a chapter called *Underground*, that starts talking about the stone chambers and the underground passageways and mines that catacomb a certain percentage of Putnam County. Then after *Contact of the Fifth Kind*, I wrote *Celtic Mysteries in New England*, and then the most recent version of that is called *Celtic Mysteries: Windows to Another Dimension in America's Northeast*.

So the first book *Night Siege* was published by Random House and Ballantine. *Contact of the Fifth Kind* was published by Llewellyn, and then *Night Siege* came out again in a second edition, which was updated all the way to the 1990s. That was published by Lewellyn, and *Celtic Mysteries in New England* was published by Lewellyn.

Chapter 10
Andrew Collins
Expert on mankind's Ancient Past, a Cygnus Visionary, and a Hardcore UFO Investigator

Did an ancient gamma ray burst from the Cygnus star constellation accelerate human evolution? Can the human brain affect a Geiger counter? These and other intriguing questions are discussed in this exclusive and thought-provoking interview with acclaimed British researcher-author Andrew Collins as we cover a wide spectrum of controversial and anomalous subject matter from UFOs to the Holy Grail, ancient civilizations, crop circles, a thing Andrew calls "alien energy," and so very much more!

For more information about Andrew Collins and his fascinating research and ideas, go to his website: www.andrewcollins.com

This interview took place back in June 2006, while Andrew Collins and his wife Sue were visiting with Doctors Greg and Lora Little at their home in Memphis, Tennessee. It turned out to be a very synchronistic day as a few years earlier, in July 2000, a Native American friend guided my wife Joan and I to an ancient Native American petroglyph site in the Bankhead Forest of Alabama. The year before, following a sweat lodge ceremony, I had the impression that I should visit this Bankhead site as there would be a certain petroglyph that I would see that I, for some reason, would need to pay attention to. At least, that's what I felt.

That day we visited two different petroglyph sites in Alabama, and both visits combined proved to be powerful personal experiences. That day I saw a cross within a circle, and got the words "Southern Cross." I also "saw" a beam coming down to the earth, from a disk in the sky with like huge rings and/or bubbles (it was like it made a screeching sound). A week later, I would see in a vision while doing another sweat lodge ceremony a cactus in the exact shape of the 'bird feet' symbols that I had seen at the Bankhead site. At that point, I knew that this was the symbol that I was to pay attention to. But until I met Andrew Collins, I still couldn't figure out how it could be significant. But Andrew explained to me how the star system of Cygnus was perceived by ancient shamanic cultures worldwide as a portal to the sky world, was associated with various birds (i.e., the swan, hawk, falcon, eagle, etc.), all over the world was connected with the symbol of a bird's foot, and, alas, Cygnus was also called the Northern Cross....and the Southern Cross was perceived as yet a twin portal to the sky world!

That same day, while we were visiting the petroglyph sites, my wife Joan had a powerful vision of three star-like beings in a triangle like formation, and ever since then she has been able, from time to time, to see energy patterns around people, trees, and various other objects. Native American medicine people have told us that the spirits had gifted her with this ability that day.

At the time of our interview, Andrew's book The Cygnus Mystery was not yet published. Therefore, I was completely unfamiliar with his research into this matter. I had also brought with me, the same day that I did this interview, seven replicas of the Pre-Columbian Chimu Peruvian whistling vessels, which Andrew and his wife Sue found quite fascinating. A group of us meditated with them, and Andrew was very impressed by the experience. In fact, four of us "saw" like a spinning vortex, and all four of us saw it spinning in the very same direction!

Andrew excitedly told me how the legendary cosmic "bird of creation," associated with the Cygnus mythologies, was also described as being connected with a mysterious cosmic or primordial sound. He talked about "bird shamanism" and Native Americans like the Chumash of California who had bird bone whistles. He was quite excited when I shared with him a paper by Daniel Statnekov, the gentleman who first discovered the psycho-acoustical effects of the Peruvian vessels back in 1972, in which Daniel noted how the ancient Chimu potters had created sound vessels that "most succinctly" duplicated the "low fluttering sound of a hummingbird in flight." In addition, Andrew noted, "Some researchers have actually argued that the hummingbird among the giant drawings on the Nasca Plain is aligned to Cygnus."

As for the beam from the spinning disk of my vision, there were illustrations in Andrew's book The Cygnus Mystery of how a jet of radiation from a disk (black hole or neutron star) has long been aimed in the direction of planet earth!

Here is the interview:

Brent Raynes: Let's talk about the many different kinds of books that you've written over the years. For example, *Alien Energy*, that Eagle Wing Books, here in Memphis, Tennessee, just reprinted I guess a couple of years ago, and many different books that explored ancient mysteries.

Andrew Collins: I'll start with *From the Ashes of Angels*, that came out in 1996. Basically this book looks at the origins of stories of trafficking between so-called angels, referred to as Watchers and Nephilim, and mortal kind, and how these Watchers were supposed to have given the arts and sciences of heaven to them. However, they transgressed the laws of heaven and were punished, and others were destroyed in a flood, including their offspring the Nephilim.

Basically what I say is that this is actually a memory of very real events that took place at the time of the neolithic explosion or neolithic revolution around, let's say between 9000-7000 B.C., in the area of the Near East. Southeast Turkey, northern Syria, northern Iraq and western Iran. This was traditionally the Garden of Eden wherefore paradise began, and basically I say that the Watchers and the Nephilim were unquestionably the priestly elite. The shamans who controlled the advance of the neolithic revolution. They set themselves aside as a priestly elite, basically, and this was almost certainly the origins of kingship as well.

The Gods of Eden is more of the same, but also included in that was the origins of Egyptian civilization, suggesting that its roots went all the way back to 9000 B.C. That was in 1998. Then in 2000 was the first publication of *Gateway to Atlantis*, relating to the origins of Plato's Atlantis, seeing it as being in the area of the Bahamas and the Carribean, with its flagship being Cuba. There were many similarities between Plato's description of the central city, the central island and Cuba, and showing that the sunken area of it was in fact within the Great Bahama and Little Bahama Bank, and that this area had suffered some kind of cataclysm, almost certainly originating somewhere in space, relating to most probably a fragmenting comet, which caused devastation of land along the eastern United States and also within the waters of the western Atlantic. Drowned large parts of the Carribean and the Bahamas temporarily with tsunamis but then more permanently as the waters rose because this cataclysm, this event, almost certainly was a turning point in the last Ice Age which caused the waters to rise up quite rapidly, and this fits in perfectly with stories found throughout the Bahamas and the Carribean as told to the first European explorers, mostly Spanish, back around the late 15th century, and originally the islands had been all one large landmass that had been split up at this time. Some of the accounts talk about some heavenly body falling to the earth.

Then in 2002, I did a book called *Tutankhamun - The Exodus Conspiracy*, which was basically the complete account of the discovery of the Tutankhamun tomb by Lord Carnarvon and Howard Carter in 1922 and 1923, and everything relating to the myth of the curse, etc. But most importantly I brought out the whole story of the fact that a papyri had been discovered inside the tomb and had been spirited out seemingly because of the sensitive political nature of them which they related to the exodus, and at this time the British were helping the Jews establish their own nation within Palestine, and obviously their claim on Palestine was based purely upon Biblical accounts. If this had been challenged by new evidence coming out of Egypt then it could have stifled or even stopped any talks that were going on.

Then in 2004 I had a book called *Twenty-First Century Grail*, which basically, aside from being a personal quest to find the Holy Grail, gives the complete and full account of the origins of the Grail, looks at it in terms of the fact that it was almost certainly the cup that Mary Magdalene used to anoint Jesus before the crucifixion, and that this was also traditionally thought to have been used to collect the blood of Jesus and that Mary Magdalene was almost certainly the person who did this and not Joseph of Arimathea. The stories of Josepth of Arimathea coming to Britain were just made up by the monks of Glastonbury Abbey to increase revenue, pilgrims, and prestige. It took the whole Grail thing into the realm of the Cathars, the persecuted heretics of southern France, their whole concept of seeing the light and how this fits in with very early concepts of Christianity found within certain apocryphal texts. Like the *Secret Gospel of Mark*, and things like that.

Then in 2006, this year, I have a book coming out called *The Cygnus Mystery*, which shows that cosmic rays from a neutron star/black hole, a binary system known as Cygnus X-3, almost certainly influenced human evolution through creating mutations within our genes during the late paleolithic era, the exact time that there was the flowering of art, astronomy, cosmology. All of these things developed as if it affected human behavior, human intelligence at this time, and probably started the ball rolling. It then went into the whole idea of civilization building the very first temples in southeast Turkey that have just been discovered, which date back to 9500 B.C. These most incredible temples, and there's no question about their date. Archeologists are saying this, and these were the precursors of everything that went on down in the fertile crescent, to create the first civilizations of Sumeria, Babylon, Syria, and also to Egypt where the pyramid builders really began that civilization as well.

Brent Raynes: So this book will tie in all of these historical developments to changes in the DNA.

Andrew Collins: Yeah. And, as I said, it pins down the source of these cosmic rays. Specifically to the Cygnus constellation. Cygnus is the celestial swan. But it was also the celestial bird or cosmic bird in ancient mythologies all around the world. And what I show is that not only was this cosmology relating to the cosmic axis, the sky pole, with the bird on top of it and the snake around the base of it, a dragon or serpent in many cultures. But a great many ancient sites, prehistoric and sacred sites around the world, from the pyramids of Egypt to mounds at the Hopewell culture in Ohio through to the Incas and the Maya, the Hindu temples in India, to some of the greatest megalithic sites in Britain, like Avebury, Callanish Dancer, called the Isle of Lewis, Wayland Smithy long barrow, Newgrange monument in Ireland, right through to these very first temples in south Turkey that I talked about- all of them reflect the stars of Cygnus, either through orientation or lay-out on the ground.

Brent Raynes: I think also there's a lot of references to the Pleiades.

Andrew Collins: Not in this book, although the Pleiades are an incredibly important constellation for calendrical purposes, particularly in Mesoamerica. Probably the earliest and most enigmatic representation of a constellation which is found in a painted cave in southeast France shows Cygnus at this time in the form of a bird at the end of a pole, in association with a bird shaman. Bird shamanism is very much associated with all of this. I began to explore it all in my earlier books *From the Ashes of Angels* and *The Gods of Eden* because the swan, throughout Europe, was a symbol of the soul in death. The swan would accompany the soul into the next life, which would be seen in terms of the north. The north was the place of heaven. This same idea was found throughout the world, but with slightly different variations. In the Near East, it wasn't the swan. It was the vulture. In China it was a magpie. Among Native American people it was the eagle, or thunderbirds. And in Egypt it was the hawk or the falcon, which were representatives of falcon headed gods such as Horus who were portrayed in the sky in the form of a falcon incorporated in the stars of Cygnus.

Brent Raynes: Now when you wrote *Alien Energy*, was that sort of at the beginning of your writing?

Andrew Collins: 1994. So that was the book before *From the Ashes of Angels.* I can't keep going back. We'd be here all day. But *Alien Energy* looked at the whole idea of the fact that UFOs were manifestations of lights, of plasma that, although independent in their own sense and in theory may be produced by the earth or in the atmosphere, seem to possess intelligence capabilities. Not just through possible telepathic links with the human mind. More than that. Obviously the closer they came the more it created hallucinatory experiences within us that would also interact with the light form to produce what we call alien abduction experiences, which I believe were occurring outside normal space time. But beyond that they had an intelligent mannerism in their own right. They're independently intelligent, and I cite various examples of people who have been lost in the middle of woods and things like this, and a light would appear that would take them virtually back to safety.

So in other words, this is alien energy. This energy itself is a consciousness within its own right. This is not to say that more traditional style UFO encounters do not exist. They do. I investigated the first ever UFO abduction in Britain, which was reported in 1977, just a year prior to *Close Encounters of the Third Kind.* But for many years, I worked with the British UFO Research Association and the UFO Independent

Network, covering high strangeness cases all over Britain. In conclusion, people were telling the truth for the most part, but what people were seeing and witnessing was often based upon their own psychism, what was going on within their own heads, how much psychic they were themselves. Because you would often find the witnesses of high strangeness cases had many, many similarities to each other. Not just in the fact that they had also experienced in their life things like ghosts, astral projection, psychometry, a feeling of information from objects, but they also had various psychological and physiological traits in common with each other. Such as, they would all burn easily in the sun, they were all ecologically minded, they had weak wrists, and many, many different traits, which we call psychogenetics. Looked at in great detail in the late 1970s, early 1980s. This was brought out in earlier material I did in magazines and journals.

So that was basically it, plus the other important thing with *Alien Energy* is that it was tied in very strongly with the crop circle phenomenon which, although from my own perspective of having been involved with that subject for many years and know many of the key people involved, I would say that unfortunately 99 percent are man-made creations. I've now spoken to the people who actually created them. But having said that there is an X Factor involved. All the answers are not simply that people created them, plus the people who do create them have the most incredible experiences making them, they have dreams about what they should portray, they feel they have to go out certain nights, they get there and they feel presences, they see strange lights, sometimes so closely that it frightens them. And other things like this, and they are as much mystified by the subject as anybody else. So there's a genuine phenomenon going on here, plus quite clearly whoever started the modern crop circle phenomenon was simply basing it on very real accounts of "saucer nests" found in places back in the 1960s. I followed that up and found that there were many, many cases around that time. There were lights and those lights were actually connected in local fairy lore, to do with spirits, and different things like this. All sorts of fascinating stuff.

Brent Raynes: And, of course, you got personally involved, as you describe in *Alien Energy*, with others doing meditations.

Andrew Collins: Yes, the orgone experiments. One of the aspects of the crop circles was the fact that we felt that this was very, very similar to the concept of an orgone accumulator, as described by Wilhelm Reich, a psychologist and experimenter basically with alternative energies which he called this energy orgone. He believed that it was present universally and that it could be manifested or brought out through certain processes. Most obviously creating different layers of organic and inorganic matter, which he would use to create boxes called "orgone accumulators."

So even though we felt that the crop circles were essentially man-made they seemed to be producing the type of phenomena that Reich associated with his orgone accumulators. Strange light phenomena, miraculous healings, a sense of well-being, a feeling of presences in the room, and various other paranormal effects which had also been associated with prehistoric sites like stone circles, barrows, standing stones and things like this. It seemed to be that the crop circles themselves were almost creating temporary temples, as we called them at the time. They were only there for just a few months in the summer and the people could go in them and they would witness all of this strange phenomena. So we wanted to try and measure that, so we did a series of experiments within the crop circles, at dawn and sunset generally, for periods of two weeks for each year, for three years in running, 1993, '94 and '95. And did controls as well by doing the same type of experiments just out in a field, plus we did others on hilltops, sacred places, and I tried to compare the whole of it together. It was scientific, and we had a lot of scientific instrumentation to try and monitor any changes on an electromagnetic level, or gravitational changes or electrostatic changes. All sorts of things like this, and indeed we got the most incredible results. Most obviously within the use of Geiger counters. We found that during meditations, or more precisely just as meditations were about to begin, almost as if people's thoughts were already collected together right before you said, "All right, now we're going to begin meditation." There were incredible increases or decreases in the amount of supposed radioactivity going on. But we don't actually think that it was any changes in the radioactivity. What was happening is that the human brain, we believe, may well have been affecting the Geiger counters to produce results as if the local radioactivity was changing. So in other words, that was what was going on. Our brains were affecting the equipment, not that there was an increase in the amount of radioactivity in the air. Plus we also found that there were incredible low frequency signals picked up by the instrumentation during meditations, which our scientific advisor at the time, a guy by the name of Rodney Hale, was technical engineer, and he could not explain at all. It just did not make any sense whatsoever.

Also it was almost like when you were monitoring things at a multi-frequency level, lots of things were going off at the same time. Geiger counters, low frequencies, plus anomalous images in photographs that were being recorded at the time as well. Plus, as far as any psychic activity is concerned, we had good psychics working in our midst, and they were picking up things that were going on at the same time as well. So everything tied together.

We initially had gone in to test any energies within the crop circles and what came out of it was a much wider understanding of what was going on, on a scientific level, during meditations, and to show that yes, when you do meditations something profound takes place in the environment and within these meditations nearby.

Brent Raynes: So you had gone from this earlier work, where you were looking at the production of these unusual energy levels, that couldn't be explained, to now coming out with a book dealing with cosmic rays and how they may have affected our human evolution.

Andrew Collins: Yeah, yeah. I am not saying that these ideas are not exclusive to the other. It may well be that there is a link, which is something that we need to look for now.

Brent Raynes: How did you become involved in this kind of area of pursuit where you have pursued what a lot of people have considered far out, unorthodox?

Andrew Collins: It's in my blood. When I was 7 or 8, I remember discussing the theories of the universe with all of the kids on the block and we'd go round and round just discussing these things all day. I tried to get people to see ghosts. We'd go down to the local park and just sort of sit out at night. We would go onto little hills trying to tune radios to white noise to see if we could pick up any UFOs that would pass overhead. By the age of about 12, I was reading the works of Sigmund Freud on dream analysis, which I couldn't understand at all. I was very interested at an early age in astral projection. Read books on astral projection by the age of 12 or 13. But then, as a teenager, you start discovering girls and going out, and I tended to forget or ignored a lot of it for a few years until I was about 17 or 18. Then I was working in London and I happened to read something on the train going to London and back every day. I started reading pulp paperbacks on UFOs. I read literally dozens and dozens of them, all the obvious people, John Keel, Brad Steiger, Brinsley Le Poer Trench, etc. And I just wanted to get involved, so I became a UFO investigator, which eventually lead me to investigate some of the most important cases in British history from the mid to the late 1970s. It was during this time that I became aware that there was a psychic element with all of the UFO encounters. The people were as important in the encounter as the actual phenomenon observed. People were important here. That started to lead me to investigate psychism and working with psychics, and at that point onwards I was so intrigued with them I wanted to try and understand how their brains ticked. And from that point onwards I've worked with psychics and I always listen to psychics. I have psychics working with me on a lot of the work that I do, because I value what they have to say because it is so much more creative and enlightening than what orthodox views will give you on it. They're not always right. In fact, they're rarely 100 percent right, most of them being 50 percent right, or it may be even less, but it still gives you enough information to work on, to look into new areas, so I would always advocate this idea. Most of the ideas for my books, even though my books are scholarly in nature, probably derived originally from some kind of personal experience, either of my own or somebody else close to me, and it sets me off on a beeline, a train of thought, which once I become passionate about and obsessive about until I get some answers.

Brent Raynes: So you're how old now?

Andrew Collins: I'm 49.

Brent Raynes: There is a lot of experimental work that you've done. I was reading in *The Gods of Eden* where you had studied cases of levitation and you felt that it was some way in the sound vibrations and there was the case over in Tibet where there were actual eyewitness accounts, one in which I believe a doctor had observed some stones being moved by Tibetans using all kinds of horns, drums, and things. They had it worked down to a science apparently, a science that hasn't been passed on to us, but a few years back you used different speakers and things trying to change the weight of an object. Have you pursued that any further?

Andrew Collins: I haven't. No. I must point out that the book reviewed all of the known accounts of sound technology from ancient sources, plus also a few more modern sources. Including the examples that you gave. I've not been able to confirm those stories anymore since the book has been published, which means that although I take at face value what was actually written, the fact is that I've not been able to confirm it. I've spoken to various people who study Lamaism, Tibetan Buddhism and they confirm there is a tradition of moving objects using the mind, but I've not been able to confirm the accounts. So I would treat it with caution until any further information is known. I have no reason to suspect that those concerned made them up, however, I would still treat with caution those accounts.

Brent Raynes: Of course, down through the years there have been stories, I think one medium that was well-known, I think back in the 18th century was D.D. Home, who levitated in front of a large group of witnesses.

Andrew Collins: It was 19th century Victorian England. Yeah, he supposedly could levitate out one window and come in another, but the problem is that when you get into this type of account, as Harry Houdini would say, it could be done through trickery, and if there is any chance at all that trickery was involved it ceases to be counted as scientific evidence of anything. It's a case of that we can't go and check it now. It just really remains an eyewitness account and as we know from people like David Blaine or any other modern magician a lot of these things can be replicated quite easily.

Sound technology, I'm pretty certain, that it existed in the past. I don't have any doubts that it did, and we've also been able to replicate it to some degree, but only in lifting very minuscule objects so far, the size of something like a pea. But I do believe that it is something that in time we will understand it better from a scientific point of view.

Brent Raynes: Where are you headed with it now, or what you would like to see accomplished.

Andrew Collins: Well, having worked with UFO encounters for almost 30 years now there's nothing in any of the cases that I've covered (some of the ones that I covered were the most bizarre that ever took place in Britain) there's nothing that firmly proves that what was occurring was of extraterrestrial nature. Nothing. Yes, you're dealing with intelligences that are not terrestrial in nature. Whether they come from inner space or outer space is another matter altogether. Surely from the point of view of extraterrestrial intelligence I would like to see, before I die (which will hopefully be a very long time away from now) proof of the existence of life outside of this planet. The so-called concept of panspermia of life everywhere, that life is being produced in other parts of the universe and being brought here through means of probably some kind of object such as a meteor, a comet, or an asteroid, and I think that we're getting very close to that now. This is an area that I go into in the book, which is about to come out in October, called *The Cygnus Mystery*, which contains all of this stuff. There is a whole chapter all about panspermia in there, and we're getting very close to it now I think.

Not mentioned within that text, but certainly mentioned within the introduction I've done is the subject of the Red Rain of Kerlala. In 2001, over a period of three months, this red blood like liquid fell as rain over parts of southwestern India, in the province of Kerlala, and it was examined by scientists in India, who after they had dismissed more obvious mundane possible explanations like it was sand from central Asia, that it was the blood of bats caught in some weird maelstrom up in the upper atmosphere, or it was spores of some kind of plant that got up into the atmosphere, that it may well have been of extraterrestrial nature. When it started it was found to be cell like in appearance and would divide under hostile environments, such as oil, and come alive and divide, and it was unquestionably cell-like in appearance. Recent work has been done at the University of Cardiff shows that it has a form of DNA which they cannot apparently identify. More work is being done now and the results of which will be published later on this year. Hopefully. It is possible that these cells are of extraterrestrial origin because just two hours before the first of this red rain fell a loud bang was heard in the air, many reports of that, and it could have easily been a meteor hitting the upper atmosphere, basically disintegrating and releasing this cell like matter in the upper atmosphere that eventually got caught up in the currents and was drawn down within rain clouds and drops of rain itself.

What's important about this is that even this turns out to be a pure terrestrial matter in origin, the fact is it is being taken very seriously by the scientific community. Articles have been published in peer reviewed journals on this. *New Scientist* in Britain is following the story all the way through. This marks a great change I think in the way that we consider the possibility of extraterrestrial intelligence, and I firmly believe that probably within the next 20 years or maybe even earlier we will have proof positive of extraterrestrial life. And when that happens it will create a domino effect which will allow us to view so many different things in a different way, everything from UFO encounters to the origins of life on this planet to all sorts of weird, high strangeness things going on on this planet.

So I look forward to that.

Brent Raynes: How about the subject of the Holy Grail? You wrote a book on that also, and you had the Grail in your possession?

Andrew Collins: Okay, there isn't just one Grail. There are many Grails. I and my wife Sue became essentially Grail keepers of Britain's most authentic Grail Cup for a period of two years. This is known as the Marian Chalice and is also known as the Hawk Stone Cup or Hawk Stone Grail, and it was actually discovered behind a stone statue of an eagle in a cave, on an estate in northwest England. It's made of green alabaster. It's actually a censer of Roman origin. Probably first century. Almost certainly comes from the Near East. In fact, there are only three places that are known in the world that produce green alabaster, one of which is in Jordan, on the border between Jordan and Israel, and another place which I think is in Turkey. In Roman times this was highly prized. This green alabaster. It is linked in tradition we think with the cup that Mary Magdalen used to anoint Jesus and also to collect the holy blood. But anyway there's various Grails around. There's the Grail in Valencia, Spain, and another one in Florence, Italy.

This might be the real one or it might not. The Holy Grail itself is almost certainly a concept. But I'm sure that along the way certain physical artifacts have been brought out to represent that and they became revered, sacred artifacts. There's no question that the Marian Chalice if it had been discovered in Mediaeval times they would have built a cathedral around it. They would have had pilgrims coming there and charging them a lot to see it. It's a very, very sacred relic, but we had it for a period of two years and it was just too much of a burden on our lives. They say that the Grail keeper must have just one focus in their life and that is to do everything within their power to protect the Grail, and in a way that's how our life had to revolve around the fact that we had this thing in our house. We took possession of it from Brian Phillips who wrote a book on it called *The Search of the Grail*, which came out in the late 1990s. He actually found it in a lot of a descendant of the person that discovered it back in 1917. He found that various things were going wrong in his life and he actually blamed it on this Grail and he wanted to get rid of it, and so we happily took it into our possession, but eventually we gave it back to him.

You just couldn't leave the house.

Brent Raynes: Afraid that someone might break in?

Andrew Collins: Yes, exactly. This was not worth it. We had two years of being Grail guardians and that was enough.

Brent Raynes: I know that you said that you do a lot of meditating.

Andrew Collins: Yes, we took it to a number of sacred places in Britain, including Glastonbury, a place very much associated with the Grail tradition. We did some key meditations with it there. I feel that we brought it alive. Much of the story of this is contained within *Twenty-First Century Grail*.

Not too many people can actually say that they became a Grail guardian in their life.

Brent Raynes: Let's talk a little more about your upcoming book *The Cygnus Mystery*.

Andrew Collins: Right. My current project is *The Cygnus Mystery*. Cosmic rays from the Cygnus constellation influenced human evolution in early history and affected human behavior and caused germ-like mutations over a longer period of time, probably about 2000 years. Now this might seem a whacky idea but as I was writing the book I discovered that a scientific think tank, known as the Meinel Institute of Las Vegas announced that they also now believe that something similar was going on in paleolithic times. Their candidate is a planetary nebula in the constellation of Draco, which is next door to Cygnus. Very, very close. This they worked out through an examination of the levels of Beryllium-10, which is a bi-product of cosmic rays hitting the upper atmosphere and changing oxygen and nitrogen into the secondary element of beryllium. Which falls to the earth and is retained within sea levels and ice cores, and measurements of this can determine the level of cosmic rays. There's no question that towards the end of the paleolithic era the level of cosmic rays hitting the earth had doubled. So to suggest that this may have been involved in mutations leading in changes to human evolution is not a mad idea. Plus I found out that as early as 1972, Carl Sagan, the great scientific writer, spoke about exactly the same thing, the idea of cosmic rays influencing human evolution, in his book *The Cosmic Connection*. He went back to the subject in 1977 in his book *The Dragons of Eden*.

It's something that I believe influenced the foundations of world religions as well. You will find this Cygnus link within Christianity, within Islam, within Hinduism, within Near Eastern religions like Mandaeans of Iraq and Iran, the Sabians, the Chaldeans of the Bible, even certain Shiite Islamic groups strongly related to this. It's behind the whole concept that heaven was in the north and that we come from the sky and that we return there in death. Somehow this is all mixed up with this whole idea of cosmic rays influencing human evolution, influencing human intelligence, but mixed up with the whole idea of panspermia as well. This connection with the cosmos. Something which is very, very important, and I think that as we go on we will begin to realize that it is more and more important.

Brent Raynes: When the tsunami hit how there was like a super wave that came through that was very powerful and a lot of people said it was just a coincidence, but still do you think there was something more?

Andrew Collins: Right. Basically what happened was that after the Southeast Asian tsunami a gamma ray burst of quite incredible power hit the earth. This was extremely short-lived. Lasted a matter of seconds really. (One author) has proposed that in advance of it there was some kind of gravitational super wave and that this would have affected the geological structure of the earth to trigger an earthquake of the type that would have formed this tsunami that caused this disaster. Now that's a theory. I am afraid that it's no more than that. Plus there have been other gamma ray bursts, including a much longer gamma ray burst this year that lasted 2000 seconds. The one at the end of 2004 was only a few seconds in length.

It's an interesting idea, but it's unproven.

As described in this interview, Andrew Collins was also involved in one of England's early UFO abduction cases. It involved many psychic elements, and he also came to have some pretty unusual personal experiences while investigating this case as well. Continue to read on.

The Aveley Abduction

Considered by some to be Britain's first and most important UFO multiple abduction case!

On October 27, 1974, an East London family had a strange experience. It was late at night, around 10 p.m., when the young married couple with their three children in the car (two asleep and one awake) noticed an odd looking oval-shaped pale-blue irridescent light some 25-30 degrees over the eastern horizon. It appeared to be traveling in the same direction as their car, seemingly "stopping and starting." At first the couple speculated that it was possibly a helicopter, but within a short time they were both calling it a UFO. The husband remarked more than once on the lack of other traffic. They seemed to be the only ones traveling on this night.

The mysterious object seemed to be an estimated 500 yards distance (or no further away), although some direction changes and a higher elevation level on the horizon were noticed. The family was a short ways outside of Aveley, in Essex, when they were entering a bend in the road at about 30 miles an hour, passing a block of four terraced houses on the right, when something felt terribly wrong. All of a sudden, the engine and tires went silent. The only sound they heard was from the radio. Then as they were driving through the bend in the road, no more than 30 yards ahead of them, there was a dense green "mist" or "fog" covering the road up to a height of about 8-9 feet. Just as the "fog" was seen the car radio began crackling and smoking. The man went ahead and pulled out the wires. Then the headlights went out.

Still traveling at 30 m.p.h., the car entered the green mist. The wife remembered the car violently jerking at this point. The couple had seen fog different times in their lives, but this green "fog" seemed very different from anything that they had ever experienced previously. In addition, it seemed very light inside the "fog," they felt very cold (the windows were rolled up), and they recalled a tingling sensation and remarked on the curious dead silence.

Next things seemed a little hazy. The couple couldn't even remember for sure if the car was still moving. It seemed as though they were only in the mist for a second or two, then there was a jolt "like a car going over a hump back bridge," and the "fog" was gone. At this point the driver realized that they were about a half mile further up the road. The coldness was gone and the car was functioning fine, except of course the radio still remained unwired.

When they returned home, the husband rewired the radio, checked the headlines, and then the two still sleeping children were carried into the house. The wife then noticed the time. Expecting the clock to read about 10:20 p.m., it instead read about 1 a.m.! They were disturbed that some three hours had passed for which they could not account for.

Ufologist Andrew Collins, who learned about this case in August 1977 and initiated his first investigation of this family's experiences beginning on the 15th of that month, would later drive this very same route from Harold Hill to Aveley, and it took him exactly 22 minutes to drive the nine miles distance.

This case became a very important one, and one which offered Andrew many significant insights into the deeper and more complex implications of the so-called "abduction" phenomenon. In a report that was compiled in January 1978 on behalf of the UFO Investigators' Network (UFOIN) and published in England's prestigious *Flying Saucer Review*, Andrew wrote: "Never before have we been able to present a fully documented account of an abduction, a car teleportation, and an important contact case all rolled into one...in Great Britain." Andrew considered this "probably the most important British case ever."

Andrew described the family as "a very normal, simple, and warm" family of Aveley, Essex. They were John, then 32, his wife Elaine, age 28, and their three children: Kevin, 10; Karen, 11; and Stuart, 7. Though John had left school at the age of 15, Andrew described him as a very intelligent and creative person who had worked many different jobs over the years, mostly carpentry and construction, but also spent many evenings as a radio disc jockey. "He expresses points very effectively and has a vast vocabulary, although keeping his typical Londoner-type personality, i.e. accent, humor and views," Andrew wrote. "He says he dislikes officialdom, snobbery and the rich."

His wife Elaine, on the other hand, was described as very quiet, left school at age 16 to become an accountant, then married John and became a full-time housewife and mother. They appeared to be very credible people.

After Effects?

Notable personality changes occurred with all members of the family following the green "fog" incident. Particularly with John and Elaine. Shortly after the incident John suffered a nervous breakdown, for which there existed no apparent cause. This occurred sometime before Christmas of 1974, and caused him to stop working, which he did until September 1975, when a job working with mentally handicapped people "fell into his lap." This had been something he had wanted to do for years, and he now felt very confident of himself. Then he resigned in July 1977 after a disagreement with the management, at which time he began working for himself "creating things," and hoping to embark upon a career in which he would teach arts and crafts. Since November 1974, John began writing lots of poems about life, written "on the spur of the moment."

In the meantime, Elaine had become much more self confident, and beginning in September 1975 attended college, something she had wanted to do for years. Kevin, the child who had been awake during the UFO/fog incident, and was also the first one to spot the mysterious light, suddenly began to improve in his reading ability, in fact soon was "way ahead of his reading age," whereas previously he had been backward in his reading at school. Additionally, John, Elaine, Kevin and Karen all stopped eating meats and got to where they couldn't even stand the smell of it. John and Elaine had tried on different occasions to eat fish and meat, but the taste made them ill. They also began eating health foods to some extent, and avoiding foods with preservatives, colorings, favoring, etc.

While before the incident John and Elaine enjoyed "a good drink" they hardly ever, as of January 1978, touch alcohol. John and Elaine also became very environmental minded and expressed great concern over how we are abusing our natural environment.

John used to smoke some 60 to 70 cigarettes a day, but before Christmas 1974 he gave up smoking completely, and now hates the smell of cigarettes.

Strange Events since the initial incident

Shortly after the UFO/fog encounter, John and Elaine began to often notice three certain cars following them around. A small red "sports" looking car, a blue jaguar, and a large white car (Ford Executive?). All of them had darkened windows.

Paranormal events also manifested themselves. At about 7 p.m., on December 13, 1977, John and Elaine were watching television, when a large portable radio sitting on top of the TV set rose into the air about three inches, and then dropped back down. Later that same evening the entire family was gathered in front of the TV when the handle on the door leading to the hall outside turned slowly as if someone was opening it. Then it shot back to its original position. Twice the back door of the house, normally kept locked, forcefully flew open. The second time this happened a smell like lavender filled the room. Anomalous humming noises, "clicking" sounds and even "morse code" type sounds were occasionally heard inside and outside their home. In October 1977, Andrew was visiting John and Elaine and ended up staying the night as it was very late and a thick fog had set in. He slept on the sofa, but during the night was awakened by what sounded like pots and pans being banged together in the kitchen. It had really shaken Andrew up. The commotion had lasted for only a few seconds. Instead of going into the kitchen to investigate, he remained under the sheets. Andrew wrote: "Suddenly I felt a very strange sensation in my feet: it gradually moved up my whole body and over my head. It was a very stimulating and soothing feeling that soon passed away. Then the sensation was felt again in my feet, and again it moved up through my body to my head. Once more it faded and went. This feeling left me really at ease and peaceful, whereas before I had been very frightened after hearing the banging."

I emailed Andrew about that personal incident, to which he replied in a recent message dated July 8th, 2006: "It was an instant calming effect that started in the toes and moved very quickly up to my head. I went from being genuinely frightened to being in a state of relaxation in seconds. Very odd indeed, and not something I have experienced since."

Young Kevin recalled seeing a strange man, apparently dressed in white, standing at the side of his bed. He said that he looked like a clown. John had recalled two experiences with ghost-type apparitions back in his childhood. In both instances, John described seeing a small boy that would suddenly disappear before his startled eyes.

The incident of October 27, 1974, was not the first and only UFO encounter described by this family. The first episode had occurred while John and Elaine were courting, perhaps around 1965-1966. They were at a seaside resort in Essex, located at Walton-on-the-Naze. They were strolling along the seafront when out over the ocean they spotted a large "flat" star-like thing flying erratically. "It was stopping, looping the loop, and darting across the sky," Andrew wrote. "It was in view for about 10 minutes before it shot off out to sea. At least 10-15 other people had been watching it." Then in 1968, John was a passenger in a car with three others riding down M1 Motorway outside of London when a "large bluish-white light" headed towards them. Andrew wrote: "...the brake lights of the car in front intensified then went out. After which the car appeared to be slowing down and John presumed the engine had cut. Then the lights and engine of the car John was travelling in, also cut. They then hit the car in front, and that consequently hit a car in front of that, whose lights and engine had also cut! All drivers left their cars and chatted together, then decided to call the police. In the confusion the light was ignored and presumably disappeared."

Sometime just before or just after the 1974 incident, John was driving along Aveley Road (the road of the UFO/fog encounter) around 8:30 a.m. when he happened to glance up through his windshield and noticed an airliner in the clear sky above. However, John was quite amazed to notice that behind and above the airliner a large cylindrical looking object, seemingly twice the size of the plane, appeared to be keeping pace with it. Then suddenly the mysterious object shot away and was lost from sight.

Then on October 7, 1977, the family was traveling from their home in Aveley to Walton-on-the-Naze, along A12 between Gallows Corner and Brentwood, when they noticed a large bluish "star-like " light moving through the sky in a similar direction as their car. "This light kept in view on the left-hand side of the car until they almost reached Colchester, some 40-50 miles from where they had first seen it," Andrew wrote in his report. "During this time the object changed speed and height and at one point was just above tree top level, at which point they could make out that it was oval in shape. Also at this point the car radio crackled and eventually the station was lost. The car's lights and engine also acted oddly at this point. Eventually the light climbed high into the sky and was seen to disappear in front of them at an incredible speed."

"Abduction" memories

John and Elaine had been asked if they had had any unusual, recurring dreams. John remembered something about being operated on (or "something similar") by "small ugly" beings that resembled "gnomes." He also remembered from the dream state something about "tests" being carried out on him. Elaine recalled a "dream" wherein she was laying on a flat wide table, feeling as if she could neither move nor speak, while standing nearby was a being of small stature in a white coat. Suspecting that these "dreams" might be masking real abduction memories or something of potential significance, Andrew Collins initiated an effort to locate a hypnotist, and soon had lined up Dr. Leonard Wilder, a dental surgeon. The first session was set up for September 25, 1977.

John later admitted to Andrew that he came close to backing out of the hypnosis session. In addition to the hypnotist, Dr. Leonard Wilder, this first session was also attended by Dr. Bernard Finch, acting as a medical adviser, and noted UFO researcher Gordon Creighton, present as an observer and a consultant, as well as Andrew and another researcher named Barry King. John was successfully hypnotized, but not actually or fully regressed. He recalled various scenes or images, like the strange image of a man with an Arabian looking headdress holding a circular red light, with hills or mountains behind him, and the consciously remembered events, but seemingly in more detail, leading up to the missing time (i.e., the radio being on fire, the green "mist" all around the car, the white beam, etc.).

The second hypnosis session was conducted on October 2, 1977. John was described as more relaxed at this time. He now knew what to expect. The hypnotist and those present remained the same, except for the absence of Barry King. During this session several interesting details emerged. John described tall peaceful seeming beings in one piece suits, with pink eyes, wearing like hoods. Also a grey looking room, laying on a table and submitting to some unusual kind of examination apparently.

John stated: "They said they need us...as hosts, and they know how, and they...help...and they (mumbles) and they are us." Dr. Wilder asked John to explain what this meant, but John replied, "Won't let me." He became silent for over a minute. Then a different question was asked.

The third hypnotic session was conducted on October 16, 1977. This time John had persuaded Elaine to come as an observer. Others present from before continued to be in attendance, in addition to Creighton's son, Philip.

Dr. Wilder did an age regression on John, going back through his childhood, stopping at ages 10, 6, 3 and then 1. Next he went back in time when John was someone else. He stated that he was Jim Bayliss, ploughing a field. The year was 1640. "The most amazing thing was that he was speaking in a very, very broad country dialect," Andrew wrote.

Then John was directed to relive the green mist incident. Speaking once again in his normal London accent, John described tall beings, about 6 foot 6 inches tall, with no visible mouths, and a smaller being he called an "examiner" who "operated the machine" that seemed to scan his body. He had apparent difficulty at this time in remembering this entity's appearance. He also described what he was told about the ship's propulsion system, that it was "very complicated" but had something to do with "ion magnetic" energy and something called a "vortex," or something similar. Dr. Wilder asked John what the purpose of their visit was, and John stated, "No visit, they are here always." Then John was asked why they were here, and he said, "To observe and to lead...through observation." Then John was asked where their bases were and John fell silent, stating later that he had been blocked from saying more.

After this third session Dr. Wilder expressed the opinion that no further hypnotic regression sessions seemed necessary. It was being noted that more details were emerging and being remembered following the hypnosis sessions than were being recalled during them.

Andrew wrote in his report in England's Flying Saucer Review: "It seemed that the more we talked together on the subject the more information would be released. As Elaine put it: 'It's like if you hit the right note, the flood gates will open.'"

That evening, on the drive home, Elaine remarked that she was suddenly hit with an urge to paint a figure wearing a headdress, with a city behind him and with hills in the background. Andrew asked John if he had told Elaine about the similar image he had described to them earlier under hypnosis, and John insisted that he had not. Andrew then instructed them both to later separately draw what they saw, and noted afterwards the results were "almost identical."

By mid-December 1977, a great deal of information had seemingly surfaced from John and Elaine's subconscious memories about the encounter.

John's memories...

John remembers how in the beginning the car became completely engulfed in a mysterious dense green "fog" or "mist." Then there was a white "shaft" of light that pierced through the fog. At first it was about six feet in front of the car, and about 3-4 feet in diameter, and then it quickly moved towards the car, growing progressively wider, until within seconds the "shaft" of light seemed to have latched somehow onto the automobile and John then feels an upward ascent. Then he blacks out, and the next thing he remembers is being on like a balcony with a railing in front of him, looking down at a lower level, approximately 15 feet higher than the car, with the car an estimated 50-60 feet distance. The car appears to be inside of like a large "hanger," and inside the car he sees a man with his head over the steering wheel, and a woman next to him whose head laid back, both seemingly unconscious. John has the strong impression that he's actually somehow looking at himself and his family!

As he watches this scene, some sort of "panel" closes in front of the car. John then notices an entity, approximately 6 feet and 8 inches in height behind him. Standing next to him is his wife Elaine, and possibly their son Kevin. Then John and the entity move off to John's left and soon they are inside of a room with a table that has lights over it. The entity then touches John's left shoulder and he passes out. When John comes to he finds himself laying on the table. Above his head, he sees what he describes as a "scan" type of apparatus about 18 inches over him, supported by two circular rods, one on each side of him. The "scan" device is rectangular shaped, 30-36 inches in length, about 3 inches in width, and perhaps 1 _ inches thick. The underside of it has a kind of honeycomb shaped design and a faint glow. The device takes about one minute to pass over his body. John notices as he does this that he feels a warm tingling sensation on the area being apparently scanned.

Then John is aware of three tall entities to his right and two small ugly looking ones to his left. The smaller ones he calls "examiners," and as the "scan" device moves over him, one examiner puts a pen-type instrument on various areas of his body. The instrument, about 8 inches in length and _ inch in diameter, never actually touches the skin. It is kept about _ distance, while the part close to the skin generates an intense white light. Again there is a warm tingling sensation associated with this activity.

The "examiner" being stands about four foot tall and wears a white gown. The gown reaches to the floor and has long loose sleeves that are drawn at the cuffs. The being has no apparent neck, is slightly hunched over, with bushy brown hair (or "fur") covering its whole head and hands, with large slanted triangular eyes, light brown nose or "beak", a slit for the mouth, and pointed, slanted back ears. Its hairy hands looked large, with only four digits seen on each hand, with claws or long nails. Heavy set these beings walked awkwardly and made occasional gutteral chirps.

The table looked to be about six feet long, 2 feet and 6 inches wide, and 3 feet and 6 inches above the floor. The surface seemed soft, with small "bubbles," and like most things inside the craft seemed grey in color.

While on the table John was unable to move. After the "scan" stopped John asked the tall entities if he could get up. "Sit there for a while," he recalls he was told, but was startled to realize that they didn't speak the words. It was a strong mental impression. Shortly though he got up and the "examiners" left the room. Then he notices that he's wearing a one piece garment, similar to what the tall entities are wearing. He also takes in his surroundings, and notes that the room is oval shaped, perhaps 20 feet in length, 12 feet in width, and about 7-8 feet high. Everything looks to be perfectly smooth like the inside of a bubble. Other than the table and two overhead lights, no other furniture seems to be in the room.

John also notices that the taller entities look to be 6 foot 6 inches tall, except the "leader" who seems to be some 2 inches taller. They all seem to be wearing a one piece suit made of material resembling lurex or synthetic felt that even covers their hands and feet and forms a "balaclava" over their heads. They have two eyes, slightly larger than ours, with pink irises and "creamy" eyeballs. No nose or mouth seems obviously visible, and John suspects that they may be wearing masks. They also seem to have only three fingers on each hand and their skin looks very pale. In fact, almost transparent. The entities also make John think of a "bendy toy" or "blow up doll" as they don't seem to have joints in their arms or legs, yet walk gracefully but with no long strides. During his entire onboard encounter, the tallest entity was the only being that John had direct contact with.

John asked these beings what they did when they went outside of their ship. He was told that they used a visor, which then was shown to him. John compared it to a welder's visor in appearance. He recalls being given this explanation: "We find this unfortunate (the use of the visor) because we see through your eyes for most purposes. There are many occasions when we cannot find suitable eyes, so we use the visor to change your lights to match our optic nerves."

John then asked why there were no colors inside of the craft. He recalls being told: "For you there are no colors but for us there are. Because of the structure of our optic unit the light we receive is reacted to in a way different to that in which your optic nerves operate. The conditions are controlled in our favor and that is why you see what you see."

John then requested to be able to look around the ship and was indeed given a tour. They walked up to a wall whereupon an oval shaped hole about seven feet tall and three feet wide opened up. John and the three tall entities walked down a "connecting" tunnel a short ways to another room. With couches and a table near a wall, John felt it was a leisure room. The room was similar in size to the one they had just been in. Then they were in another tunnel and next entered what resembled a laboratory, where they explained that they did "research." After awhile they went up a vertical tube into a larger room, what John knew had to be the control room. Four more tall beings were seated at a crescent shaped unit with panels along its top surface. The beings had their backs to John, and appeared to be busy working controls, passing their hands above some sort of instrumentation.

John was ushered over to a couch where he laid down. It was comfortable, covered with miniature air cushions, and about six feet long. Some 18 inches above his head was a dish-shaped object some 15-16 inches in diameter. Soon a single dimensional picture, some 5 feet long and 2 feet and a half high, was projected on the wall in front of him. Over the next few minutes he was shown hundreds of images, pictures of plans, maps, drawings, and charts, all in a rapid fire fashion. Object overhead seemed to supply "verbal accompaniment," narration for the images. When John complained that it was all "going too fast," he was told, "Don't worry, it is all being remembered by your mind."

John doesn't consciously remember much about what he was shown, but stated that he did recognize a map of our solar system, and recognized Saturn "because of its rings." During this time he remembers hearing the word "Phobos", and admitted that he didn't know then that Phobos was the smallest satellite of Mars.

John was then led to a darker area of the control room where a hologram was projected. He observed a complex of pointed grey metallic looking cones protruding from an alien landscape, with mountains or hills behind them. He was told that this was how their planet looked in its last years after it had been ruined by pollution and natural problems. In front of this scene a figure could be seen.

Wearing a hooded robe, the figure looked very old, had pink eyes, and held a round object that glowed red and yellow. John was asked to touch this object. When he did he felt some sort of strange sensation moving up his arm. He felt that it had something to do with their planet's energy, though he couldn't recall being given an explanation. He did state that he felt privileged to have seen this. Then the "leader" told him that it was time to leave but that they would meet again one day. Then soon he finds himself back behind the wheel of the car, and soon he's moving down the road again.

Elaine's memories...

Elaine and John's memories dovetail quite precisely in many respects. Elaine also recalls the green fog or mist, the white beam of light, feeling the ascent, and blacking out. Then she finds herself on a balcony standing next to John and looking down at a hanger looking area. She remembers seeing the car, with John, herself and Kevin standing in front of it. And, if she remembers correctly, Kevin was also standing near her on the balcony. Then she was led away, recalls descending a short distance, and a hole appeared in the wall. Behind it were two "examiners" (her description matches those of John's) and she was led into the room. Kevin however was taken away against her will by a tall entity and an examiner to another part of the room out of view. Elaine was led then to a flat table and made to lay down and a strap was put across her legs and arms. As she struggled two "examiners" began conducting tests, one doing the testing while the other assisted. With a kind of "pen," about 4 inches in length and 3/4 inches in diameter, her whole body was examined, beginning with her feet. The interior of the "pen" glowed with a purple color, which seemed to change in luminosity. Little by little the examination procedure continued until they reached her head. Particular attention seemed focused on her left side around where her kidney would have been.

The "examiners" seemed to be humming or singing like to themselves during the procedure. Continuing to struggle and still very scared, one tall entity adviser her that they couldn't do anything with her like this, and so a tall entity them approached her and placed a middle finger on her forehead and the two others on the outsides of her eyes, during which she passed out.

After awhile Elaine came to and noticed that the straps had been removed. Nonetheless, she was unable to move. She then noticed that she was wearing a long gown with a tight hood rather like those worn by the tall entities. The material looked almost transparent and resembled crinkly cellophane.

Next Elaine recalls walking down corridors with walls covered in honeycomb design. She was accompanied by 2 or 3 of the tall entities. At one point, she noticed John in his one piece suit walking in the opposite direction with two other entities. Neither of them acknowledged the other.

Soon she too found herself inside what she recognized as a "control room." She was led across the room to another entity that was seated. The being swung around in his seat and faced her, took her hand and helped her up to a seat at his level. "That wasn't too bad was it," Elaine believes the being said. "It was nothing to fuss about." At this point, Elaine realized that they weren't "speaking" to her. She was puzzled, and felt even more uneasy. After awhile the entity asked another being standing nearby to "play her some music." Elaine described how the tall entity began to twiddle its hands slowly and she heard a soothing sound, a sound that made her think of a high-pitched harp. She wasn't sure how the music was being produced but noticed that once finished she did feel relaxed. Around about this time too the entity seemed to sense Elaine's concern for her children, turned to her and said: "Your children are safe. You value your children. We do not reproduce. We do not have children. We reproduce through you. You are our children."

Later Elaine was led across the control room to a dark area where she was told to lie down on a couched area and watch the screen. Over her head was a dish shaped device with a concave octagonal shaped inside. Elaine was also shown many maps, charts, pictures and drawings. Se described the experience as like "having the contents of an encyclopedia pumped into one's head all in one go." The images flashed on and off very quickly. She only remembered one, a star chart that she recognized as showing our solar system, but instead of the traditional nine planets there were eleven! Then the screen went blank, and Elaine was led to another area where John and Kevin were also. This was the holographic experience it seems that John had also described. She remembers how the entity explained: "This is the seed of life, our past and your future, our whole existence. Accept this from us for yourself, your children and your fellow kind." Elaine saw John and Kevin already touching the mysterious ball as she was being told to do it also. So she did, and then the "leader" told her it was time to leave, but that she would see them again.

Soon the family appeared to be in the hanger area again, standing on like a catwalk that circled around the car. The catwalk appeared to be some 4-6 feet higher than the car. Between the catwalk and the car were layers of several steps. The car was also facing the opposite direction it had originally been in, and was sloping downwards. The "leader" appeared and the entity who had played the music as well. Elaine believes she heard the "music man" refer to the "leader" as Lyra, and heard the "leader" call the "music man" something like Ceres. Both entities said goodbye to Elaine. She looked at the car and the children were already inside and John was about to get in. As she stood there taking this in, she feels that she may have given the impression of being reluctant to leave as she was told that she could stay if she wanted to. She felt though that they didn't really mean it, and figured later that they were simply testing her. But as she stood there the car "fizzled" away, dematerializing through the wall, and as this was happening the room became very bright. When the car had completely disappeared, Elaine began to worry. She was told not to worry though, that she could catch up. Then she saw the car traveling along the road around a wooded area and then found herself getting into the vehicle as it was still moving. Shutting the door she noticed that the interior light was on. The car experienced some kind of jolt, and Elaine looked around and asked if everyone was in the vehicle.

Though descriptions of the tall entities and "examiners" tallied very precisely with John and Elaine, their descriptions of the examination rooms varied considerably, though both described a "pen" type device attached to wires, but related differences in size and color. Both told of a control room, how they were shown maps, drawings and charts on a screen, and also experienced an incredible hologram.

John asked if they had any computers to which they seemed amused and replied that they had an organic computer which could control the craft when required. In addition, they explained, they could link their minds directly with this computer if needed, bypassing the use of manual control.

The entities also explained that they had their own system of communication, but that when conversing with humans they could somehow pick our words from out of our minds and redirect them to form a communications link with us. Presumably they possess no language or vocabulary themselves, but function on an emotional level, and can somehow process the equivalent of a thousand of our words in a fraction of a second. In addition, when they first make contact with a human they will allegedly scan that brain for emotional acceptance. They even reportedly admitted that they could then project an image acceptable to ones emotional level.

Andrew again recalls this case in his book *Alien Energy*, adding that John came to conclude that he and his family never actually physically were onboard a real spacecraft. He feels it was an alien contact, but it was in "some form of astral domain," and that the alien intelligence responsible could convey their knowledge and ideas in a way that would be acceptable. He called them the Watchers, presumably an alien race of great stature who formerly inhabited our planet long ago. Andrew wrote: "I therefore find it intriguing that in European occultism the term *eggregori*, Greek for Watchers, was the name given to balls of etheric light that watched over the affairs of mankind. Perhaps John might have been closer to the truth than he could ever have imagined."

Recent Notes on this case from Andrew Collins:

Though initially the pseudonyms of John and Elaine Avis were used, I learned in an email from Andrew Collins on July 2, 2006 that their real names were John and Sue Day. When I met Andrew while he was visiting Dr's Greg and Lora Little at their home in Memphis, Tenn., on June 10th, we discussed this fascinating case. As we had been talking about shamanic elements of similarity with UFO contact situations, Andrew told me how these witnesses had nightly OOBEs that he had found similar to what shaman's described. I asked him about it and in this email he wrote me: "...it is true that the sometimes nightly journeys of John and Sue Day, where they went to some kind of collective consciousness somewhere out there in the universe in order to communicate with the Watchers, the perpetrators of their abduction, mirrored exactly the experiences of shamans achieving similar astral journeys. In their case they believed they went to the sky-world, or a place of light, where the souls of the ancestors resided. Yet the contact is more-or-less the same, even though abductees almost always achieve their altered states of consciousness without the use of stimulants or sensory deprivation."

In an email dated July 8th I learned additional details. Andrew wrote: "The couple split up many years ago, as they both entered separate lives. The wife, Sue, ended up becoming a pagan witch and midwife who served the Allies in Iraq during the first Gulf War. ...John has many strange dreams, but generally things have calmed down over the years. He is still psychic, and very much in tune with the environment. He is a sculptor, artist and maker of child's doll houses and lives a reclusive life with his second wife in the wilds of Scotland. He still doesn't drink any alcohol either."

"The family are very credible, and what is important is that they have always attempted to analyze what happened from a grounded perspective, suggesting even that the whole thing had been an astral experience after they all entered the green mist.

"In my opinion, the whole incident happened instantaneously for the family and car, but outside usual space-time for the rest of the world, leaving them with a three hour time loss.

"I am sure I could eventually work out that something like this is possible on a quantum level, using Einstein's Special Theory of Relativity."

I asked Andrew to describe his apparitional experience at John and Sue's home back in 1977, which he related in an email dated July 14, 2006:

"Myself and Barry King would camp round at the Day's home every Friday night to see whether any paranormal phenomena might occur, and sometimes it did. You know about the pots and pans episode [described last issue- editor]. Another night John, Barry and I sat up chatting until the early hours. So as not to disturb his wife, Sue, who was asleep, John remained with Barry and I as we bedded down for the night. John and Barry were in sleeping bags on the floor, and I was on the sofa.

"I slept, and was then awoken around seven o'clock that morning by the sound of the door handle moving behind my head, at which I craned my neck to see in the dawn light the door opening just feet away. I thought that John or Barry had got to the toilet upstairs, and were returning to the room. A tall silhouetted figure stood momentarily in the doorway, before moving quickly out of sight as if walking away. It was at that moment that I glanced on to the floor and saw that both John and Barry were clearly present and both fast asleep.

"I became slightly anxious, but assumed that the person had to be Sue, the only other adult in the house. This was despite that no sound of anyone going up the stairs followed the figure's disappearance, and these were right by the door. It could not have gone anywhere else as it had stood in the house's tiny reception area, which leads only on to the stairs.

"It was then that very suddenly and unexpectedly I was engulfed by an extremely pungent smell like rotten eggs, which stifled me, and then instantly I fell back to sleep and woke up around 10 o'clock.

"The whole thing eventually came back to me, and I recounted what had happened. Sue assured me that she had not come down at all, which made sense as the figure was in my opinion male. Moreover, Sue is quite short.

"It was definitely no one in the house, and an intruder can be ruled out as the doors to the outside would have been locked (they almost always are in Britain). The strangest aspect was the pungent smell, which we know is associated very strongly with UFO entity cases.

"The person/entity was unquestionably physical, and not etheric."

Chapter 11
Allen West, Ph.D
The Evidence of Ancient Cosmic Impacts and Catastrophes!

Allen West, Ph.D, is an author and retired geophysical consultant to oil-and-gas and mining companies in the U.S., Canada, Mexico, the Middle East, and South America. Allen has been involved in many projects searching for petroleum, silver, and gold, including Spanish treasure. He retired after nearly three decades to become an author, and that led to the discovery of new evidence for an impact event 12,900 years ago. Allen provided some of the funding for the research and helped organize a 26-member international research team from 18 universities. Details of the research are found in the book, *The Cycle of Cosmic Catastrophes*, as well as in a scientific paper published in the Proceedings of the National Academy of Sciences.

(See that PNAS paper at http://www.pnas.org/cgi/reprint/0706977104v1)

Brent Raynes: Please give us somewhat of an overview of *The Cycle of Cosmic Catastrophes*, a book that you co-authored with Richard Firestone and Simon Warwick-Smith.

Allen West: The book has three parts to it. The first part is the story of the discovery of the clues and the search for answers. Of course, it has been a long-standing mystery about what happened to the mammoths and the mastodons and the saber-toothed tigers. I remember as a child hearing stories that described how the mammoths just suddenly disappeared from the planet and of thinking to myself, 'Well that seems awfully odd. What happened to them?'

So that was the mystery, and the first bit of evidence that we found, which is described in the first part of the book, came from Bill Topping, one of the co-authors of our PNAS scientific paper, who had been working in Michigan at a site called Gainey, a Paleo-American campsite. He had wondered about what had killed all of the animals, and he also knew that the Clovis culture vanished at the same time, although humans survived, unlike the mammoths. Their culture disappeared and after that time there were no more Clovis points around, which were a very distinct type of spear points.

In the sediment at Gainey, he found what we call magnetic spherules, or micro-spherules, that look like little ball bearings, highly polished and intensely magnetic. He found hundreds of thousands of them in this layer where these Indians had camped in Michigan. He knew that typically these magnetic spherules come from space, so he began to think that since this happened at the same time that all of these animals disappeared, maybe there was a connection.

That was the initial impetus for the story. So the first part of the book takes the reader through all that we went through of getting that initial clue and finding other sites in North America and extending the search into Europe and finding the same things, these micro-spherules. It's the story of how we found one marker after another until now where we have fourteen different lines of evidence that all point to a massive cosmic impact having taken place.

So that's the first part of the book, the story of how we put all the clues together. The second and third parts deal more with how the theory evolved to explain what it was that we were finding.

Brent Raynes: Yes, it's a fascinating scientific detective story really.

Allen West: It is, and just like a detective, we had a big murder mystery on our hands. Millions of animals got killed and we had a few of the bullets, as tiny as they were. The question was: Who did it and what happened?

Brent Raynes: I had always imagined that something like that if you were at ground zero then you were fried and that with these events hundreds and thousands of miles at a distance then it was a gradual thing, but that wasn't really the case though.

Allen West: The interesting thing is that these were like thousands of nuclear bombs going off. That's what we found was the best explanation. With the atom bombs that went off in Hiroshima and Nagasaki, people survived and in fact, people survived fairly close to it. Lots of people didn't, but some just through serendipity did, and that, in a sense, is what happened to a lot of these animals. Some of the species were killed off and some miraculously made it through, including us.

Brent Raynes: Even though the sites were such widespread distances apart, like from New Mexico to South Carolina, and there must have been who knows how many life forms at that time, Indian, the saber-toothed tiger and the mammoth and so on that died from those fragments that were flying through the air.

Allen West: Exactly. Then, of course, there was more than just the explosion itself and the flying fragments. One of the curious things of it is that it appears to be that the biggest explosions happened in or over the big ice sheet that was covering Canada. Then we think that one of the most troublesome parts of it was that suddenly, and I mean it may have been within a matter of hours or days, the temperature plunged. All of a sudden, animals that were used to living in Arizona had to suddenly get used to living in the climate normal to Alaska, and many of them weren't adapted to it, so we think that a lot of animals probably survived the actual initial blasts only to die from starvation. One of the big implications of this is that with that kind of climate change, the animals might have made it through for some length of time but chances are high that almost none of the plants did. You can imagine the same scenario when you think about what happens in most places when it turns into winter. All the plants die and they go into hibernation until spring.

Well, that's okay; animals today make it through such things. But, what if nearly all the vegetation burned up and there were months and months of an "impact winter." Then there never would have been anything to eat for many of the animals. So we really think starvation probably killed many more animals than did those things that were flying through the air, like the tiny ball bearings.

Brent Raynes: Right, which were flying at an incredible amount of speed.

Allen West: Absolutely. Equal to probably rocket speed -- faster than most jets can fly by two or three times. Even though they were small, you can imagine that if something were going that fast and hit you in the arm or the eye, it would definitely damage you.

Brent Raynes: So how did you become involved in co-authoring the book?

Allen West: This whole story has been one of unusual coincidences, which C.G. Jung called synchronicity, and I think that's a pretty good term for it. Things that, on the surface, have no apparent cause-and-effect relationship, and yet they were crucial to making this story happen.

Bill Topping made the original discovery in Michigan, and Richard helped analyze the evidence, but the theory that they developed turned out to be incorrect, or rather, incomplete. They thought that a supernova had done it, and so they published a short paper that was not received very well. In fact, very quickly, people disagreed strongly with parts of the theory. So even though Richard and Bill had made an important discovery and thought that there was something to it, they dropped the story for a couple of years.

Due to health reasons, Bill dropped out and did not continue with the story. Even though he's a co-author of our scientific paper, he really hasn't participated in the more recent research, but he was the one who set it in motion. Richard is with Lawrence Berkeley National Lab, and he has been with the story almost from the beginning. He was the second to come in.

By that time, I had retired from a career as a geophysicist. Since I had long been interested in extinctions, my agent had gotten me a book deal to write about them, including the dinosaur extinction. So during the research, I came across the paper published by Richard and Bill and thought, "Oh my gosh, this sounds altogether like an impact." They thought that it was a supernova, but it sounded to me like an impact. Not long after that, I contacted Richard, one thing led to another, and I became the third to join the story. Right away, I went to a Clovis site that's here in Arizona, very close, and found the same things there that they had found in Michigan. That led us to realize that this was a massive event to have gone across most of the continent. It had to have been very, very big.

I had some time on my hands and I had some money that I could pay for the research, so I visited many more sites and found the same evidence everywhere.

Over time, Richard and I began to work out more aspects of the theory. Eventually, I asked Richard to join me in co-authoring the book, and he agreed. I pretty much went out and collected the evidence, analyzed some of it, and Richard analyzed a lot of it, too, and together we evolved the theory and put it into the book.

After that, because of all my years in business, I realized that we needed a team with lots of people from different areas of expertise to analyze all of this, so I began contacting people and asking if they were interested. Gradually, we assembled a team who saw the evidence and realized that it was something unusual, too. And that was an important part of it because as you know from reading the book that it's an immense subject that crosses a lot of scientific disciplines, so it's impossible for just one, two or three people to have enough expertise to answer all of these questions. That's why we ended up with 26 co-authors on the scientific paper we published.

Brent Raynes: Yeah, I don't know if I've read a book in my whole life that has explored something that was this important and used all of these different disciplines and was involved in it themselves.

Allen West: Yeah, isn't that amazing. The impact event had an effect on just about every aspect of life 13,000 years ago, and the chilling part of this is that it's the only impact that we know of that happened while anatomically modern humans were around. This has happened within our history, even though it's technically prehistoric. Our evidence suggests that it is quite likely that these things happen more commonly than scientists believe because they're the type of impact that leaves very little trace. So it could have happened thousands and thousands and thousands of times, and yet for the most part, there would be virtually no remaining evidence of it back beyond a few hundred thousand years.

Brent Raynes: Wow. Of course, with the age of the earth, 13,000 years ago was just not that long ago.

Allen West: That's right. A geologic eye blink.

Brent Raynes: It's incredible that all of this happened and we're just now kind of putting it together, so to speak.

How about Plato's story of Atlantis? Based on this, could there have something to that story?

Allen West: Yeah, absolutely. I will say though that as a scientist you have to make distinctions between theories that you have good evidence and theories that you don't, and of course, there is no widely accepted concrete evidence for a civilization as sophisticated as what Plato described, though one may have existed. But what I will agree to is that there were almost certainly very well developed groups of people living back then. The Clovis people were very organized, and they were clearly just as bright as we are. They were completely modern humans. I'm sure that they were extraordinarily successful in their environment whereas we couldn't be equally successful in their world. In fact, they'd probably do better in ours than we'd do in theirs.

There is one thing that makes me think there's some truth to Plato's story. It's because what you see is that the story that Plato told, in its general details, is extremely similar to the stories told by fifty different groups of native peoples living around the world, and that just can't be coincidental.

Brent Raynes: Right. You detail a lot of these stories and legends in the book that just seem to give testimony to what you're finding about a fire from the heavens and great floodwaters.

Allen West: Absolutely. That's one of the most interesting things. However, there are a number of scientists who collect cultural stories and they say, "Well they're allegorical," or that they just aren't true. When they hear these ancient stories, many of the cultural scientists say, "Well they're just describing a local flood that might have happened once in 500 years." However, when they come across Native peoples today who have gone through some kind of severe flood like that, they don't typically tell their children around the campfire that all the animals died and that everybody on the planet, except a few, were killed. So you have to think that whatever they were referring to was something absolutely extraordinary and well beyond the kind of thing that any human culture goes through very often.

Even those the old stories seem to fit, we can't say for sure that those stories apply to this impact event, because we actually think that there have been impacts in between 13,000 years and today. Not as serious as that one, but they still would have caused local devastation. For example, the impact in Tunguska, in Siberia, destroyed thousands of square kilometers of forest, and anything living in it would have been pretty much toasted. So if that kind of thing happened today, then obviously the natives would tell some horrendous stories about it. So we can't be sure than these 50 stories apply to this event, but I would say that the chances are quite high that a substantial number of them do. As you saw in the book, they all have similarities. All of them have several parts to the stories, and while the details might vary considerably, there are certain things that are common to all of them. They almost always say that something fell from the sky. It was either a star that fell or rocks that fell, huge clouds that fell, or rain, but something fell from the sky. Most people were warned in advance, but they didn't listen and so they got killed. Most of the animals got killed, too, and only a few people survived and they went on to repopulate the world.

It seems extraordinary to me that there would be such a similarity in those stories without there being, most likely, some single event behind them all.

Brent Raynes: So based on what you know at this point, you and your co-authors propose that a supernova and, say, asteroids and comets that are perhaps pushed off course, some maybe hitting the sun causing solar flare activity, and of course things crashing directly into the earth itself would have been all interrelated in this?

Allen West: Absolutely. Yeah. However, the one thing that we're certain about, about which we have the most evidence, is that there was an impact. Exactly what caused it and exactly what went along with it is less clear, but when you have impacts on earth and other planets, you would expect that some part of that is going to hit the sun. In fact, comets that come in, and break up, frequently do that. They might run into a planet like Jupiter, and some of the fragments are going to be orbiting the sun and could hit the sun too, so we expect that there would be flares. But we don't have any real evidence for that. It's just consistent that those things one would expect to happen during a major impact.

We think we were hit by a fragmented comet or comets, but we don't know exactly what kicked those comets out of orbit. We theorize that it was the supernova, but we don't have any evidence to tie the two together, except that we do find potassium 40 in a thin layer or sediment across North America, but there are other explanations for that other than a supernova. So as one part of the story, we have solid evidence for an impact, although we don't know exactly what the object or objects were or where they came from. We just have solid evidence that something hit us. What's more speculative is: what was the chain of events that led it to hit us?

Brent Raynes: Looking at some of the aerial photographs taken say around Myrtle Beach, South Carolina, they are just amazing when you look at them and you say something definitely tremendous happened.

Allen West: Exactly, and I think that most people who have never seen the Carolina Bays look at that and it definitely has a "wow" factor to it. You think, "Oh my gosh, that doesn't look normal."

Brent Raynes: Of course, when you're looking at it at ground level you don't get the same perspective.

Allen West: That's it. You can't see them from the ground. In some cases, you can see that there's a lake, but you don't see the rim and the elliptical shape until you're in an airplane.

Brent Raynes: And I might just throw this in that I recently read on the Internet that it was believed that a lake was found up around that Siberian blast in 1908 that they think was perhaps an impact crater.

Allen West: Right, I saw that too. I think that they've got a ways to go to convince a lot of scientists. I know I heard some people saying that there are lakes like that that are just in the permafrost anyway, and most people say that they're going to need evidence. How do they know that lake was formed by the blast? So, that's part of science. You can come up with a theory all right, but then you really need to come up with evidence before people will accept the theory widely. They may say it makes sense, but always you have to come up with the proof.

Brent Raynes: In the appendix of your book, you have a section entitled "Find Your Own Stardust," where you write about taking a supermagnet and searching for particles.

Allen West: That's right.

Brent Raynes: So how deep do you dig?

Allen West: You know, interestingly enough, you can find it right on the surface in many places on the coastal plain in North and South Carolina, Georgia, and Virginia. You can find not just the magnetic grains, but the carbon spherules too, which are shown in the book. They're easier to see than the magnetic grains and they float on water. If you take a big bucket of water, put the sediment in it, then these things will float to the top along with charcoal and sticks and everything like that. So once you dry what comes up, then these spherules will roll down a plate. So they are direct evidence of this impact, and in many places in South and North Carolina, we can go out and take a shovel full, go down 6 or 8 inches, and throw a shovel full in the bucket and these things will float right out.

Brent Raynes: Wow, I didn't think that it would be that close to the surface.

Allen West: It varies, of course. If you're up in the mountains, the top of the ground in places was exposed to the surface 13,000 years ago, and so anything that would have fallen back then would still be right on the surface. At most of the sites that we went to, they're typically buried three to six feet down, but in many cases they're close to the surface, and rarely are they deeper than 3 or 4 feet.

Brent Raynes: So if a person was to dig down, there's what they call the black mat which is a layer that's darker than the normal sediment and if you have that supermagnet then you can pick up things, and if you have a Geiger counter, get readings.

Allen West: Absolutely. However, with the Geiger counter, there has to be a lot of uranium for it to be very sensitive. It's quite subtle to detect uranium, so the supermagnet is the easiest way to do it. The other easy way is to throw some dirt in a bucket and look at the carbon spherules with a little microscope or a magnifying glass, and it really takes those for both types of evidence, the magnetic grains or the carbon spherules. When you do that, you can take a look at something that was part of a massive event that killed off 30 or 40 million animals 13,000 years ago.

And there's more. The interesting thing too is that, and it's touched on just briefly in the book, we now have considerably more evidence for microscopic diamonds. We just got done testing at Murray Springs, Arizona, for the carbon spherules, plus the layer that's under the black mat. The sediment right under the black mat at Murray Springs is just absolutely loaded with these tiny diamonds. Unfortunately, they're too small to see without a laboratory electron microscope -- they're smaller than a piece of dust floating in the air, but nevertheless there're just millions and millions and millions of them. Actually, if you're in North Carolina and walking across the surface, in many places they're in the surface sediment, and you can step on more than a million diamonds with every footstep that you take. There're that many of them.

By the way, I should say one more thing. The black mat is not everywhere. It has been at maybe a third of the sites that we've been to. So sometimes you can dig down and not find a black mat. Yet, in the impact layer, you'll find the magnetic grains and the carbon spherules, and there're not many of each one of them. You can't visually see them looking at the sediment- you'll need a microscope. So, there may not be any evidence of a black mat, yet there will be all of these other markers.

Brent Raynes: That's incredible.

I don't know if you had a chance to look at the article by Andrew Collins, a British author who had written a book called <u>The Cygnus Mystery</u>, and he wrote about how from Cygnus X-3 there's a cosmic plasma blast, which he has compared to a cosmic gun barrel and we're kind of like in its path.

Allen West: Yeah, aimed right at us.

Brent Raynes: Apparently it's not always the same levels of intensity, and he believes that there were genetic mutations in DNA, and that there were events like what you have described too.

Allen West: Absolutely. I've followed his work over the years. He's written several books, one of them about the Carolina Bays; it has those in them, and other things too. I don't find anything that he suggests that's implausible, though I can't say whether it's right or not. Frankly we don't have much evidence for that side of the story, as to what actually caused these things, but I think that his theory is legitimate. Scientists certainly, without a doubt, have found Beryllium-10 and other cosmogenic isotopes that are formed by cosmic radiation. They found them in the ice core, they found them in the ocean cores, and they all date to about 35,000 years ago. In fact, just recently we had a poster that we presented at AGU (see http://ie.lbl.gov/Mammoth/Impact.html) on the mammoth tusks that have the meteorites in it, as described in the book. Do you remember the part of the book where it describes the mammoth tusk containing what look like pellets from shotgun blasts?

Brent Raynes: Sure do.

Allen West: Okay. We have analyzed some of those little bits of metal and they have a geochemistry that is extraterrestrial; they have high levels of nickel relative to the iron, low levels of titanium. That perfectly matches a number of classes of meteorites, and does not match any typical terrestrial geochemistry. And there appear to be burn marks. Curiously enough, we thought that this was from the 13,000 year event, but when we carbon dated those things, it turns out that the bulk of the tusks are 34,000 to 35,000 years old. That supports what Andrew Collins had been saying, that there was a cosmic catastrophe about 35,000 years ago. That's a perfect match with this evidence. The ocean cores and the ice cores all show evidence of a cosmic evemt just the way he said, and now here we have radio carbon dated tusks with meteorites stuck in them that date to exactly the same time.

Brent Raynes: Fascinating. And these tusks also that had these effects were not just from like Alaska and the Canadian area, but also in Siberia.

Allen West: Exactly. That's the bison skull that is mentioned in the book. It came from Siberia. The tusks mostly came from Alaska, and yet they both date to roughly the same time.

While we don't have any smoking guns, we've definitely got some bullets from it!

Brent Raynes: You've come up with an impressive body of evidence.

Allen West: It's certainly exciting. This is what makes science fun, when you find some of these things. When we got into it, there was no way that we could have predicted it. You can't go looking for something like this. You kind of stumble on it, and so much of science is done that way. You come across things by accident. Because of that, I tell people I can't take any credit for it. The only thing that I did was pay attention when I stumbled across these things. It's been extraordinary.

Brent Raynes: It's been a lot of hard work, I'm sure. You have to read the book to really appreciate the journey.

Allen West: Yeah. The journey included quite a few dead-ends, too, but like somebody said, "A dead-end is just a place to turn around."

Chapter 12
Timothy Green Beckley
Publisher, Reporter, Movie Producer, and UFO Paranormal Researcher and Experiencer!

Timothy Green Beckley, editor, publisher, movie producer, UFO-paranormal-conspiracy researcher, began reading FATE magazine back in 1957, at age ten, the same year he sighted two UFOs over his New Jersey home. He hasn't stopped thinking, researching, investigating and writing about the subject of UFOs and things that go "bump in the night" since (he also had some classic paranormal experiences back in his childhood as well) and is today regarded as an internationally acclaimed authority on practically all things strange, unexplained and paranormal.

Brent Raynes: Your interest in the realms of the supernatural, unexplained phenomena, and UFOs really goes back to your childhood. Living in New Jersey, you grew up in a haunted house with poltergeist phenomena. Could you recount a little about that for us?

Tim Beckley: I guess the paranormal probably came pretty easy for me. My mother had an unusually high level of interest in the subject. I won't say that she was psychic, but she seemed to believe in a lot of this and read a lot of the literature that was available at the time.

Around the age of six, I recall having like poltergeist phenomena occurring spontaneously around the house. Lights would go on and off, doors would open and close. This would not be on a nightly basis. I wouldn't want anybody to think that it was the Amityville Horror. It wasn't by any means, but things did occur from time to time. I remember in particular I was seated at the dinner table and this big dish slid across the table and kind of floated to the floor, and it didn't break. Maybe it didn't break because it was a heavy dish. I don't know. I mean, you could read something into this. Whatever you want. But it occurred.

We also had the peculiar phenomena of a baby crying around the house. I remember one night in the middle of the winter hearing the sound of a baby crying and my mother and I went to the back door, opened it up, and there in the snow, leading down to the few steps to the driveway, was what appeared to be little baby booty prints, and we followed them in the back and they just disappeared in the snow.

My godmother, who was a real staunch Catholic and not prone to believe in any of this stuff at all apparently was there one day and she heard the sound of a baby crying (I guess maybe she had been babysitting me at that point) and opened the door and there was a woman with a baby in her arms, rocking the baby and the baby was crying. My godmother knew that there was no such person in the house (there was only my grandparents) so she got kind of spooked and closed the door, and when she opened it again there was nobody there. Later on we found (I guess my mother and somebody did some research) and we found that there was an incident going back, I don't know what year, but this was during some epidemic, maybe around 1914, 1918. There were thousands of people dying around the world, and apparently a mother and her daughter had died in the house. They had a wake and they put the baby in the same coffin as the mother. So maybe this was the ghost that we were encountering, if it was a ghost indeed. But there were supernatural things happening in the Beckley residence I would certainly say.

The next thing that happened would have been some out-of-body experiences. Maybe at the age of seven or so, where I actually found myself floating in the air (not in my physical body but I guess in my astral form) and I could see that the room was filled with all of these strange colors. I remember seeing vivid colors and hearing celestial music. Don't ask me what it sounded like. I don't remember. But I remember that's what happened at the time, and then a little while later I found myself back in my body, and I actually remember tumbling or being drawn back into it and I awoke in a really, really cold sweat. This happened a few times, and then later on in life I did have some astral projection experiences that were more controlled than this.

Anyway these things were happening, and at the age of ten I had my first of three UFO sightings.

Brent Raynes: Right, and I recall from reading a previous interview that even though you were just ten you knew that this was something unusual.

Tim Beckley: Well, with the UFO sighting there was no doubt about it. That's even clearer than any of these other experiences that I just told you about. I've told this story so many times it's almost like repeating a record really, but it was a warm summer evening in 1957. We were all sitting outside because in those days nobody had air conditioning. So we all sat outside until it cooled off. It was just after twilight, as I recall, and somebody had come up the stairs where I was seated with four or five people sitting around chatting, and somebody pointed out these two objects in the sky.

Now I can't tell you that I saw any landing gear. There were no little men and I was not abducted. But there were two bright lights up above the clouds. I would estimate that they were maybe 30-35 feet in diameter, very brightly lit objects, or orbs I guess you'd call them. You can't say objects because I didn't see any metallic hull or anything like that. One of them was across the street over an abandoned factory building and the other one was directly over the house, and they kept rotating in the sky so that the one over the house would go over to where the one over the manufacturing building had been, and that one would move over to the house, and they would kind of like circle overhead. I think this went on for a period of maybe 15 minutes or so, until the one across the street it looked like someone had pulled the light switch because it just disappeared.

The next day there was a little item in the newspaper to the effect that other people had witnessed these lights and the authorities were saying that they were nothing more unusual than weather balloons. Well, even at the rather tend age of ten, it kind of struck me funny because I knew these weren't weather balloons. It wasn't something that was bobbing and weaving in the air current. They were much too large and they did seem to be under intelligent control. So I don't know what they were. I cannot tell you that they were from outer space, but they were up there in the sky. It fascinated me and I remember writing to the newspaper with my concern that the authorities were saying that there was a conventional explanation and I was pretty sure that there wasn't, and that kind of led to my coming out of the closet UFOwise. I started putting out a little newsletter called *The Interplanetary News Service Report* and the first issue I had printed by a fellow by the name of Alan Katz who lived in Middlesex, New Jersey and he had a mimeograph machine and printed like 50 copies of the newsletter, and it was me and a fellow by the name of Edward J. Babcock Jr. who did a book early on called *UFOs Around The World*, and we were the first researchers to actually give credibility to the idea that there were UFO sightings not only in this country but all over the world, and we had contributors from maybe twenty different countries. We printed this book. In those days there were no fast copy places like Kinko, Staples, or any of those other places, so you had to do everything yourself. You either had a ditto machine, which was this terrible liquid like purple. It wasn't even liquid, it was like alkaloid, so that you couldn't print maybe more than 75 copies and then it would evaporate on you, and then the next step up was a mimeograph machine. So I went out and bought a mimeograph machine and Jerry Clark cut my stencils. He was the assistant editor of *The Interplanetary News Service Report*.

Brent Raynes: This is the Jerry Clark, known today as Jerome Clark?

Tim Beckley: *The* Jerry Clark, whether he wants to admit it or not, he cut my stencils, and Lucius Farish was the assistant director of *The Interplanetary News Service Report*, even though Lucius and I have not spoken in years. He did not like the fact that I was associated or friendly with Gray Barker and Jim Moseley. He didn't like Jim Moseley because he had run an expose on George Adamski.

A lot of us active in the field today got started as teenagers. There was a whole confederation of teenaged UFO researchers. Gene Steinberg put out *The UFO Reporter*. I believe that was the name of his publication. He does *The Paracast* today on the Internet. Allen Greenfield, of course, was a good friend and associate as was Rick Hilberg, or Ricky Hilberg in those days. And so we all kind of got started together.

Brent Raynes: Well back in 1967, when I got started I had a little publication called *Sauceritis* which I mimeographed, and I corresponded with Lou Farish back in those days quite extensively, and Loren Coleman was on my little board of directors. (laughs)

Tim Beckley: Is that right? Huh. Well, we must have been all pretty handsome and pretty young in those days I guess.

Editor: It goes back a ways.

Of course, you became active pretty quick. There was Harold Salkin back in the mid-1960s.

Tim Beckley: Harold is one of the unsung heroes in the field. Harold was out of Washington, D.C. He shared the choirs with Clara John who actually ghost wrote Adamski's book *Inside the Spaceships*, and they put out a publication called *The Little Listening Post*, which was a very, very chatty newsletter about maybe six or seven pages. It was kind of like the Paul Harvey of ufology. Everything was broken down real fast, very accurate, and it always seemed that whenever you got *The Little Listening Post* something was going on even if nothing was going on.

Harold, just by synchronicity or coincidence, and of course we know there is no such thing, but anyway his mother lived in the next town over from where I was, in Highland Park, New Jersey, and when he was in town visiting his mother he would call me on the phone and we would chat and we got together, and maybe I was 16 or so at the time. I had this old I guess Remington manual typewriter and we knocked out an article for *Saga* magazine. It was one of the best that I ever wrote which was the astronaut sightings and encounters, long before anybody else was writing about any of this.

Brent Raynes: Right. That's been reprinted in your recent book.

Tim Beckley: It's in our book *Strange Saga*. Anyway, Harold and I had gone to the NASA headquarters in Washington, and even though James Oberg has called me a liar on this, we spent three days at NASA headquarters, we went through their files.

They were very kind to us. They showed us every single transcript that we wanted to see. We culled out of the printed transcripts, page by page by page, and they also gave us a sheet that stated on top "UFO Photos Taken By The Astronauts." We got prints of all of these things. I wrote an article for *Genesis* magazine, of all places, which is one of the men's magazines. I was a movie review critic for *Hustler* magazine. I don't know if most people realize that. I wrote for a lot of men's magazines in those days, and in Genesis I wrote this piece with a lot of photographs that had never been published before that date.

Oberg says that I made it up, but I didn't make this up. I didn't lie. He's just B.S.ing again. He believes what he wants to believe and I know what I know. We didn't make any of that up. All of that testimony of the astronauts and what they saw was right there in the documents.

There were so many UFO groups back in those days. We exchanged publications with 125 different UFO organizations around the world, back when there were actual physical publications.

So anyway, Harold Salkin was not only the co-editor (although they never used their names), he actually helped NICAP get started. He donated I think the first $1000. that NICAP ever saw. He helped Major Keyhoe write that famous *True* article and at the same time he was helping out with the voice of NICAP he was also Adamski's unofficial publicist, Dan Fry, Wayne Aho, and other New Age contactee types. Whenever they came to Washington, Harold would get them on radio and TV. He never got paid doing any of this. Again there's no money to be made on UFOs per se.

In fact, I remember back during the Vietnam War Era, Harold had booked me in the large YMCA in Washington to give a lecture and I had brought all of my slides down and everything, and it was in the middle of a demonstration and there were five people in the audience. I still went ahead with my lecture. Police had the whole area blocked off and I could see through a big picture window as I was giving the lecture the police were tear gasing people and people were running in all directions. I said to myself, "Probably some of these people who are running actually came to hear the lecture and were not war protestors." (laughs) I'm sure that out of the 500 or 600 people that were being scurried down the street with the tear gas, I'm sure that there were a couple little old ladies in there who were bent on getting to the Y to hear my talk, but they never made it to the front door. I don't even know how those five people got in, to be honest with you.

Then Harold moved up to New York and we started writing for the tabloids. My publishing company, Global Communications, was a news feature service that supplied articles to magazines and newspapers all over the world. Not just on UFOs but on a lot of different subjects, and the tabloids were our big market. Most of the articles, even though the stories did not contain our name, many of the articles in *The Enquirer*, which *were not made up*, were written by us. In fact, we had a couple of headline stories in there which we even got pretty large sized bonuses for, back before *The Enquirer* decided that not enough people were interested in UFOs and dropped that from their format to go totally celebrity.

Harold died just recently. He was in the military, you know, during World War II. He was kind of a combat stringer for the Associated Press. That's why when he got out of the military he knew all of these guys who worked for *Voice of America*. I actually was on a show that had the potential audience of a 130 million listeners on the *Voice of America*, and they actually had programs on UFOs. Many were censoring it in this country but we got to talk all about this stuff and it went out all over the world.

Brent Raynes: Did you ever meet Bob Pratt?

Tim Beckley: You know, I don't know if I did or not. We were stringers. Free-lancers. We did have a pretty close relationship with the Enquirer people down in Florida and went by there a couple of times. My main contact was a fellow by the name of Cliff Linedecker, who actually wrote a couple of books on psychic phenomena, including I believe a book on country western singers who had metaphysical experiences, ghost encounters, and so forth.

I met a number of the people there, but I don't know if I ever met Bob Pratt. I did correspond with him and, of course, I sold his book. His book *UFO Danger Zone* was certainly a very well researched volume. One of the best, I would say, in the field, although I don't necessarily agree with his conclusions that UFOs are menacing or hostile. It seems like a handful of sightings out of tens or thousands of reports don't necessarily make an accurate conclusion.

I will say one thing. People think that *The Enquirer* was yellow journalism and that they made up stories. They never made up anything that I am certainly aware of.

I remember being at a MUFON Conference, one of the few that I've ever gone to, and Tracy Torme was there, and of course Tracy did *Fire In The Sky* and his father was Mel Torme, the famous singer. I had written an article about Torme's UFO sighting, which was not particularly spectacular. He was out walking his dog near Central Park one day and there was an object in the sky, and I mentioned that to Tracy as a way of introducing myself and he said, "My dad said that was the most accurate article ever written about him." All *The Enquirer* ever did was use exact quotes. We would provide them with the tapes of the interviews, with the witnesses, and pretty much all that they would do was take the quoted material. There was very little introduction, very little between any paragraphs. It was just stated word for word, none of it was made up, despite what other UFO researchers, who are not in the know about most things, would have you believe.

People ask me, "What do you think UFOs are?" I say, "Well UFOs are unidentified. It doesn't necessarily even have to be flying, and there's probably more than one phenomenon." It's obvious that we're not talking about one thing here. Brad Steiger has his list of 17 different UFO origins and theories, so I'm sure that some are spiritual phenomena, some physical craft from other planets (although

I don't think there are many of those here, but maybe every once and awhile). Then others of them are intelligently controlled earth lights. I have written about this, and you've written about this as well, and I wrote about this subject extensively in my book *Our Alien Planet: This Eerie Earth.*

Brent Raynes: Right, it could be earth energies or Keel's old ultraterrestrials.

Tim Beckley: That seems to be a popular explanation or theory these days and a lot of people are taking credit for it, not realizing other people who came before them. Allen Greenfield should actually get quite a bit of credit. I remember doing an interview with him for Ray Palmer's magazine. He was one of the first to talk about alternate realities or other dimensions.

Brent Raynes: It's amazing how many of the current crop of ufologists don't even know when you mention John Keel or Jacques Vallee or Allen Greenfield who you're talking about.

Tim Beckley: Well, I would hope that they would know who John Keel is.

Brent Raynes: Well, of course, after the movie came out you do have more people, and he also went on Art Bell, but before that a lot of people really didn't know.

Tim Beckley: I think I'm one of the few people who talks to John every other week or so, but we don't talk that much about UFOs. We've been kind of personal friends over the years.

Brent Raynes: He's certainly presented a lot of very interesting data and I've talked to him on the phone a few times too.

Tim Beckley: He doesn't like to give interviews.

Brent Raynes: No. He doesn't. You have to settle for a little comment here and there that he might let you share but not an interview.

Tim Beckley: I guess he figures he's interviewed out. Whatever he's said he's said many times.

Brent Raynes: Yeah, he's told me to go get one that has already been published and re-use that.

Tim Beckley: I guess another great influence in my career as a writer and publisher was Gray Barker. Gray published *Saucerian Publications* out of Clarksburg, West Virginia, and of course Gray was best known for his book, *They Knew Too Much About Flying Saucers*. Now I believe that it was in the 5th or 6th grade that I had to do a book review, and what book did I pick. It was, *They Knew Too Much About Flying Saucers*, of course not knowing at that point that Gray would be the publisher of my first book and that after he passed away I would buy from his estate the remainder of the copies of that particular title. It impressed me not only because of its contents but also because of his writing style, and I always wanted to write like

Gray Barker (laughs) and I guess that some would say that I accomplished that, for better or for worse, or whatever.

And for some reason, which I can't remember off hand, at one point he wasn't doing a column anymore. I wrote to Ray Palmer and said I'd like to do my own column, and so in the late 1960s I started doing a regular column for *Flying Saucers* magazine called *On The Trail Of The Flying Saucers*, which ran for maybe five or six years. Then I did a couple of columns for *Search* magazine, which was one of Palmer's other publications. Of course, Ray was the man who kind of started UFOs and was responsible for the Shaver mystery. I became fairly friendly at least in correspondence with Richard Shaver. He was a character, as everybody knows, and people ask me, "Well, what is the truth about Richard Shaver's claims," and I just look at them and say, "I don't know." Obviously, the inner earth and the whole idea of a subterranean world holds a great fascination with people.

In fact, people don't realize this but being in the UFO publishing business like I am there are more books sold that deal with UFOs being of Nazi origin and originating from the inner earth. People are not interested in UFOs from outer space.

Brent Raynes: Oh really?

Tim Beckley: That is the least popular theory. In fact, any time that I have tried to publish anything serious, and any time I have gotten a good review in *The MUFON Journal* I know that is the kiss of death as far as book sales go. Of course, there have obviously been some exceptions, like the Betty and Barney Hill book, *The Interrupted Journey* and some of Frank Edwards's early books, but those are few and far between.

Brent Raynes: That's just the opposite of what I would have thought.

Tim Beckley: Well there you go. I've certainly published my share of what I would consider serious UFO books. One of my favorites was by Jenny Randles, *From Out Of The Blue,* about Bentwaters, the UFO landing at the NATO base there and the contact and so forth with the US military, and we sold the paperback rights and the book just barely paid off in very small advances and sold less than 15,000 copies in paperback, which is why publishers do not publish UFO books because they just don't sell in big numbers.

With a few exceptions over the years, UFO books don't sell in big numbers. So they don't publish them. It's not a censorship thing. It's a bottom line.

Brent Raynes: And it's been that way for a long time.

Tim Beckley: Yeah, a long time. The coming of Barnes and Noble and Amazon destroyed the middle level publisher. Guys like me, who would have a new title and would print two or three thousand copies, a very small run, but we had wholesalers who would distribute them and we had over 3000 mom and pop metaphysical/New Age/alternative stores around the country who would scoop these things up. They would never sell more than a couple of copies of each title, but there were a lot of them, but little by little they went out of business, and today there are very few left.

Very few wholesalers and distributors who specialize in this type of thing and not very many stores anymore, and the stores that are still around their income is mainly derived from selling crystals and incense and such.

Brent: Yeah, I saw a real nice crystal in one of those stores recently for about $2000.

Tim Beckley: Oh yeah, some of them are really high priced, but some of them are museum quality pieces. They're really nice. Even in the mail order business, that's what people seem to want. That's what they're looking to buy. They don't want a serious book on UFOs.

Brent Raynes: Now you were involved with many people who were involved in the forming of the Congress of Scientific Ufologists, and of course one of the biggest ones was in New York City back in 1967.

Tim Beckley: I was indeed Jim Moseley's assistant with that, and I actually introduced Roy Thinnes to the audience. He was of course the star of the TV show *The Invaders* about aliens invading the earth.

Brent Raynes: I remember that show well. I used to watch it every night it was on.

Tim Beckley: Yeah, it was pretty good program, and Roy came down, Jim paid his expenses. Most people don't realize this. They think Jim made a lot of money on that, but he broke even, because a lot of people ended up getting in for free. Things got screwed up and the elevator was opening up on the wrong floor and people were coming in by the droves and not paying the big admission of two dollars.

There were quite a variety of speakers like Venus from the planet Venus, Dr. Frank Stranges, Howard Menger, and in fact Dr. Condon of the infamous Condon Report was there. He was in the audience taking notes.

Brent Raynes: And of course John Keel was there.

Tim Beckley: Now that's pretty funny. John Keel was to give a talk at a closed session to Jim's group, the Inner Circle, and people think that there is a kind of bootleg tape that people have passed around of John's lecture at that conference, but what most people don't realize is that it was broadcast on the radio, on WBAI, so it really wasn't a secret lecture because probably thousands of people heard it on the radio.

Brent Raynes: Oh, so this tape I've got over here on the shelf wasn't an exclusive after all. I have a tape I think Al Greenfield supplied me with years ago of a talk that Keel gave at that conference.

Tim Beckley: There were about 12,000 people who attended that conference. The hotel held about maybe 2,200 people. Long John Nebel, the original all night talk show host, had a UFO speaker on every night for a week before the show. He really packed 'em in and drew in the people in those days. If you were a speaker on the Long John Show you could pretty much be assured of a pretty good turnout the next day, or whenever the lecture was going to be. In those days it was a pretty spectacular show, a lobby full of vendors, book sellers, and artifacts of one type or another.

Brent Raynes: You were a regular there for quite awhile on the Long John Nebel Show.

Tim Beckley: Somebody just sent me a listing for the *New York Times* of 1965 of an appearance that I made on *The Amazing Randi's* program. Now most people don't realize, or care to realize, that with Long John's switch from WOR to, I believe it was WNBC they needed somebody to take Long John's place, and so for about two years *The Amazing Randi* was host of an all night talk show there. His program was not devoted to the paranormal and UFOs, though he did do some programs on the subject. The only thing was that if you went on Randi's program Long John would not let you on his show, so for quite a few years some of us were kind of blacklisted. We couldn't do Long John. But then after awhile, when Randi went off the air, it didn't matter too much.

Brent Raynes: Then, of course, there were the celebrities.

Tim Beckley: There were two reasons that I got around to doing the celebrity interviews. As I said I was a stringer for *The Enquirer*, so I met all of these celebrities and in those days they were not just interested in Courtney Love and Britney Spears and Brad Pitt. They covered many celebrities, including those who were relatively obscure and hadn't done anything in awhile. We did people lots and lots of people, and of course one of the questions I always asked a lot of the celebrities was, "Have you ever had a UFO sighting?" "Have you ever lived in a haunted house or experienced anything supernatural?" And a lot of them did.

Bill Shatner told me a story about having a UFO encounter in the Mojave Desert where a UFO appeared overhead. I guess that he got separated from a motor cycle group that he was with. He was all dressed in leather and had a helmet on and it was like in the middle of the afternoon, 102 degrees, and the motorcycle conked out, and the UFO appeared overhead and led him out of the desert. Kind of like a Moses trip or something. (laughs)

Brent Raynes: I always wondered if that was a true story there.

Tim Beckley: Well, that's the story he told me. He told it to me backstage at the Ten Thousand Dollar Pyramid, which is where I did the interview with him, and somewhere here on an audio tape I still have it. Some people have heard it, and other people have lifted the story, and all of these stories have made the rounds.

Brent Raynes: Also David Bowie.

Tim Beckley: You see, I promoted quite a few rock and roll shows and met quite a few of those stars back in those days. My friend Walli Elmlark was the White Witch of New York, and she also wrote a column for *Circus* magazine which is kind of a hard rock version of *Rolling Stones*. She met all of these different rock stars and I would hang out at her apartment and since I was writing for some of the magazines too I met them at press conferences and socialized with them. Of course, this is when they were on their way up the ladder to success although they were more anxious to meet with the press and tell their stories and all. And when I did meet with David he was signed to RCA Records and he was doing the Ziggy Stardust tour. I met him and he was dressed up as Ziggy Stardust. We never did talk a great deal about UFOs. He did tell me that he believed in UFOs and was interested in the aliens and stuff like that, but he was good friends with Walli and in one of the books written about David Bowie's career there is three pages about Walli's dealings with him because for awhile he was heavily into the Wicca. Then he got into Buddhism, and I don't know what he's into now. But rumor has it that he had UFO sightings in England while growing up and then was actually an editor of a UFO newsletter when he was a teenager, but I don't know what that newsletter was.

Brent Raynes: And then May Pang, who was John Lennon's former girlfriend.

Tim Beckley: At one point with May Pang, we did a couple of radio shows discussing John Lennon's UFO sighting up on The Dakota, because she was living with him at the time and they were both naked on the balcony overlooking Manhattan. He called her out to the balcony and they watched these strange lights in the sky. It was a UFO over Manhattan.

I talked to John Lennon a couple of times on the phone. There was a band that was his back up band that was called *Elephant's Memory* and we had a Halloween Concert and an occult program at the Hotel Diplomat, which is where *Kiss* did their first show, and John Lennon showed up, and Andy Worhol. It was a pretty good party, and I guess he came because *Elephant's Memory* were our headliners. I didn't get to talk with him, but I did see him there. But when I did get to talk with him on the phone he was very much into this fellow by the name of Dean Kraft who had some psychokinetic ability similar to Uri Geller. He could move objects across the room, and Yoko Ono and John told me about how he had apparently passed his hand over this candy dish that was on their coffee table and a couple of pieces of candy came over the top of the candy dish and kind of squiggled out until they fell onto the floor.

There was a big article written about Kraft in, of all places, I think it was *Cosmopolitan* magazine. He was very well known at that time, and he was written up in *The Enquirer* and he had quite a notoriety for doing psychic healing. He was very well known for that. He moved down to Florida. I went to his wedding. I haven't been in touch with him for years, but I believe he's still in Florida and still doing healing work. He also wrote a book.

Brent Raynes: I know that John Lennon had also met with Uri Geller in New York.

Tim Beckley: Well you know Uri and I were fairly good friends. I had an office just off of Central Park and Uri around the corner a couple of blocks away and he had just landed here in the United States and was looking for publicity, and so we did a couple of articles for *Saga* magazine and a couple of the papers and weeklies in Manhattan.

I saw him do a couple of things that I thought was fairly incredible. I was in his apartment one time with the science editor of *Argosy* magazine. Now *Argosy* magazine was one of these men's adventure publications. Real little cheese cake, but basically articles about people's wartime experiences, or kind of He man stuff I guess you'd call it.

The science editor of Argosy was a fellow by the name of Herbert Bailey, who was a pretty good friend of mine. But anyway I had introduced Herb to Uri (we were in either Herb's apartment or Uri's, I forget for certain) but he told Herb to hold his key in his hand and told me to take my key and put it on the desk across the room, and he said, "Let's see what happens." So he started stroking the key that Herb had in his hand. It was no slight of hand trick. He didn't change the key out. It was Herb's key to his front door. In fact, I remember later on he was kind of upset because he couldn't use it in the door anymore. The thing bent about I would say about a little bit more than a third of the way. After they were finished doing this, Uri said, "Take a look at your key across the room." I picked it up from the desk and it was bent a little bit. Not as much as Herb's was, but it definitely had a little bit of curl to that tip.

Mohammed Ali was a big UFO buff actually. We went down to his home at Cherry Hill and he wanted us to bring slides and movies, because he wanted to see if it was like anything he had seen in the sky.

He claimed over twenty-one sightings and he tied it in with his religious beliefs. I first met him after the *Daily News* ran a report about Mohammed Ali sighting two bright lights over Central Park while he was out jogging one morning. Harold was a big promoter and he'd get on the phone and call anybody and Harold got Angelo Dundee on the phone and said, "We'd like to come around and talk to the Champ about his UFO sightings." So Dundee said, "Well he's out there jogging through the park around 6 a.m. Come and join him." So we got out there at 6 a.m. and I was in a little better shape in those days and jogged maybe a quarter of a mile with the Champ and he told me about his UFO sightings and so forth, and invited us down to his home in Cherry Hill. We went there a couple of times to show him the UFO movies and pictures, whatever he wanted, and he even did a drawing for us, which I've used in my book, *UFOs Among The Stars*, of one of the UFOs that he had seen which looks exactly like an Adamski craft. I think he was into the Adamski ships in those days. He must have seen an Adamski photo or two or read an Adamski book and that was his cup of tea. He had also seen this huge mother ship parked up above his training camp in Deer Park, Pennsylvania. He invited us up to see if we could see it as well, which we never did, but also took Uri Geller with us. Ali was at first interested in meeting Geller, but Ali is the type of person who is not going to share the spotlight with anyone, even if there's only three people around he's the one who wants the attention, and I can't say that Uri is too much different than that either. He likes a little bit of attention as well as all of us do, you know.

Anyway we took Uri up there and Ali knew who he was. I guess he had seen him on the Johnny Carson Show. It turned out that Ali is an amateur magician so he got his tricks out, like the one where you cut the rope in half and you magically put it back together, and a couple of other tricks with a ring and such that I don't remember exactly, but Uri got a little bit peeved at that because he thought that maybe Ali was trying to put him down. So we kind of slipped away from the main group and went over to this big rock where he (Ali) would stand up on the rock or next to the rock and ring a bell that was on the rock when he wanted people to gather around. Anyway, there was a guy there who was Ali's sparing partner, and I wrote this up in *UFOs Among The Stars* and in *The Enquirer*, and I had a photo of the guy, but anyway this sparing partner of Ali's had this medallion around his neck like a St. Jude or St. Christopher's medal. It was pretty heavy. It wasn't a cheap medal. It was a piece of silver. So Uri takes his thumb and he pushes his thumb into the medal and takes it away maybe two or three seconds later and there's an impression in the guy's medal, like he had indented it with his thumb.

That seemed to be a little bit beyond a little magic trick. He didn't take the medal off of the guy's neck or anything like. He just pressed it and there's an indention in the medal obvious for all to see.

Then Melinda Ali, who I believe was Ali's second wife, was curious about this more so than Ali seemed to be that day and Uri did an experiment with her where he took his hand and put it over a ring that she was wearing, and I couldn't tell you exactly what kind of a ring it was. I don't think it was an expensive diamond or anything like that. He put his hand over it and started kind of touching on her hand, but nothing too overt. He wasn't touching the stone. He didn't have any utensils in his hand or anything like that, and then after a few seconds he said "Let me know if you feel anything strange or anything different," and then after a few seconds into it she said, "Ouch, my hand is getting warm," and then a few more seconds after that he took his hand away, the ring itself was still there but the stone inside the setting was gone. So how he accomplished that I don't know, and as far as I know she never got the stone back. She seemed pretty awed by that.

So is he an entertainer? Yes, in his own way. Is he a magician? No, I think whatever he's doing he's pretty legitimate about it. Maybe not a hundred percent of the time, but whenever I saw him I don't think that there was any overt attempt to create a fraud there.

Brent Raynes: Now back in your travels, back in the 1960s, you went to one of the better known windows, or UFO sighting locations, over in Warminster, England, where you met Arthur Shuttlewood, and that was when you saw one of your other UFOs.

Tim Beckley: That would have been my second of three UFO sightings. I was invited by my friend Brinsley La Poer Trench who wrote the book the *Sky People*, and a book on the inner earth, which we have in print now. He was an interesting character, and in fact he was a member of the House of Lords and he was responsible for trying to get a little bit of interest going with the members of the British Parliament to get them to release whatever information that might be available on UFOs. This was long before Nick Pope.

Anyway, they organized a UFO study group made up of members of Parliament and the House of Lords, people like Lord Hill Norton who was the former head of the British Fleet, a former Admiral. I was invited over to deliver a talk to the group, and then afterwards, after giving this little address I got to meet everybody and shake hands, I took a little side trip out into the country and went to Stonehenge, and not far from there is the town of Warminster where Arthur Shuttlewood was the editor of the daily newspaper there, *The Warminster Journal*. This was, of course, the seat of all UFO activity in England at that time. Hundreds of sightings, including I think Mick Jagger was one of those who had observed something in the sky hovering over Cradle Hill, and Starr Hill was another area that people would gather to witness these sights. It was quite a remarkable phenomenon that was happening there.

I met with Shuttlewood and we went out to the field at Starr Hill where a lot of these sightings were taking place. It must have been about 11 o'clock in the evening and almost directly overhead. He says, "Here's one of them now." What could I tell you. It looked pretty much like a street lamp in the sky. We were 5 or 6 miles out of town and nothing around there. It didn't appear to be moving around or doing anything peculiar, and that's probably why it didn't really catch my attention, but Arthur having witnessed probably dozens if not hundreds of sightings said that this was one of these objects. So he said, "Let's see what will happen." He goes to the trunk of his car and picks up a big torchlight. Not a little flashlight but a big torchlight and starts blinking at the object. Now it wasn't in Morse Code or anything like that. I don't even think he knew Morse Code. But every time that we would blink at this object in the sky it would seem to do a little bit of a somersault or tumble around, as if it were acknowledging our presence in our trying to signal to it with this light. This went on ten minutes or so, if I remember correctly, and then clouds came over and we didn't see the object, and then we eventually left. It was a pretty cloudy night.

In the history of UFOs, many of these intelligent lights whether ghost lights or whatever, they do seem to be responsive to humans who attempt to communicate or signal to them. This is something again I cannot tell you that it was a ship from outer space, but it was something that seemed to acknowledge our presence and our effort to try and signal to it. There was another fellow there who was a retired World War II Air Force pilot by the name of Bob Strong. Now Bob set his camera equipment up there at Starr Hill and Cradle Hill, on a tripod, and this guy had a huge photo album of all kinds of UFOs. I mean, bat shaped things, a whole string of objects going across the sky, cigar shaped craft, and he had photographs of these things, and you know what the darned thing was half of the photo album was missing because someone would say, "Let me borrow that photo. I want to make a copy of it. I'll give it back to you," and so it just depleted his collection in no time. But an amazing collection of photographs, some of which were published in Shuttlewood's various books.

Brent Raynes: Wow, what a story. Lots of stories!

Tim Beckley: Yeah, lots of stories.

Brent Raynes: So your ultimate conclusion of it all is that there is no one single theory.

Tim Beckley: Yes, that is what I'd have to say. My conclusion is that there is no one conclusion, and there probably never will be a conclusion. I've been doing this, gosh, I wrote my first FATE magazine article I think in 1962. I bought my first issue of FATE in 1957. I would have been ten years old. I read all of the books by Keyhoe, and I guess that I was impressed enough to start a career, you know? It's been a career that's had it's ups and downs.

And people have to realize, and I don't think that a lot of people do, that I have my own personal opinion on all of these things which means that it happens to coincide with the books and ideas that I publish, because basically I'm a publisher, a successful publisher, and that's what publishers do, even if they don't happen to agree with the content of all of their titles. This is something that most people can't seem to get through their head, that just because I publish a book by somebody who says he was visited by beings from Alpha Centauri or something, it doesn't necessarily mean that I think they were from Alpha Centauri, but I think that there is a need for publishing a book that other people have written about these experiences and let the readers sort it out for themselves.

So my conclusion is that there is no conclusion.

Also we hear about Disclosure. There is no disclosure and there will not be a disclosure. The only way that there will be a disclosure is if these objects land and make themselves known. There is not going to be any release of any information from the White House or the Air Force or any other military or governmental group because I don't think that they've really reached any conclusion on this. If you go back and read a lot of the famous things that happened the military is made up by a lot of people who believe and who disbelieve just like there is in civilian life.

Brent Raynes: Right. I remember John Keel some thirty years or so ago writing that he felt that the military was just as perplexed by the phenomenon as we were.

Tim Beckley: Is there anything to MJ-12? There might have been some people in the early days of the subject who thought that they had to adopt such tactics, but I doubt if anyone is around today who is aware of any of this information. Maybe higher up in the CIA they had access to certain data and certain reports that haven't been released yet, but what kind of reports would it be. We know that these things have hovered over missile silos, they've interrupted computers, electrical devices, and so everything you see in Close Encounters and science fiction genre has happened in real life. So we know that this stuff goes on, so what's the difference if we have another half dozen sightings over military bases where these things have screwed up our radar or something like that.

There's more evidence to indicate what they are than where they originate from. They could originate from anywhere. A lot of them could be just environmental phenomena.

Chapter 13
John Burke
Electromagnetic Phenomena at Ancient Sites

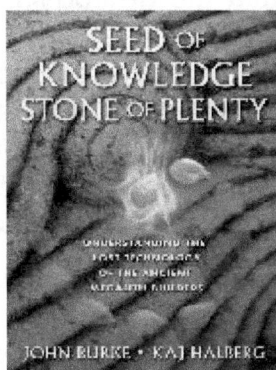

John Burke (the "B" in BLT Research Team) and his colleague Kaj Halberg, have written a startling and highly thought-provoking book entitled *Seed of Knowledge, Stone of Plenty* (http://www.bltresearch.com/JohnBurkeBook.htm). In this exclusive interview, Mr. Burke shares with us exciting details of the field work and the lab work that makes up the foundation of this book and the mind-boggling conclusions that were reached.

Brent Raynes: Your book, *Seed of Knowledge, Stone of Plenty*, which you co-authored with your colleague Kaj Halberg, makes an absolutely exciting and sensational claim that "old-world engineers" constructed standing stone circles, pyramids, mounds and dolmen using a "secret" that ties in their structures, local geology, and geomagnetism so that they seemingly could affect human consciousness and plant growth. How did you and your colleague come to embark upon such an unusual quest and ultimately to make such a startling discovery?

John Burke: By accident. We were working in England in 1993, partly in collaboration with Nancy Talbott, on trying to figure out why such a disproportionate amount of the world's crop circles were occurring in such a small area of England. A geologist friend of mine had suggested he'd like to see a map of the geology that underlay the area. I found that it was mostly chalk aquifer, with strong seasonal fluctuations of the water table. Now, water running through chalk can create a strong electric charge. Using standard scientific instruments, my co-author, Kaj Halberg, and I were able to confirm that that was exactly what was taking place at Silbury Hill, the largest manmade mound in Europe circa 3,000 B.C., with an estimated 14 million man hours in the building. The owner of the B&B at which we were staying suggested that we take our instruments to Avebury Henge (the forerunner of Stonehenge and half a mile from Silbury Hill), insisting that we would get some interesting readings there. We tried it and he was right. We found an intriguing pattern of magnetic alignments that wound up taking 5 weeks of work and 1,000 measurements to understand. But what we found was that the 66 remaining standing stones were magnetic and that their north poles were all aligned in the same direction, pointing at the next stone in line. This could not have been by accident.

Next we realized that the geology below both Silbury Hill and Avebury Henge was special in another way. Both were placed atop "conductivity discontinuities", something that sounds far more technical than it is. A conductivity discontinuity is simply the intersection of two zones of land, one of which conducts natural electrical ground current relatively well and the other less well. At such sites the normal daily fluctuations of the earth's geomagnetic field are magnified several hundred percent, and with them the telluric currents that flow through the ground.

The way in which Silbury Hill and Avebury were designed and built further amplified this energy. Once we started looking at other places and other countries we found out that this was the rule rather than the exception. Overwhelmingly, the ancient megalithic architects all over the world chose to build on conductivity discontinuities, and then designed and built these enormous structures in such a way as to further concentrate the natural electromagnetic energies present at those sites. You do not need to get on a plane and fly to a foreign country to experience this. Two thirds of the American population lives within a few hours drive of such sites and one of the appendices in our book lists dozens of such sites, with directions, hours, etc. The other appendix tells you how you can duplicate our work while visiting these sites.

We wondered how an ancient people without our fluxgate magnetometer, electrostatic voltmeter, and ground electrodes could have discovered such energies. But then we stumbled into a spot in the Black Hills of South Dakota that was both a geomagnetic anomaly and a vision quest site, dating from the days of Crazy Horse and his visions. That's when we found that many sensitives, such as shamans, can sense these energies as well as our instruments.

Furthermore, we began examining the chronology at megalithic sites around the world, whether pyramid, henge, or mound and found that they overwhelmingly were built during a time of food crisis, and that after their construction the crisis seemed to have vanished. Now, at the time I was working for a company that enhanced agricultural seeds with an artificial version of such energies and obtained advanced yields as a result. I asked myself if the same thing might have been true for the ancient builders. So we began bringing seeds to the sites and the results were startling.

Brent Raynes: Sounds intriguing. Please tell us more!

John Burke: We have used our instruments to examine henges, mounds, pyramids, and stone chambers in England, Guatemala, and across the U.S. While we did not get to France, and the oldest megalithic structures (circa 4,800 B.C.), a Belgian engineer named Pierre Mereaux spent 30 years surveying the region with the same types of instruments we used and came up with findings that precisely matched the pattern we found. For example, stone chambers we have examined in New England, starting just one hour north of New York City, are structurally and electromagnetically identical to ones built from Ireland to India over a 6,000 year period. You cannot argue they were a cultural phenomenon because there was no one culture across that time span and geographic range. But they are functional. They are always sited on conductivity discontinuities, have a negative magnetic anomaly right at the entrance, and electrically charged air inside.

In most locations we used two or three instruments. Our fluxgate magnetometer will measure the vertical axis of the earth's magnetic field anywhere, and this is the axis that changes dramatically each day in the pre-dawn hours and sets up natural electric currents in the ground which we can measure with our specialized geological ground electrodes. You stick a pair in the ground connected by a hundred feet of wire, have the wire run through a standard volt meter, and you can measure the current running through the ground between those two points. Our third instrument, and perhaps the most useful, is an electrostatic voltmeter, which will measure the electric charge of the air or an object.

Working at the New York chambers, we brought in samples of the same primitive varieties of corn used by Native American farmers from 700 A.D. onwards, about the same time period as the chambers were built. We would get statistically significant improvements in the growth rate and germination percentage of these seeds as compared to seeds left 100 feet outside the chambers and in the lab back home. The climax of this investigation came when we put 9 samples of 100 seeds each inside several chambers and had them grown out to harvest organically by the same Harvard-trained ethno-botanist who had supplied the seed. The samples left in the chambers yielded double to triple the amount of corn vs. the samples placed outside. When you combine these results with the fact that most megalithic structures seem to have been erected at a time of food crisis, it becomes compelling evidence that there was a functional purpose to these things that would explain how you could mobilize a population to invest such vast resources in building them.

We got similar results at North American mounds and earthen pyramids. And at the oldest Mayan city of Tikal, the oldest limestone pyramid (circa 600 B.C.), known as the Lost World Pyramid, produced visually stunning improvements that we show in the book, and the degree of improvement was in proportion to how powerful the electric charge was in the pre-dawn hours of a given day, as measured by the electrostatic voltmeter and the ground electrodes.

While I have not been able to measure the sites we discuss in South America and Egypt, the geology, the engineering, and the chronology all fit the pattern. This is a case based mostly on circumstantial evidence but the amount of it is overwhelming, and to claim it is all coincidence, frankly, begins to seem ludicrous. Every statement in *Seed of Knowledge* is backed either by personal, direct measurement with standard scientific instruments or by one of our 300 references from peer-reviewed journals or books from academic or university presses. This is solid science here. We even understand and have measured the biochemical processes taking place inside the seeds that triggers these remarkable transformations. And there is some direct evidence, detailed in the book, that ancient farmers actually brought their seed to these sites.

On the one hand, this all seemed very surprising. Yet, on the other hand, I began to think of it from a modern perspective. After all, these ancient builders had the same brain we do, they just worked in different media. In our modern world the biggest structures we build, by far, are hydroelectric dams. And why are we willing to invest such gargantuan amounts of time and effort to build them? Because we know it will be worth it in very concrete terms. From them we get *electricity*, the lifeblood of our industrial civilization. By comparison, I wonder if our ancestors weren't willing to also invest mind-boggling amounts of time and effort creating pyramids and such in order to achieve a very concrete reward: *fertility*, the lifeblood of any agricultural civilization.

Brent Raynes: Earlier today (03-31-07) you explained to me that many of us live close to similar sites and that you encourage people to go out and explore and investigate such places for themselves. Could you please share with us how anyone interested might also embark upon a similar quest of exploration?

John Burke: In one appendix to *Seed of Knowledge, Stone of Plenty,* we list details of many dozens of such sites open to the public in the U.S., Canada, and England. In the other appendix, we explain how you can use similar instruments or seed yourself at these sites to confirm or refute our work. After all, it isn't accepted science until the work has been replicated, so there is important work that needs to be done by others. So far I have worked with one university biology student who confirmed the growth differences between control seed which she kept in her lab and seed she sent me and which I placed in a rock chamber for her.

Anyone wishing to do similar work can contact me at
seedofknowledgestoneofplenty@yahoo.com.

Even without seed or instruments, there is work to be done using the human brain as the sensor. I personally experienced a powerfully disorienting sensation during a lunch break in the Black Hills of South Dakota when I unknowingly leaned my head back against what turned out to be a highly electrified vein of quartz. The Black Hills are the second biggest conductivity discontinuity in the United States and were always sacred land to many tribes. Some vision quests still being conducted today clearly consist of sitting an individual alone atop a sufficiently strong magnetic anomaly for an all night vigil. Dr. Michael Persinger, a Canadian neuroscientist, has confirmed that the magnitude of magnetic changes we have found at these sites conforms to those he has found capable of creating visions in volunteers in his lab. Finally, the largest conductivity discontinuity in the U.S. is on the west bank of the Rio Grande at Albuquerque. This land is today the Pictograph National Memorial because it contains thousands of rock carvings which are considered by anthropologists today to have been made by shamans illustrating their trance hallucinations. I measured very powerful and extremely odd surges of electric current in the ground there. When the ranger at the Visitor Center heard what I was finding, she said to me, "You know, periodically I get these "New Age types" coming in here and telling me they just love to go sit up in the rocks and feel the energy. I thought they were a bunch of flakes, but you're telling me there might be something to this."

Chapter 14
Marie D. Jones
UFOs, Psychic Phenomena, and Quantum Physics

Marie D. Jones, author of the newly published *PSIence: How New Discoveries in Quantum Physics and New Science May Explain the Existence of Paranormal Phenomena*, has been involved with the paranormal for most of her life, including over fifteen years as a trained field investigator for both MUFON (Mutual UFO Network) and CUFOS (Center For UFO Studies), and a member of Fate Magazine's research community. She also formed two UFO/paranormal research organizations in Southern California.

Marie is a licensed New Thought/Metaphysics minister and pastoral counselor, holding a Master's Degree in Metaphysical Studies. Currently she is pursuing a Doctor of Divinity status. She has studied Wicca, Hermetica, goddess traditions, mythology and comparative religion.

A screenwriter, magazine writer and book reviewer, and the author and co-author of over three dozen inspirational books, this prolific writer maintains a personal website at: www.mariedjones.com. Also a blog at: psience.blogspot.com.

Marie welcomes emails: info@mariedjones.com

Brent Raynes: Marie, I really like your recently published book, PSIence. The theoretical physicists should find your own investigative and scientific journey to isolate a (to borrow a term from their field) "Theory for Everything" quite thought-provoking and potentially important. There's a wonderful overview of the latest and the fascinating variety of physics theories to be found in your chapter "Quantum Physics 101," as well as your inclusion of much parapsychological, cryptozoological and ufological data, emphasizing their potential interconnections, all of which to me shows great insight and clarity of focus on your part.

Please share with our readers some about yourself, how you came to write this book, and what you hope that this book and its message will convey to its readers.

Marie Jones: I've always been interested in the paranormal, and in metaphysics, from the time I was old enough to read, which was about age 2. My whole life has been about looking into things, trying to find connections and patterns. I'm a curious kid at heart, always wanting to know what's under the rock. I read five or six books a week, and I devour ideas voraciously. I tend to be a concept-oriented person, as are most writers, always envisioning (and chasing down) the overall bigger picture. Over the last ten years I'd been reading a lot about quantum and theoretical physics, and how some of the most cutting edge research was pointing to an underlying truth about reality that seemed connected to human consciousness and perception. And, as always seems to happen to me when I get "hooked" on a subject, other books began falling into my lap on the same subjects, and people sort of mysteriously appeared in my life with more pieces of a puzzle I was beginning to feel a tremendous desire to put together. That led to the writing of this book, which I hope will serve as a potential springboard for further inquiry and open-minded discussion. I want readers to get excited about these concepts, maybe even expand upon them and delve deeper into them on their own time. Ultimately, I hope the book conveys that we have the potential to understand much of what we deem reality if we keep an open mind and look for connections where others might fail to see them.

Having grown up the daughter of a scientist, I have a tremendous love and respect for science (my next book is about super-volcanoes!) and believe it can indeed explain everything we see around us, including the supernatural and paranormal. The problem lies not with science, but with scientists who haven't caught up yet to what nature is trying to tell us, to what human experience is trying to tell us. The supernatural is simply the natural not yet understood, to paraphrase Elbert Hubbard.

Brent Raynes: Can you share with us some of the most interesting, personal case investigations of UFO and paranormal phenomena that you've been involved with yourself?

Marie Jones: As for cases I've investigated, three stand out the most. One involved a guy who entered a very unusual fog bank and experienced missing time. His experience sounded very much like the Time Storm reports of Jenny Randles' research. The guy was incredibly articulate and intelligent, yet when he would discuss this event, he would become almost childlike, very afraid, very apprehensive. Yet he did not want to use hypnosis to try to find out what happened during the missing time. This was at the hey-day of abductions, and I was friends and colleagues with Yvonne Smith at the time, who was just starting to work with abductees. What made this case so interesting for me was the fact it took place on a military base and a couple of years later, my husband and I were passing through the same area and encountered a weird orange fog, but we didn't lose any timeÉat least none that we know of! Sadly, I lost contact with this person, who had become a friend, after I moved to L.A. a few years ago, then back to San Diego.

The second case involved family members who had had UFO sightings before. One day they were driving in a remote area of the county (San Diego) and came up to a very slow car they could not get around. At the first opportunity to pass the car, they did so, only to find that the occupants of the slow moving car were anything but human. They described them as having extremely long, drawn out faces, almost mask-like, but real, with eyes that just stared blankly ahead. Weeks later, these same family members experienced other UFO sightings and had their home and business buzzed by black helicopters. After about a year, their alien encounters seemed to come to an end and we could never quite figure out why, other than the fact that the area they lived in was at the time being developed and became much less remote. Their experiences, though, were highly unusual because they - three family members - all had repeated sightings and was my first experience with contagion- I had my own sighting at the same time in La Costa, although I am still not sure what the heck I saw. It was an object moving through the dusk sky at rapid speed, one end flipping over the other end! It looked like a big square slinky!

The third involved a poltergeist case that really launched my total obsession with the occult for about ten years. It happened when I was a teenager. It was a friend from my junior high school days who was living with a poltergeist, and I reluctantly stayed overnight once and felt the presence of something move across my body the next morning. But what happened later was the kicker. Me being the bold and curious person I am, I decided I was going to perform an exorcism, since the family's church would do nothing to help. So I went to the library and got all these books on demons and rituals and I went home and one night I attempted to do a circle in my bedroom. I was a teenager, mind you, and I did this ritual to call forth a spirit and had a very scary experience that convinced me I was not cut out to be an exorcist. That's about all I can tell you!

Other cases were very much run of the mill, except for one rather hilarious case I encountered when I was leader of a MUFON group in northern San Diego- a series of sightings that turned out to be a hoax, yet we managed to get our group on the local news (we wanted some press!) and the reporter, who was like the "hot guy" on local news at the time, came out and saw the hoax himself and fell for it! So much for the media!

Brent Raynes: From your research, what have some of the most important realizations or lessons been for you about these phenomena?

Marie Jones: Much of the phenomena involve energy in some form or another. Energy being manipulated, transformed, mutated, changed, amplified, altered. It always seems to come down to some form of energy that we have not yet learned to master or understand the mechanics of. Ghosts, UFOs, vortices where time stands still, it all seems to suggest that something, or perhaps someone, is working with energy in a way we are only beginning to understand at the quantum level, where things like entanglement and non-locality and wave-particle duality are the norm.

In the quantum world, things happen that are far more bizarre than a ghost or Bigfoot. I mean, we are talking about something being both a wave and a particle, and that two particles that have been in contact continue to affect one another across vast distances instantaneously - faster than the speed of light. That a thing may not be real until we observe it and "collapse its wave function" so that it goes from a wave form to a solid form we can label a chair, or a dog, or a HummerÉWOW! Or that the entire universe may be nothing more than a holographic image being projected from some other level of reality, in another dimension! The quantum is paranormal, yet it's reality at the smallest, most fundamental level. It's spooky action at a distance, as Einstein called it. It's magic, but magic we are beginning to take from the level of theory to provable law. Most startling of all is that at the quantum level, we the observer have a direct affect on the experiment's outcome, meaning that there is a deep connection between everything, which physicist David Bohm called the "implicate order" that underlies the visible, knowable "explicate order." Reality, it seems, has two levels. The one we see and the one just behind the one we see. Like Dorothy in Oz and the man behind the curtain!

Not to mention that much of what we deem paranormal is simply a matter of perception. Look at what a person living two hundred years ago would think of a teenager listening to an iPod. That would appear as magic, being able to hear music in your ear coming out of a little tiny box. Or television? Totally paranormal to a Neanderthal! Things that seem normal to us would be considered paranormal to primitive people. Things that seem normal to an advanced civilization now seem paranormal to us. It's all relative, and all a matter of perception.

Brent Raynes: What do you say to those who might argue that you're attempting to connect too many dots, that UFOs are simply "nuts and bolts" physical visitations of extraterrestrial craft and your review of data on poltergeists, ghosts, Bigfoots, chupacabras, Electronic Voice Phenomena, near-death and out of body experiences, etc., etc., is a feeble and misguided attempt to try and isolate relationships where none exist. After all, to many they are separate fields entirely.

Marie Jones: I would remind them that guys like Einstein and Bohm understood that there was a connectedness behind all things, so I am in good company. As a writer, though, I get to boldly go where no physicist has gone before and take the concepts I present one step beyond the outer limits of the twilight zone! The ideas I present are just that, ideas. I offer no proof and don't claim to have found the truth, just a potential piece of it. Besides, one would have to be quite feeble-minded to NOT see that all reality HAS to be connected, otherwise there would be two realities, two truths, and scientists themselves will be the first ones to tell you, there can only be one overall truth. One reality. Not billions, one for each person on the planet, although our perceived reality certainly is individualistic.

What concerns me is that people working in separate fields tend to think inside the box, to be compartmentalized in their beliefs and thought processes. So my book is clearly not for the close-minded or compartmentalized mind! The biggest problem in science is the inability of scientists from divergent fields to come together and compare notes! But you know, the same can be said for many paranormal researchers, who get so caught up in just one niche area of research, they forget the forest for the trees.

And if anyone ever dared call me feeble-minded to my face, they'd get a good dose of New York Italian whoop-ass, so let that be a warning! LOL!!!

Brent Raynes: Can you summarize for us what you what you think the Theory of Everything comes down to here between UFOs, the paranormal, and quantum physics?

Marie Jones: Well, whatever TOE or GUT these folks decide on, if it doesn't include paranormal experiences, it is not a real TOE or GUT, because leaving out the real experiences of millions of people throughout history is not good science. It's arrogant and ignorant to just flat out deny that this stuff is going on. But we see this kind of arrogance and ignorant denial right now with global warming (although more minds are waking up to the truth), so what the heck do we expect when it comes to the paranormal? Believe me, when more scientists think they can explain the paranormal, they will accept it. AND when more scientists have their own experiences, they will accept it. AND when more scientists can speak more openly about their belief in the paranormal without losing funding or tenure or their jobs or their reputations, they will accept it and research it whole-heartedly. Can you even imagine how many scientists must really want to dig into this stuff, but cannot because of academic politics? But there are plenty of mavericks bucking the system and writing books and doing research. So things are definitely changing!

My feeling is that the Holy Grail everyone is seeking is going to be just exactly what Bohm said- that there is an implicate and explicate order to reality and that everything is connected and everything influences everything else, past, present and futureÉMy fave is the Zero Point Field, a field of pure potentiality from which everything else springs forth and takes manifest form, as it's been referred to. As for the actual mathematical equation physicists come up with to cover all of that in one theory- it's not my job! I suck at math.

Brent Raynes: What do you hope to see happen in these various fields of exploration in the future?

Marie Jones: More open dialog, more working together, more dedication to professionalism and a respect for science on the part of the paranormal community, more willingness to go out on a limb on behalf of the scientific community, and especially more books that explore and expand and excite. Every week there is another stunning news story that suggests the quantum world is the place we need to focus on to find the answers to questions about the paranormal. Last week, for example, a story came out about an experiment where some physicists at the University of Ithica in New York MADE AN OBJECT MOVE JUST BY LOOKING AT IT. And now these mavericks are going to prove that they can put one thing in two places at once. THIS IS SCIENCE!!! Yet how "paranormal" can you get? Teleportation, psychokinesis, Indian Gurus reportedly in two places at the same time. HELLOOOOOO!!!

Chapter 15
Greg and Lora Little
Portsmouth Bound:
Looking for an Atlantean Replica?

We arrived in South Shore, Kentucky, across the Ohio River from Portsmouth, Ohio to be greeted by a torrential downpour, high winds and lightning. Although we didn't know it at the time, the tornado siren had been sounded around 4:30 p.m. in downtown Portsmouth. All the way up from Tennessee and traveling up through Kentucky it had been very pleasant weather, even though it had been cloudy. We were hurrying to arrive in the Portsmouth area as soon as possible because Allison Kalb, the wife of the Mayor of Portsmouth, had been in touch with Greg's wife Lora and had revealed that a very significant ancient earthworks site that Greg had previously written about in Mound Builders: Edgar Cayce's Forgotten Record of Ancient America (2001) [co-authored with his wife Lora and with John Van Auken] and in his most recent The Illustrated Encyclopedia of Native American Mounds & Earthworks (2009), was not "obliterated" completely as had been previously reported and believed.

This was certainly exciting news as this particular earthworks was the one that was very similar in appearance to Plato's description of the center of the city of Atlantis which had been described as having a high hill with a flat top (upon which a temple had been constructed), was surrounded by three water rings, and was divided up into a cross-shaped pattern with three bridges and a canal that led to the ocean. However, in this case the canal was replaced by an "embanked walkway" that led 1.5 miles to the Ohio River (perhaps a symbolic substitute for the ocean). In Edgar

Cayce's trance readings he stated that "the mounds that were called the replica or representative of the Yucatan experience, as well as the Atlantean and in Gobi land."

"Indians who lived in the heart of the Mississippian Era mounds believed the earth started as a huge circle of land surrounded by water," the authors of <u>Mound Builders</u> wrote. As Greg and Lora have pointed out, that "walkway" just mentioned continued on the other side of the Ohio River, ran another five miles into what is modern Portsmouth, to two huge horseshoe shaped mounds. They point out that at the center of England's Stonehenge there is a "horseshoe" arrangement of stones strikingly similar to Portsmouth's "horseshoe" earthworks. (One unfortunately has a school built on top of it, but the other is still quite intact and in a park) "In addition, the 'ceremonial causeway' leading from the center of Stonehenge is similar to that found in Portsmouth as well as at many other American sites," these scholarly authors added.

The next morning, Sunday, July 12th, 2009, we were greeted by beautiful sunshine. We arrived at about 9 a.m. at K.C. Hardin's Greenhouse and Garden Center in South Shore. Mr. Hardin greeted us warmly and led us through three gates out past his barn to what we now could see was a huge central mound! In years past, a large amount of its upper portion had been removed. Still what a thrill it was to see and walk around the remaining mound. Though not nearly as tall as it used to be obviously, it was still noticeably on elevated ground, and enormous in size. Greg and Lora excitedly looked at a blow up that Greg had had made of the Squier and Davis 1848 survey map of the site and together they were able at times to identify and at other times logically guess certain physical features in the landscape indicative of the rings and the four walkways. At one point as we stood atop this mound, Greg had, he would tell me later, a brief and unexpected clear vision of what it must have looked like. In that "vision", he could see the "walkway" all the way over to the horseshoe mounds.

Little did we know at the time how that brief "vision" foreshadowed startling events that would occur to us, as well as twenty-one other people from across the nation who were gathering to meet us in Columbus, Ohio to go with us on an A.R.E. (Association for Research and Enlightenment) sponsored tour of Ohio's incredible ancient Indian Mounds and geometric earthworks.

That evening, at the Baymont Inn and Suites off of Mediterranean Avenue in Columbus, we all gathered in a small meeting room on the first floor. Chairs were arranged in a circle and going around the room each person introduced themselves and shared with everyone some information about themselves, including what they hoped to learn from the tour experience. It was soon apparent that this was a very intelligent, outgoing, and friendly group of people. In fact, quite a few of them had served in various backgrounds of teaching and education. Lora brought everyone up to speed on everything that was scheduled, the latest updates, what to expect, how to dress, and, most important of all perhaps, what was to be served on the next menu. She kept us in the know, and she also helped the bus driver reach our many destinations (which were often in some very remote places down very narrow roads), which involved unexpected detours and critical locations that were not marked as they should have been by road signs. And our bus driver, God bless America, pulled us out of some tight spots that I probably would have been afraid to have attempted with my pickup truck! At any rate, Greg presented an overview on the mounds and earthworks, showing numerous pictures and illustrations that he projected onto a movie screen. As usual, he gave a great talk. Then it was my turn, and I stepped into the center of the room and showed them a set of fully functional replicas of the pre-Columbian Peruvian whistling vessels, explained about the significance of whistles in ancient ceremonies, and then gave a demonstration of how they sounded.

Monday morning, July 13th, our tour began. We headed out for our first ancient Native American site. Our destination was nearby Newark, where Greg explained to us that we were about to behold some of the most incredible and best preserved ancient earthworks anywhere around. And if he didn't say it, I'm sure he'd have included also that they were among the most mysterious earthworks to be found anywhere too. Attributed to the ancient Hopewell culture, one of the most magnificent and enigmatic centerpieces of this group of earthworks was the enormous walled octagon shaped enclosure, whose interior covered 50 acres! Connected by a narrow set of parallel walls to a circle whose interior covered some 20 acres and whose walls ranged from 8 to 14 feet tall, this awesome geometric earthwork was used to make lunar and solar observations, and even had alignments that incorporated the 18.61 year cycle of maximum and minimum moonrise and moonset.

We also walked to the center of the Great Circle Earthworks, which once had been called the Fairgrounds Circle as the local county fair used to set up there. Consisting of a 9 foot high wall, with a 7 foot deep moat on the inside, the interior consists of 30 acres. At the center is what has been described by archeologists as a large bird effigy mound, but when Greg and Lora accompanied British science writer Andrew Collins to the site in 2004, he concluded that it was a bird's foot effigy mound instead. It was here that Joan and I smudged the mound and our accompanying ARE entourage of friends. Although Joan and I had been with Greg and Lora to this mound back in 2001, on another ARE sponsored mounds tour, I was now able to look at the effigy mound from the perspective of a bird's foot. I had read Andrew's book The Cygnus Mystery and indeed he was absolutely correct. *It did resemble a huge bird's foot!*

Tuesday morning, July 14th, in the city limits of Columbus, we stopped shortly after 10 a.m. to see a 20 foot tall Adena era conical mound, known as Shrum Mound, located off of McKinley Avenue, close to the Scioto River. While Greg walked a group of folks to the top of the mound and explained what was known about the site and these ancient people, Joan and I found a shaded area on the back side of the mound.

Brent Raynes with Peruvian Whistling Vessels

An Appreciative Indian Spirit?

It was a sunny and pleasant day. Joan took our small deer skin drum and sounded four beats in each of the four directions to call in the spirits, and then we lighted the white sage in our seashell. Soon everyone had gathered around us on the grass in a semicircle, some leaning up against a nearby stone wall. I instructed everyone to relax and sit with their back's straight, to close their eyes and take three deep breaths. I had them to visualize a medicine wheel and instructed everyone that we would briefly visit each of the four directions individually and try for some sort of message, guidance, or insight each time. Afterwards Greg complimented me from his nearby spot on the ground stating he had found the slow beat of the drum very pleasant. Then he added that he seldom meditated, joking that he meditated with his eyes open, but at any rate he wanted to share something quite extraordinary that had just happened to him! He said that soon after Joan had smudged him with the sage, (and before I began the drumbeat) an opening had appeared to him from inside the mound to his left. A Native American man came up to Greg from the mound. He was tall, strong, bare chested. It all happened suddenly and quickly, Greg pointed out. He spoke a different language, but Greg somehow knew that he was saying something like "Thank you for bringing these people here. This is a good thing you are doing."

Greg said that it was like he could see inside the mound, like it was illuminated, and he could see clay pottery that this man's people had buried with him, but that none of this really mattered to him anymore. Greg just instantly knew things about this man. He died at age 35. He had been a fierce and mighty warrior. He had killed many of his enemy. But later on in his life he had become a beloved leader of his people.

A lady sitting right next to Greg stated that she had sensed a protective Indian presence behind her.

From here we headed out for Chillicothe to do lunch and then that afternoon we visited nearby Mound City, a Hopewell burial site and ceremonial center consisting of 24 burial mounds surrounded by a square earthen wall enclosure. Although an impressive site, Greg told Joan and I privately at one point that he felt nothing there. After Shrum, which was such a good feeling experience, Mound City just felt dead.

That evening on the outskirts of Chillicothe, we attended a powerful outdoor play at the Sugarloaf Mountain Amphitheatre entitled "Tecumseh!" Based on the life of the legendary Shawnee leader Tecumseh, one odd historical footnote (which was included in the play) is how he accurately "prophesied" the New Madrid earthquake. It was to be a signal to other Indian tribes to band together and to push the whites out.

Mysteries within Portsmouth's Horseshoe Mound

Wednesday, July 15th, we headed out for Portsmouth. We arrived there around 11 a.m. at the large Horseshoe Mound. Joan and I entered this walled enclosure first and while Joan began smudging around the walls of the mound and the opening, I faced the four directions with my functional eagle bone whistle replica, blowing three times in each direction. Then we decided we should have smudged ourselves at the beginning and so I asked Joan where the feather was. She said she had laid it on the small Indian blanket that we had laid on the ground. I looked and it wasn't on the blanket. Joan then looked and she couldn't find it either. I looked over the blanket and surrounding grass again. We both felt that we had done a thorough search of it. Still no feather, so then we decided we'd just go ahead and smudge each other fanning the smoke with our hands. I smudged Joan and she smudged me. As we were finishing up I glanced back down at the blanket *and there it was!*

It's a good sized feather, about a foot long. How did we miss it, we wondered?

Joan felt strongly that everyone who wanted to should enter the mound site in a line, doing a simple toe, heel Indian style dance. She gave them a quick dance lesson and then led the way. Once inside they formed a circle and sat down on the ground. Joan smudged everyone and again I blew the eagle bone whistle in the four directions. Then everyone relaxed and meditated for a few minutes. Afterwards, Greg wanted to know if anyone had seen any "lights" or heard anything unusual. One man meditating nearby stated that he had "seen," out from the area of his Third Eye, a sun-like image. Joan said that with her inner vision she "saw" a sun-like display with a ring of light around it, with a beam that she felt, she said, "was coming into my heart." Greg then shared that he had heard a humming sound like—a vibration—seemed hard to explain. Lora also felt a strange vibration that seemed, I gathered, to come up from the ground into the body. Both were sitting with their backs close to the back wall of the horseshoe mound.

Greg said that he had seen flashes and then a sun-like light. That evening though, after supper, Greg paid Joan and I a visit to our room. We were talking about the events of the day when, out of the blue, Greg began to share with us what he experienced and "saw" before the hum and lights. He said it was like he was walking from the huge mound with the concentric rings, walking down to the Ohio River, and the ground at the site and within the walkway was white. On each side of the wide road he was walking were these wide walls and 20 to 40 feet out from the walls were the trees, the forest. He got to the river and then he just found himself across that body of water walking up the hill to the horseshoe mounds. From there he could look around at it all, plus the mound with the rings, and the rectangular walled site across the Ohio River, across from where the Scioto River enters the Ohio.

"And I was an Indian," Greg then exclaimed with a laugh. He said he had something on his head, and in his hand. His walk, it seemed, was part of some sort of ceremony.

Greg wasn't the only one who experienced a "past life" kind of memory while inside the horseshoe mound. Long time ARE member and author Ann Jaffin shared this experience:

On our recent ARE mounds tour of Ohio, I received a gift of understanding. I picked up a past life for my husband, Stan. Over the years, I've traveled the world often with ARE groups. Stan never objected to my going but he never wanted to go along. The exception was Bimini. He loved this beautiful little island in the Bahamas where Cayce said to look for Atlantis, and visited it more than a dozen times. Not being a diver, it was the mounds that attracted Stan. These mounds are located in remote, uninhabited east Bimini and are very difficult to reach. Wielding his machete, I called him "Indiana Jaffin" as he carved numerous paths through the mangrove swamps to 11 different mounds, including the magnificent 450-foot-long effigy mound of a lemon shark.

Given his disinterest in foreign travel and love of the outdoors as well as his physical strength and athleticism, I had speculated that Stan may have had more than one lifetime in early America. On Thursday morning our group visited the unique horseshoe mound in Portsmouth. The mayor's wife kindly allowed us to enter this restricted area for a meditation and a ritual. After the meditation I remained seated and did not rise to get tobacco to offer to the four directions. Stan is not usually drawn to group activities and I was quite surprised when he rose, took some tobacco, and made offerings to the cardinal points. As I watched him turn and make the offering, in an intuitive flash I knew that he had been a builder of that mound. Very, very briefly I saw him as he had appeared then.

There is perhaps an irony to his association with a horseshoe mound. Both of us love horses and ride as often as we can. We had long known that we had a lifetime together among the horsemen of the Asian steppes. No wonder that Stan chose to go on a tour that took him home.

After the group meditation in the horseshoe mound, I stood in the center of the group's circle and I spoke to them about this site and the importance of the rituals and ceremonies that were conducted at this and other ancient sites. Greg later explained that he's heard me talk many times before, but inside this mound something was different. He couldn't hear me except when I was facing him. He said it was strange, as my words seemed kind of muffled like, as though they were being absorbed and sucked up into a vacuum of some sort. Later I played him a recording I did inside the mound, just after the feather incident, when it was just Joan and I there. I was using the tape recorder with hand held microphone that I often use for doing interviews. It picks up sounds very well, and though there was a school nearby, a helicopter that frequently flew over, there was a lawn mower and a weed eater, people and traffic nearby, all you can hear is my voice. I asked Joan a question. She was standing nearby, but on the tape you can just barely hear her voice, and you definitely can't tell what she was saying.

The following week I phoned Allison Kalb, the wife of the Mayor of Portsmouth, to discuss our visit and to find out more about these ancient sites. I was telling Allison about the feather incident that had occurred at the horseshoe mound and she told me that Joan had told her that same story over lunch later that day at a restaurant in Portsmouth named Damons, located at the Ramada Inn. "You know, while she was telling me that I had the weirdest experience," Allison said. "I've thought a lot about it since then. But I started feeling really strange. She was talking about that and it was almost like everything started getting really far away. I could hear what she was saying but it sounded real far away. I've never felt like this before. I can't even explain it. It was almost like an out-of-body thing or something. I kept thinking: 'I'm going to pass out,' but I was trying to concentrate so hard on what she was saying."

"I was afraid that you all could tell. I thought: 'I feel so strange.' I just felt like I was going to black out. I can't even explain it. I have never felt like that before. I thought, 'Am I having a panic attack?'"

I asked, "So her voice sounded far away too?" and Allison replied, "Yeah. It was like I could see her lips moving. I could hear what she was saying, but it was like I was in a tunnel or something. I can't even explain it."

I next described to Allison the sound dampening effect that we had experienced inside the horseshoe mound, how Greg had said that unless I was looking directly at him he couldn't hear me, and that it was sort of like my words were being sucked up. "See. Oh my gosh," Allison said. "Yeah, that's how I felt when your wife was talking, and we were down at the Ramada, sitting there eating, and I thought, 'I feel like I'm in a tunnel,' and I'm watching her mouth move but I'm having such a hard time hearing her, and she wasn't far away from me. It just sounded really, like you said, like the words were being sucked up."

Joan and Allison were sitting directly across from each other at a long table. There was only three or four feet between them.

Many people have described strange things happening to them at the horseshoe mound site. "People have reported that they have seen little glowing lights over the mound, like little balls of dancing light floating through the air," Allison told me. She also described how ghost hunters have even visited the horseshoe mound and the surrounding site and reported quite a number of unexplained occurrences.

Portsmouth and the immediate surrounding area held many fascinating surprises for us.

Thursday morning, July 16th, we left Chillicothe's Comfort Inn at 9 a.m. First we went to see the four conical burial mounds at Mound Cemetery in Piketon. Then we proceeded on to Seip Mound, described as one of the largest earthen mounds built by the Hopewell culture. There we smudged and on top of this enormous mound we blew six of the Peruvian whistling vessels. The lady who had felt the protective Indian presence back at the Shrum Mound told me how it was as though she "saw" the face of an Indian man at this site. She said he had like a peacock feather headdress. She also envisioned Indians surrounding the mound. As we were leaving, Joan told me that she sensed an old Indian man with a staff taller than him standing near the opening in the earthen wall in front of Seip Mound. She "saw" him as having skins on and felt he was like a caretaker. He seemed to be watching all of us, she said. That afternoon we headed for Fort Hill, where many of us got a real physical workout climbing up to the top of this ancient site. Some opted to stay behind and again blow the whistles with Joan at a picnic area at the bottom. After that it was on to Miamisburg, where we spent the night at the Comfort Suites Hotel.

Friday morning, around 7 a.m., we headed out bright and early for Fort Ancient. We toured their wonderful museum, a lot of us also did business at their gift shop (I noticed one person purchasing a booklet on sage) and then we went back outside and looked at the mounds, earthen walls, and went to a lookout spot that afforded a great view of the surrounding area. Our bus even passed some people doing an archeological dig.

Joan Raynes in Horsemound, Portsmith, Ohio

Confirmation?

Then we returned to Miamisburg to visit one of the two largest conical mounds in the eastern U.S. Joan smudged each person as they were about to go up the stairs to the viewing platform located at the top of this 65 foot tall mound, while I held out a small plastic pouch for anyone who wanted to have a pinch of tobacco mix to make an offering to the four directions. This was going to be our final Indian Mound visit on this tour, and this was to be everyone's final opportunity for a smudging and to make an offering. It was at this time that a young lady in our group approached me and told me that she didn't know quite how to ask me this and wondered if I knew it already, but that at one of the recent site smudging and meditational events these human shaped shadow forms, as best as she could describe them, had appeared around me. They came up to around my shoulders (I'm about 5' 9" tall) and at first there was like one, then two, then three, and it seemed that pretty soon there was a pretty good sized group of them. At any rate, she said that she just wanted me to know that the spirits were listening to me, that when I called them in that they indeed did come. I must admit that listening to her share this story with me gave my arms goose bumps.

Bullwinkle's Top Hat:
Were the Spirits Friendly?

After our visit at this great site, we all headed into Miamisburg to do lunch at Bullwinkle's Top Hat. I chuckled to myself, wondering if Greg had had a hand in the selection of this restaurant. In his book <u>People of the Web</u> he actually mentioned Bullwinkle J. Moose in a subtitled section in chapter 5 entitled "The Spirits Are About To Speak – Are They Friendly Spirits? ...Friendly? Just Listen." But from what I knew of the arrangements, Greg didn't have a hand in the restaurant selection at all. Maybe Trickster Coyote was playing a synchronistic little mind game with us.

Indeed were they friendly? We certainly felt like they were!

After another delicious meal (much more than the average person should eat at one sitting), we headed back to Columbus, where we'd spend the final night of our tour. But on the way back we were to stop at Columbus's Ohio Historical Center where acclaimed archeologist Bradley T. Lepper would lead us on a personally guided tour of their archeological displays. Greg said that in the field of archeology Bradley Lepper was his hero. A few years back, Lepper had announced to the world the existence of the remains of an apparent 56 mile long straight line walled walkway from Newark's Octagon to Chillicothe's High Banks Circle and Octagon site. When we were visiting Mound City, most of us walked down to the Scioto River and Greg pointed to the fields across the river from us, to the locations of where this Circle and Octagon had been. Unfortunately, it was demolished by white settlers like thousands of other sites, but pictures from the air still show its outline on the ground below. It looked very similar to the Newark site and was used the same way it seems, but while the circle was 20 acres as well, the octagon was a smaller 18 acres.

We heard talk that this site might be reconstructed. Hopefully this is so, but due to the present economic crisis this looks very unlikely any time in the near future. Both Greg and Mr. Lepper expressed concern about the future of archeology in Ohio. There were impending cut backs, anticipated lay offs, parks and museums were opening fewer hours to save money (this was a problem in planning our tour), and Greg was disappointed to see how this museum's archeological section had been greatly reduced in size while the existing space was being used for other things. We expressed our collective concern to Mr. Lepper that these wonderful treasures were going to become less and less available to the public. I think we also wondered (at least some of us) if the public at large fully appreciated the significance of all of this. I remember talking about the archeological treasures of Portsmouth with Allison Kalb and what a great shame it was that so little of the original sites remained intact, that what was originally there had been just as spectacular, if not more so, than England's cherished tour attraction Stonehenge. She quickly agreed, saying that she really didn't think that most area citizens really comprehended and fully appreciated what had once been there.

Brent Raynes in the Science Fiction Museum
Seattle, Washington, 2004

GEORGE HUNT WILLIAMSON'S THE SAUCERS SPEAK'
OTHER VOICES

In 1951 George Hunt Williamson was doing anthropological field work among the Chippewa when he began to hear the many legends of the "Hairy-Faced Men," "Gee-By's" (ghosts), along with countless tales of the "Gin Gwin" or that which shakes the Earth. These "Earth Rumblers" might also be known as "Flying Wheels" or "Flying Boats."

The author of Other Tongues Other Flesh began to realize that such "tales" were common place among many other native tribes. This fascination with "Flying Saucers" lead to actual radio contact with Extraterrestrials that was repeated time and time again in front of credible witnesses. His privately published report on these ongoing communications attempts to "speak" with beings from other worlds has – over the years – been duplicated by others and has been the subject of highly classified debate in scientific circles.

OTHER VOICES (ie Saucers Speak) includes Wiliamson's full findings as well as a complete update which includes no less a famous individual than the late Senator Barry Godwater who often stated that both the U.S. and Russia had "picked up such (unknown) signals before..." and that "NASA is doing research into this." In recent times, ordinary citizens have heard messages over their households radios and have even received strange pictures on their television sets that have NOT been aired by any normal broadcast facilities.

Order OTHER VOICES for just $15.00 + $5 S/H

OTHER TONGUES OTHER FLESH REVISITED
BY BROTHER PHILIP
(PEN NAME OF GEORGE HUNT WILLIAMSON)

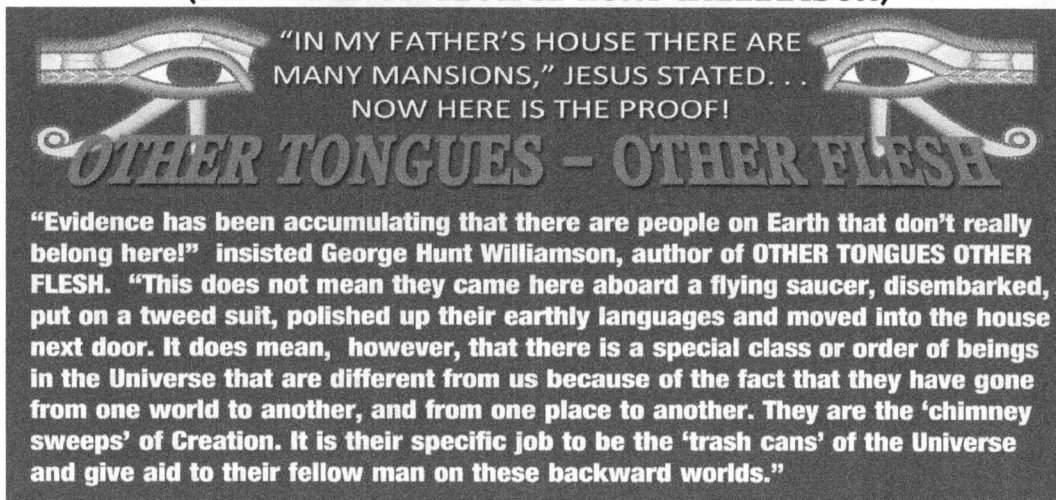

"IN MY FATHER'S HOUSE THERE ARE MANY MANSIONS," JESUS STATED. . . NOW HERE IS THE PROOF!

OTHER TONGUES - OTHER FLESH

"Evidence has been accumulating that there are people on Earth that don't really belong here!" insisted George Hunt Williamson, author of OTHER TONGUES OTHER FLESH. "This does not mean they came here aboard a flying saucer, disembarked, put on a tweed suit, polished up their earthly languages and moved into the house next door. It does mean, however, that there is a special class or order of beings in the Universe that are different from us because of the fact that they have gone from one world to another, and from one place to another. They are the 'chimney sweeps' of Creation. It is their specific job to be the 'trash cans' of the Universe and give aid to their fellow man on these backward worlds."

Order OTHER TONGUES - OTHER FLESH REVISITED
for just $24.95 + $5 S/H

INNER LIGHT, BOX 753, NEW BRUNSWICK, NJ 08903

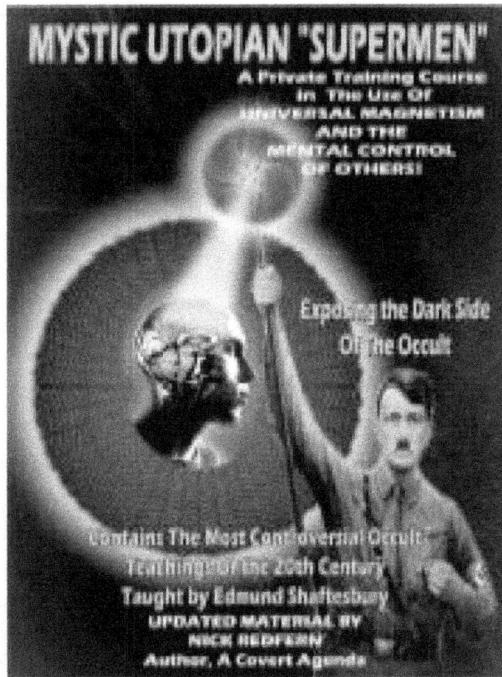

www.ingramcontent.com/pod-product-compliance
Lightning Source LLC
Chambersburg PA
CBHW081228090426
42738CB00016B/3228